FIREFIGHTING
Antiques & Memorabilia

James G. Piatti &
Sandra Frost Piatti

Schiffer Publishing Ltd

4880 Lower Valley Road, Atglen, PA 19310 USA

"Hear ye! O! I pray ye,
Lord masters claim your buckets."

—The call of the town crier
New Amsterdam
After a fire c. 1658

Dedication

To firefighters everywhere:
the brave and
the fallen

Copyright © 2001 by James G. Piatti and Sandra Frost Piatti
Library of Congress Card Number: 2001090303

Designed by John P. Cheek
Cover design by Bruce M. Waters
Type set in Americana XBd BT/Korinna BT

ISBN: 0-7643-1411-4
Printed in China
1 2 3 4

Published by Schiffer Publishing Ltd.
4880 Lower Valley Road
Atglen, PA 19310
Phone: (610) 593-1777; Fax: (610) 593-2002
E-mail: Schifferbk@aol.com
Please visit our web site catalog at
www.schifferbooks.com
We are always looking for people to write books on new and related subjects. If you have an idea for a book, please contact us at the above address.

This book may be purchased from the publisher.
Include $3.95 for shipping.
Please try your bookstore first.
You may write for a free catalog.

In Europe, Schiffer books are distributed by
Bushwood Books
6 Marksbury Avenue
Kew Gardens
Surrey TW9 4JF England
Phone: 44 (0) 20 8392 8585
Fax: 44 (0) 20 8392 9876
E-mail: Bushwd@aol.com
Free postage in the UK. Europe: air mail at cost.

Contents

Foreword

Imagine fire apparatus in the days of hand- and horse-drawn equipment. Firemen running down a muddy street pulling a heavy hand-pumper, or a team of horses galloping along with a shiny steamer in tow, black smoke coming out of the stack. All of the uniforms, accessories, and equipment used at the time are now highly collectible.

The firemen's helmets, lanterns, speaking trumpets, and even the actual hand pumpers and steam fire engines are valuable antiques today.

James Piatti, one of the world's foremost collectors of firematic antiques, is extremely knowledgeable about these scarce objects. A fire collector for many years, Jim has built up a wealth of information on all aspects of fire collecting.

From extremely rare engine lights and helmets, to more common books, badges, and everything in between, Jim either has it or knows where it can be found. Jim is a recognized authority on fire collecting, having written a number of books and many articles on the subject.

His personal collection is vast and even includes an 1859 Button hand pumper, as well as a full-size Amoskeag steam fire engine. He began collecting early and was fortunate enough to be able to buy or be given items that are quite scarce and expensive today.

Jim specializes in the hand-drawn, horse-drawn, and early motorized era of firefighting. Although a volunteer firefighter, he has little interest in modern firefighting equipment, preferring to go back in time to the days of old, when firemen wore high eagle helmets and fire chiefs used ornate speaking trumpets.

In this, his most recent book, Jim collaborated with his wife Sandra, whose expertise in the field of art has brought an added depth of knowledge to this presentation.

Marvin H. Cohen

Marvin H. Cohen is past National Secretary of SPAAMFAA (Society for the Preservation and Appreciation of Antique Motor Fire Apparatus in America); winner of the William L. Robinson Award, the highest honor that the SPAAMFAA can give; past President of the Monhagen Hose Company of Middletown, New York; and a Director of the Orange County Firefighters Museum.

Preface

We have attempted, in this book, to provide a comprehensive guide to firematic antiques, memorabilia, and collectibles. While firefighting collectibles range from the earliest items, like buckets used in bucket brigades, to china mugs saved from current firefighter celebrations, our focus will be on items which would more likely be termed antiques or memorabilia—that is, items that are fifty or more years old.

While reading this book you will come across the term "firematic." It means: of or pertaining to things related to firefighting.

Acknowledgments

It is our great pleasure to recognize the special people who have helped make this book possible. Thank you to Liz Jocham for the very professional assistance you provided in preparing the manuscript. To Michael J. Novak we offer thanks for his photo of our daguerreotype. And to Molly Higgins, whose great skill as a photographer has made our book a work of beauty— we are so grateful. Donna Baker, our editor, deserves many kudos and our everlasting thanks. Also we must mention Marvin Cohen, an old friend, whose expertise in the field has always been a source of knowledge and an especially positive influence.

Introduction

There is mighty speculation as to the origin and practices of early firefighting and firefighters in America. Though colonial records are few, some do exist and those pieced together with the scholarship of latter day historian Augustine E. Costello (who, in 1887 wrote *Our Firemen, A History Of The New York Fire Department, Volunteer and Paid*) provide us with a possible picture. We shall attempt, using these sources and others, to pass on the likely scenarios.

Fire leapt onto the stage of America's earliest history. In 1608, fire reduced the desperate survivors of those first terrible months at Jamestown to a people without winter shelter or provisions. Not long after, in 1623, fire became the mortal enemy of the Mayflower colonists as well. Reporting a warehouse fire, their governor, William Bradford, said, "This fire was occasioned by some of the sea-men that were roystering in a house wher it first begane, making a great fire in very cold weather, which broke out of the chimney into the thatch, and burnt down 3. or 4. houses, and consumed all the goods and provisions in them. The house in which it began was right against their storehouse, which they had much adoe to save, in which were their commone store and all their provissions; the which of it had been lost, the plantation had been overthrowne."[1] In essence, he said, we barely survived this fire.

Thatch, wood, and wattle (common building supplies of the time) made excellent kindling for vigorous fires, the colonists repeatedly learned. And the means for fighting fires? One can only imagine a frantic and hastily formed group of neighbors with sundry containers or maybe wooden buckets running to and from a source of water.

In 1630, the selectmen of the city of Boston—finally smarter—instructed, "Noe man shall build a chimney with wood nor cover his house with thatch."[2] This would be America's first fire regulation. Sometime later, in New Amsterdam, similar regulations were coming to the fore. Under famed and notable one-legged governor, Peter Stuyvesant, the following fire related rules and regulations were established:

· New wooden chimneys and thatched roofs were forbidden.
· Old chimneys were to be kept swept and inspected.
· Four fire warden-police were appointed.
· Fines were established for noncompliance.

· Fire ladders, hooks, and buckets were to be purchased and maintained with fine monies. And further, by 1657, each householder was required by law to keep fire buckets in his home. To that end, all were taxed and city shoemakers set to the task of making some 250 buckets.

Many improvements—and important ones—came a short while thereafter with the establishment of the first volunteer Fire Company in New Amsterdam. Eight volunteers were chosen (this soon became fifty) and were established to form a "rattle watch." These men, teasingly called "the Prowlers," patrolled the city from 9:00pm until sunrise and sounded an alarm on their rattle to bring forth citizens in the event of a fire. In case of a fire, ". . . they directed neighbors and passersby into bucket brigades, with one line passing the filled buckets from the water source to the fire and the other passing the emptied buckets back to be refilled."[3]

Later, citizens were required to leave full buckets of water on their doorsteps and at the town pump for the use of the evening fire watch. When a fire had been fought and the buckets were empty, all were thrown in a heap in the town square, at which time the town crier could be heard shouting: "Hear ye! O! I pray ye, Lord masters claim your buckets."[4] Young boys would then scramble wildly to grab and return a rich man's bucket, for a glass of wine, a sweet cake, or a coin might be the reward. Fire buckets were made large enough to hold approximately three gallons of water and were, at first, marked with simple identification; later, some came to be elaborately and beautifully decorated. These are highly prized today.

Back in Boston, rules governing building supplies proliferated. The general assembly of the city of Boston passed laws dealing with fire protection. They said in part, ". . . henceforth no dwelling-house, shop, warehouse, barn, stable or any other housing more than eight feet in length or breadth, and seven feet in height, shall be erected and set up in Boston, but of stone or brick and covered with slate or tyle . . ."[5] Bucket brigades were again the only means of fighting fires.

The beginning of the eighteenth century saw additional innovations, such as the mutual fire society (the banding together of a group of people foresworn to aid each other in the event of a fire) and the more enduring fire insurance company. In 1711, less than a month after a serious fire, ". . . Boston was divided into several districts each under the care of new municipal officers to be called "fire wards." The act of the General Court that created the fire ward read as follows: "an act providing in case of fire for the more speedy extinguishment thereof, and for the preserving of goods endangered thereby"[6] These fire wards were to carry a staff of office and a badge and were to have authority over everyone at the fire scene. They were charged to put out fires, protect and salvage goods, and identify wrongdoers for future prosecution. (Surprisingly enough, arson seems to have been a common crime in early America.) Standard equipment amongst them: a bed key for the dismantling of beds (a most precious possession), and a salvage bag (a large commodious bag into which valuable possessions could be quickly stuffed).

When the city of New Amsterdam had reached 1,200 houses and contained approximately 8,628 souls, two new fire engines arrived from London. "Richard Newsham of London applied for the first patent for his 'new water engine for quenching fires' in 1721. This engine is said to be capable of pumping over 100 gallons (455 l.) a minute and to possess more cranks and winches than any earlier engine."[7] What a profound improvement, one might note, over the three gallon bucket! Newsham's engines were man-powered by the hand and foot action of ten to twenty men and could play a stream of water upwards of fifty-five yards.

The first volunteer engine company in New Amsterdam was marked by the arrival of these fire engines from London. Established in 1737, Engine Company #1 endured until the year 1864. But the award for the nation's very first volunteer engine company, however, must go to Ben Franklin's Union Fire Company, which was founded in Philadelphia just one year earlier. Soon volunteer fire companies began to proliferate throughout America. And the century and a half following the founding of Franklin's company could well be known as the heyday of the volunteer firemen.

As cities enlarged, compacted, and grew upward, there developed a greater need for fire protection. Fire companies formalized, enlarged, and became competitive. The term "companies" here is significant, as these volunteer firemen owed their allegiance to individual fire companies—not to towns, cities, or districts. Each company had a sense of individual identity that quickly fostered competition and—despite company names like Friendship, Humane, and Protector—vicious rivalries often ensued. It is easy to imagine contests of speed, agility, accuracy, and strength at a fire scene. Inspired sometimes by cash prizes offered by insurance companies (for the first company to reach a blaze or put a stream of water on the fire), such contests could turn ugly and violent. There are reports of fires having been abandoned while the men engaged in a raucous, wild, and bloody melee. One can easily imagine the result as to the fire!

The fire companies had originally organized for a common goal—to fight fires—but gradually this activity and everything associated with it became a multi-faceted, long lasting, and politically influential social institution. The firehouse and firefighters were a source of pride to the community. Songs were written, melodies sung, statues made, and lithographs printed, all glorifying the firefighter. It is well known that there was great social prestige attached to belonging to a fire company. In his red shirt and black helmet, or his parade hat and cape, the "fire laddie" was greatly admired. There were balls, dances, and picnics. There were parades. Daytime parades often featured spidery-wheeled, mirrored hose carts that glittered in the sun. Garlands of flowers bedecked fire engines and ladder trucks while proud cadres of firemen marched to the cadence of a band. Night parades were ablaze with firelight. There were hand held torches and lanterns, there were helmet torches, and—perhaps most beautiful of all—there were hand drawn fire engines

7

with gumdrop-bright, red and blue glass engine lights illuminating their way. Oh . . . the ladies must have swooned, while the gents and children delighted at the sight of those glorious parades! Memorabilia associated with parades are special treasures to the fire antiques collector.

But, improvements came along. Man-powered hand pumpers were no match for the tireless, giant, steam-powered behemoths that emerged on the scene in the middle of the nineteenth century. Nothing lasts forever and the volunteer fire departments resisted change. ". . . Those devoted to the traditional system rejected suggestions that horses should pull apparatus or that steam engines be introduced."[8] However, " . . . in the 1850s many innovations were being made in firefighting equipment. The industrial revolution now began to affect firefighting. The conversion from man-drawn, man-pumped 'engines' to steam-powered horse drawn 'bulljines' was underway—much to the angry dismay of the dedicated volunteers and to the heartfelt relief of insurance companies and many concerned citizens."[9] The Civil War also played a role here, as it had taken the lives of many heroic firemen and with those men died much of the knowledge and practices of the old firehouse system. Eventually the steamers came and were motorized. Larger cities had paid departments. For all practical purposes, the end of the nineteenth century marked the final end, too, of the grand heyday of the "fire laddie."

Clearly there is evidence galore recording the activities of these latter day, nineteenth century firefighters. Some of this evidence is in the form of documents, much is in the form of artifacts. In these artifacts—of any era—we delight. But whether objects of volunteer or paid companies, these helmets, badges, programs, belts, engraved trumpets, alarm equipment, ledgers, extinguishers, fire marks, hoses, nozzles, builder's plates, scrimshaw, toys, engine lights, silver ewers, salvers, fine paintings, folk paintings, and so on define the terms "firefighting antiques, memorabilia, and collectibles." These objects make our hearts merry and are the objects of our everlasting search. Perhaps you will join us.

Endnotes

[1] Dennis Smith, *Dennis Smith's History of Firefighting in America 300 Years of Courage* (New York: The Dial Press, © 1978), p. 3.

[2] *Ibid.*

[3] *Ibid,* p.5.

[4] Augustine E. Costello, *Our Firemen, A History of the New York Fire Department Volunteer and Paid* (New York: Knickerbocker Press, 1977), p. 12.

[5] Donald J. Cannon, Ed., *Heritage of Flames* (Artisan Books, © 1977), p. 16.

[6] *Ibid*, p. 24.

[7] Arthur Ingram, *A History of Firefighting and Equipment* (Secaucus, New Jersey: Chartwell Books Inc., © 1978), p. 10.

[8] Donald J. Cannon, "Firefighting in America" (U. of Penna. Hospital Antiques Show brochure, © 1980), p. 27.

[9] Smith, p. 56.

Firefighting Collector's Tips

Thoughts on Collecting

Jim: Thirty years ago when I started collecting, people would ask, "Why do you collect this stuff?" Those of us who did collect turned out to build large and valuable collections. At that time, we were able to buy some of the more historical pieces at a reasonable price. New collectors to the field will have an opportunity, too. Items that are reasonable today will be tomorrow's treasures. Examples include new fire engine toys, recent movie items, and current cartoon figures in fire outfits.

Sandy: When I married Jim, firefighting collectibles were a new thing to me. If I thought of them at all, I thought of them as a "man thing." Today, I have a whole different outlook. I see that many pieces have great historical value. Some go beyond the categories of "collectible" or even "memorabilia" and enter the realm of "true antique." Some are also enjoyed as art. Today I am pleased to be able to join with Jim in the search for these valuable and exciting firefighting items. I believe that my background in art has had a positive influence on our collecting and on our understanding of this field of collecting as a whole.

Where to Buy

The best place to begin your search for firefighting collectibles is at local antique shows and shops. As your collection grows, attend fire collectible shows such as The Spring Thaw Auction and Sale in Allentown, Pennsylvania, SPAAMFAA (Society for the Preservation and Appreciation of Antique Motor Fire Apparatus in America) conventions, The Firehouse Magazine Show and Flea Market, and various muster-flea markets held around the United States. Firematic items can sometimes be found at car shows as well. Schedules of major shows are published in the *Maine Antique Digest* and *The Antiques and The Arts Weekly*.

Other possible sources include garage sales and group shops. Also, several dealers publish yearly lists full of quality fire collectibles, memorabilia, and antiques.

Auctions are another major source of firematic items, but please remember: always attend the preview and examine all items carefully at that time. Set a price in your mind and do not go above it. "Auction fever" can

be very costly! Another caution: once you buy an item there are no returns—items are sold "as is."

A new source for firefighting memorabilia is online auctions; notable among these is eBay. Thousands of fire-related items are listed every day. In order to participate, you must sign up and receive a password. Auctions last from three days to two weeks. If an item has a reserve price, you are notified and can bid accordingly. Of course, with online auctions one cannot examine the item personally and this may be a problem. You can, however, e-mail questions, and many sellers will give a three day return privilege. It should be noted that auctions end at a specific time and most action occurs during the last two minutes.

Values

Establishing values for firefighting items can be difficult. First, the demand far exceeds the supply. A valuable item is rare, but a rare item is not always valuable. I will use parade and convention ribbons as an example. Some ribbons are exceedingly rare, yet so many varieties and types were issued that their value is limited. In essence, abundance breeds disdain.

Availability

Certain items are readily available, including low front helmets, ceramic items, ribbons, badges, and postcards. If an item is a once-in-a-lifetime find, it should be purchased. I am reminded of advice I once received from a famous collector. "In regard to unusual items," he said, "you may have to settle for a higher price and lesser condition for that once-in-a-lifetime find. Should a higher grade item become available you can always upgrade."

Demand

As with all collectible items, certain pieces are "hot." This increases demand and value. The problem is that these items can "cool down" and their prices will then reflect this change. Presentation fire trumpets are an example of this: in the early 1980s they were worth twice today's value. Other examples include engine lights and parade hats. Your collection should not be for investment. Buy what you like and can afford. If the value of your collection grows, all the better.

Age

Age is not always a major factor. For example, certain paper and convention items from the 1800s are in large supply and are not exceedingly valuable.

Condition

Items shown and discussed in this book range from above average to excellent condition. As a rule, items in mint condition may be worth several times more than an item in good condition. An important consideration with firefighting collectibles is that they were originally *used*, so finding items in mint condition is difficult.

Auctions

Buying at an auction, whether online or live, presents difficulties not found in other methods of purchase. In most buying situations, prices are comparatively fixed, whereas at auctions the purchase price of any one item may vary drastically due to many factors: reserve pricing, geographic location, buyer's premium, and the tendency to succumb to "auction fever"—the fear that someone else will buy this item, causing you or another collector to keep on bidding.

Panic Buying

Panic buying is a bane to all collectors. Here is a common scenario: you find you haven't bought anything in a couple of weeks and you're at a large antique show. Frustration sets in and you buy on impulse. A week later you look at your purchase and shake your head, wondering how you could have been so stupid. One should make every attempt to avoid "panic buying."

Cross-Over Value

Any antique with a collectible value in two or more fields of collecting has, in a sense, a heightened value. Furthermore, such items often have the greatest value in the collecting area to which they most specifically pertain. For example, shaving mugs with firematic designs would be very collectible to both firematic collectors and shaving mug collectors, yet would most likely bring the highest price from shaving-mug collectors. Similarly, toy collectors will pay higher prices for fire-related toys than will fire collectors. However, folk art dealers have driven the price of firematic fire buckets to astronomical heights by paying up to $90,000 for a pair.

Original Parts

Pieces should have original parts and finishing. Refinishing and/or the use of reproduction parts will most often decrease an item's value. Original finish indicating that an item has been used is preferred.

As a final note, this book is a price guide and should be used to assist you in determining value. I am available for questions and comments about this book and continue to be interested in purchasing fire collectibles. Please contact Jim Piatti at P.O. Box 244, Oakland, New Jersey 07436. I can also be reached at 973-962-6470.

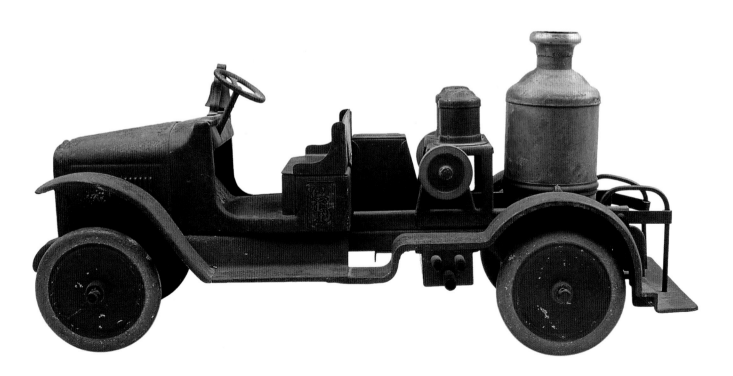

Chapter One
Alarm Equipment

With the removal of most street fire alarm boxes and the increased interest in house gongs, registers, central station equipment, and indicators, prices in this area are skyrocketing. When collecting alarm equipment, it should be noted that Gamewell Fire Alarm Company material is most valuable.

In 1851, the city of Boston voted to award a contract for the installation of a central alarm office, forty-five alarm boxes, and the apparatus for striking signals on the sixteen city alarm bells. The following year the system was inaugurated.

In the first boxes, a notched code wheel was turned by a crank handle in the front of the box. This soon gave way to a spring-driven, clockwork-type mechanism which drove the code wheel when activated by a lever. If the lever were pulled more than once, an incorrect signal would result. Therefore, instructions on the base stated: "PULL HANDLE DOWN ONCE, THEN LET GO." Examples of these boxes are valuable and rare.

As the systems expanded, another problem arose. When two or more boxes on the same circuit were pulled, they interfered with each other's signal, causing a jumbled alarm. In 1889, a successive box movement was developed. The alarm from one box on a circuit would have to finish before another box on the same circuit could send its signal.

The original hand-cranked boxes gave way to boxes locked with a key. The keys were issued to policemen and responsible citizens or kept at easily accessible locations. In 1900, the Gamewell Fire Alarm Company's Cole Key-Guard appeared with the instructions: "BREAK GLASS, OPEN DOOR, PULL HANDLE DOWN ONCE, LET GO." In 1922, a quick-action door was made available, replacing the Cole Key-Guard. Many of the alarm boxes in service today are of this type.

After World War II, telephone alarm boxes began to appear, with a direct phone to fire headquarters inside. The 1950s brought radio transmitter boxes, which eliminated the need to run wire from the box to the alarm office.

There were a number of manufacturers of fire alarm boxes, but the products of the Gamewell Fire Alarm Company predominated.

House gongs hung on the wall in the firehouse and rang out the number of the activated fire alarm box. These gongs measured from six to eighteen inches in diameter and ranged in style from plain to very ornate.

According to an early Gamewell catalog, they were available in walnut, oak, or mahogany cases, if so ordered. Also available was a brass fire annunciator bell, mounted on a cast-iron base. These came in sizes from six to twelve inches in diameter and are not as desirable today as those with wood cases.

An indicator is an electromagnet device which hung in the firehouse. Revolving number wheels turned to indicate the number of a fire alarm box when an alarm was activated.

There are a few varieties. One type indicated the number of the box only; it had no gong. Another included a gong that rang out the number being displayed. A third variety contained an indicator and a notifier bell that needed to be hand-pulled; this advised firemen that a box was pulled and told them to check the indicator for the box number.

American Fire Alarm Telegraph cast iron box, 1869. $750-$1,200.

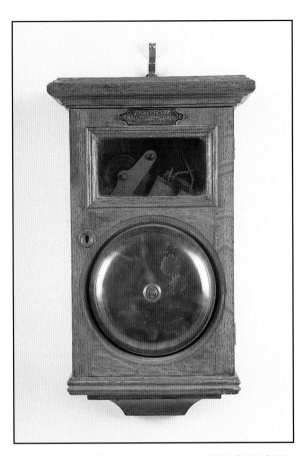

Gamewell 6" oak cased gong, c. 1900. $760-$900.

United States Fire Alarm, walnut cased 8" gong, c. 1910. $2,500-$3,000.

Right: Date-Time stamp with Chelsea clock, c. 1910. $1,200-$1,500.

Left: Gamewell cased indicator, c. 1900. $2,000-$2,500.

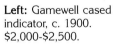

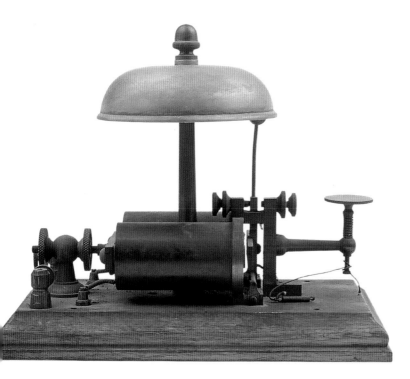

Alarm tapper, c. 1910. $350-$500.

Tin toy fire alarm box, manufacturer unknown. $350-$500.

Gamewell punch register, c. 1900. $300-$500.

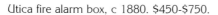
Utica fire alarm box, c 1880. $450-$750.

Three New York City Fire Department keys. $15-$25 each.

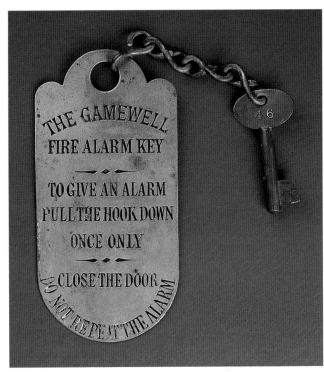

Gamewell fire alarm box key with instruction tag, c. 1890. $400-$500.

Gamewell fire alarm box, c. 1880. $750-$1,000.

Gamewell auxiliary fire alarm box, c. 1900. $100-$150.

Gamewell fire alarm box, c. 1890. $500-$700.

Promotional double deck giveaway playing cards with Bakelite case, from Gamewell Fire Alarm Company. $400-$600.

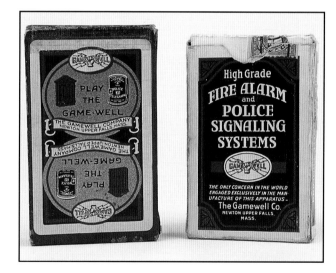

Two decks of promotional playing cards, c. 1910. $250-$350 each

Star Electric Company advertising knife, c. 1910. $200-$250.

Advertising compass, c. 1880. $350

Chapter Two
Apparatus Parts

Apparatus parts are sought after by two types of collectors: one is the person trying to restore a rig to its original condition, the other is the general collector looking for an addition to his collection. Looking for parts to complete a restoration can be a frustrating experience. I have seen owners of apparatus carrying around a list of "wants" for years.

Axes are hung on fire engines and are important tools for fighting fires. Today's fire axe differs in shape from most early American axes. Early axes had a sharp pick on one end for prying and a round blade on the other end for chopping. The round blade was replaced in fire service by a square-edged blade, which was a more effective tool in fighting fires, although the round-blade style was retained for parade use for many years. The handle of an axe may help determine the age of the axe, since prior to the Civil War axe handles were absolutely straight and immediately after the war they were changed to curved.

In order to distinguish their apparatus from all others, the men from Philadelphia Hose Company Number 1 came up with a novel idea. In great secrecy, they designed a bell that moved and rang by means of a spring. Its sound not only cleared the way, but signaled their location to members of the company who were not at the hose house when the alarm came in. Thus, between the years 1788 and 1800 a tradition began that lives on today with the use of bells as warning devices on fire apparatus.

Fire engine bells were made in many sizes, They were made of brass, bronze, and bell metal (copper and tin), and may have been nickel or chrome plated. The most desirable are those from hand- or horse-drawn equipment and those few that are engraved with a company name.

Many bells on early horse and motorized apparatus were mounted, so that the whole bell swung back and forth by means of a rope pulled by an officer. Other varieties include hand- and foot-operated rotary bells manufactured by the New Departure Manufacturing Company, and stationary bells with the clapper pulled by a cord.

In recent years, with the cost of apparatus rising rapidly, many fire departments have been ordering equipment without bells. In other cases departments will transfer a bell from a retired truck to a new piece of equipment. These practices have led to a scarcity of fire engine bells. As a result, bells produced fairly recently are now collectible, rapidly increasing in value, and difficult to obtain.

Gauges were often the only mechanical device salvaged from scrapped fire engines. The most desirable gauges are those from the steam era; they have the manufacturers' names on the dials. A particularly rare gauge of the 1800s was one produced by the Amoskeag Steam Fire Engine Company, which had an illustration of a steamer on its face. Gauges from motorized apparatus are also very collectible, especially those from Ahrens-Fox apparatus.

In order to prevent seams from bursting, American manufacturers of fire hose bound the stitched seams of hose with twenty to thirty copper rivets to the running foot, thereby eliminating the leaks caused by weakness and rotting. This idea was patented in 1817 and began to be manufactured for every fire company in America. However, by the last quarter of the eighteenth century, new technology had made leather hose obsolete. Full lengths of American made leather hose can sell for in excess of $1500.

Name plates from old fire apparatus could be found around the firehouse long after the apparatus was removed from service. Name plates were made in several varieties; most were silver-plated brass. Some bore the name of the engine and the number, others had the name of the manufacturer or a combination of both. Dedication plates bore the names of members of the truck committee and town fathers. It is known that old-time "fire laddies" prized the name plates from apparatus just as seamen valued the stern ornaments and figureheads of ships.

In the motorized era, builder's plates ranged from small brass serial number and patent plates to heavy cast plates. These are highly collectible. Many collectors are saving name plates from modern apparatus. Since many modern apparatus manufacturers have gone out of business, these are an excellent investment.

The first fire nozzles were attached directly to eduction pipes. These nozzles were usually six to seven feet long and made of brass and copper. With the introduction of hose and the ability to get closer to the fire, nozzles were shortened.

There are two varieties of nozzles: those with shut-offs and those without. Nozzles with shut-offs are more collectible and command higher prices. Nozzles with apparatus manufacturers' names stamped on them are equally valuable.

Some unusual types of nozzles are those over four feet long, those with gas-cock shut-offs, ladder pipes, deluge guns, and cellar nozzles.

Builder's plate from hand pumper,
Sizelman and Sickler, c. 1855. $750.

Builder's plate, Wm. Jeffers
and Company, c. 1850. $650.

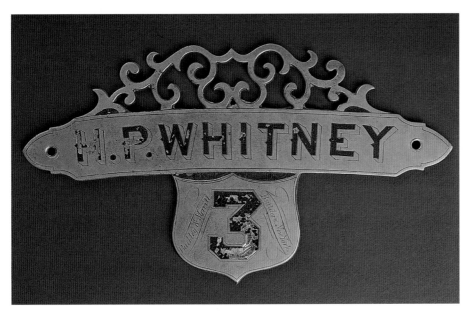

Engine plate, H. P.
Whitney Hose Company,
c. 1880. $500.

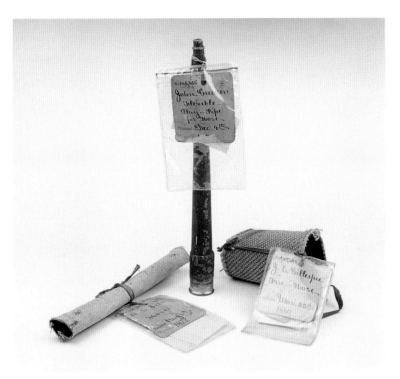

Patent models. Left to right: fire hose, 1872. $350; play pipe (nozzle), $800-$1,000; fire hose, c. 1880. $350.

Engraved bell from Hunneman hand pumper, New Orleans, Louisiana, 1843. "Mississippi Two." $1,500.

Unusual adjustable hand pumper nozzle, 5' tall. $1,500-$2,000.

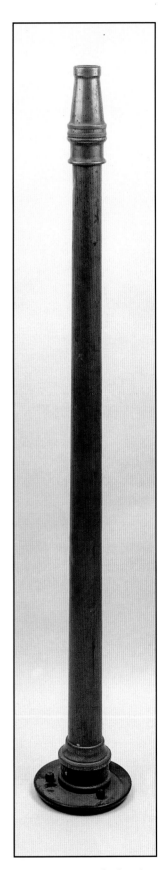

Six foot play pipe for hand pumper. $1,500.

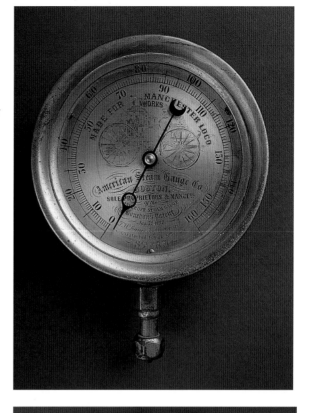

Early Amoskeag steamer gauge, c. 1870. $750.

Tournament nozzle, c. 1880. $1,000-$1,200.

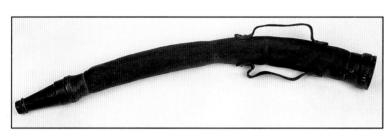

Early leather nozzle, c. 1850. $550-$750.

Amoskeag builder's plate from steamer, c. 1900. $750.

LaFrance apparatus builder's plate, c. 1890. $500.

19

Builder's plate, 1903, Augusta, Maine hose cart. $375.

Builder's plate, Silsby Steam fire engine. $750.

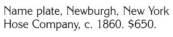

Name plate, Newburgh, New York
Hose Company, c. 1860. $650.

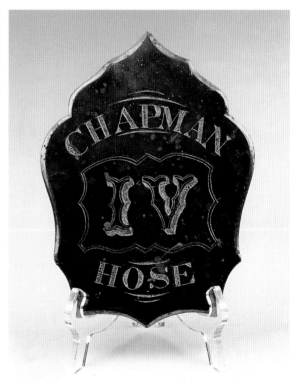

Presentation hydrant wrench, c. 1910. $175.

Engraved "Engine 31" bell,
10" diameter. $650.

Left to right: American
LaFrance motor meter,
c. 1920. $375; American
LaFrance bell finial, c. 1930s.
$200; American LaFrance
radiator cap, c. 1920. $200.

Hood ornament, fireman profile. $200.

Early engraved hose coupling. $300.

Ahrens Fox fire engine gauge. $175.

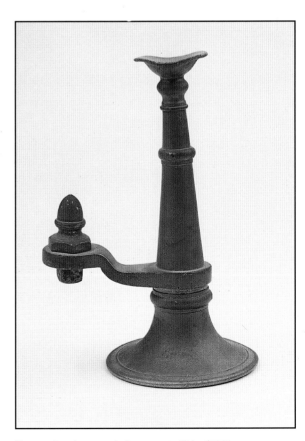

Decoration from early hose cart, 8" h. $750.

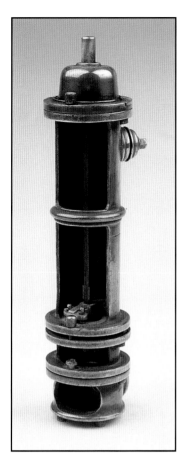

Salesman's sample fire hydrant
(working). $1,250.

Viking-style axe head with interesting decorative work, c. 1860. $275.

Viking-style parade axe with
decorative keystone and initials,
c. 1870. $750

Salesman's sample fire hydrant. $375.

Chapter Three
Badges and Ribbons

Uniform badges have always been highly prized collectibles. Their size, unique designs, and availability have put them in high demand. Those made of precious metals command premium prices, as do those that are highly decorated or have presentations.

A major problem in the early 1800s was rowdyism at fire scenes. To prevent persons who were not firemen from entering the fire lines, the legislature of New York ordered the Common Council in 1855 to design a badge to be displayed in a "plain, conspicuous manner for the breast." While on duty, every fireman was required by law to wear his badge. The badge was made of "Prince's Metal" and bore a number which was kept in the records of the fire department to identify the owner. This practice was successful and fire companies all over the United States followed suit.

In 1860, this badge gave way to badges of different shapes: a helmet-front shaped badge showing a hand pumper for an engine company; a round badge with a four-wheel hose cart for a hose company; and an eight-sided badge with a ladder truck for a hook and ladder company. Each badge also showed a large number for the company and a smaller number for the wearer. Many other fire companies followed these designs. Today, these different shaped badges are the hardest to find. Firemen's badges are still in use today, of course—current badge catalogs show literally hundreds of different styles and variations. When a fireman was promoted, attained a certain number of years of service, or retired, he was often given a presentation badge, hand crafted of either gold or silver by a jeweler. These badges were engraved on the back, personalized with his name on the front, or a combination or both.

In the past, and for approximately 150 years, ribbons were issued for various events. Some ribbons were very simple, some were very ornate. Some had metal badges, fancy embroidery, and celluloid pictures. These ribbons were hung proudly from the uniforms of the firemen in attendance. Please note that a tremendous quantity were issued between 1880-1915, lowering their value.

Left: unidentified fire insurance patrol badge. $400. Right: fire alarm box shaped Paterson fire line badge. $395.

14k gold presentation badge with diamond, from Wheeling, West Virginia, c. 1900. $1,500.

Left: New York City Hook and Ladder Company badge, c. 1860. $600.
Right: early Brooklyn Western District badge. $450.

14k gold front piece shaped badge, c. 1890. $450.

Left: New York City engine company badge, c. 1860. $225. Right: Chicago fire lines badge. $450.

14k gold New York City twenty year active service presentation badge with diamond chips, c. 1910. $1,000.

14k gold, Hartford, Connecticut fire commissioner's badge. $350.

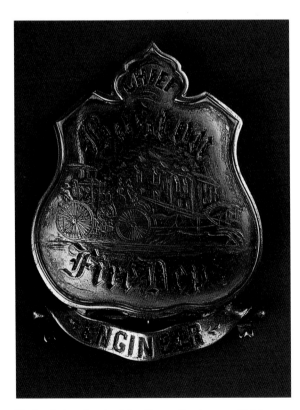

14k gold New York City twenty year service engineer badge, c. 1910. $1,200.

Die for an early fire badge, c. 1860. $300.

Badge belonging to John Damrell, who was Chief Engineer, Boston Fire Department, c. 1870. $2,500.

Fire insurance patrol badge, Philadelphia,
Pennsylvania, c. 1900. $375.

14k gold chief's badge,
c. 1920. $500.

Sterling silver, Brooklyn Western District, fire
commissioner's badge, c. 1850. $1,500.

14k gold presentation badge. $850.

Sterling silver, Newark, New Jersey Chief Engineer's badge, c. 1870. $450.

Presentation badge, West Hoboken, New Jersey, c. 1890. $450.

Assorted early badges. Left: early New York City fire lines badge. $350. Center top: New York City engineer's badge. $375. Center bottom: rare Washington City Fire Department badge with unfinished capitol building. $600. Right: fire patrol badge, c. 1890. $375.

Photographic badge, convention souvenir, 1906. $50.

Left: Hand painted convention ribbon, 1892. $100.

Right: Celluloid fire line badge, Worcester, Massachusetts, 1915. $75.

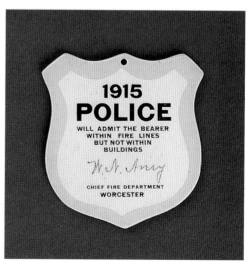

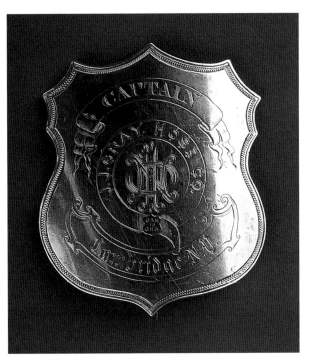

Sterling silver presentation badge. $250.

14k gold badge with diamond, Leonia, New Jersey, c. 1910. $1,000.

14k gold early lapel badge (steamer), c. 1900. $175.

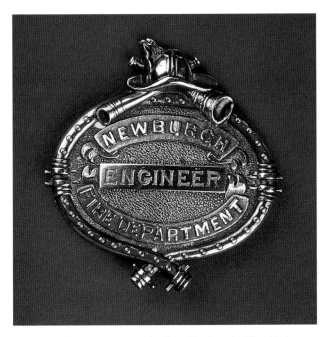

Sterling silver presentation badge, Newburgh, New York, c. 1880. $375.

Chapter Four
Ephemera

The dictionary defines ephemera as "short-lived." Any item (usually made of paper or something similarly fragile) not expected to last past the time of issue falls into this category. Readily available and reasonably priced, ephemera is the answer for collectors who do not have a lot of room or are on a tight budget. Some of the major areas of collecting ephemera include:

Advertising

The world of advertising is an extremely competitive field. In order to sell a product, every possible gimmick has been used. Colorfully decorated signs, posters, thermometers, mirrors, tins, and ashtrays (most collectible examples contain illustrations of firemen, fire engines, rescues, or burning buildings) are a few advertising pieces that might be of interest to collectors.

Perhaps the most visual examples of advertising were logos produced by insurance companies, alarm companies, fire engine manufacturers, beer companies, and tobacco companies.

Today's advertising items are often made of plastic and the quality does not compare with those of yesteryear, which included fine lithographs and items made of metal, mother-of-pearl, or celluloid.

It should be noted that, with the increased interest in fire-related items, reproductions do exist. Examples of reproductions include glass paperweights, tin signs advertising fire engine manufacturers or gasoline companies, and trade cards. More of these items appear every day.

Books

Age alone does not determine the value of a book. Rather, the demand for a particular book or topic determines its value. In recent years, a resurgence of interest in fire-related books has caused prices to escalate. Even fire books published in the 1970s are now eagerly sought by collectors.

Fire books have been published for over one hundred years, but they were printed in small quantities, making them scarce today. During the 1890s, many histories of volunteer fire departments were printed as they were replaced by paid departments. These books contained some historical facts but the focus was on including the names of the firemen, who were its best sales prospects.

After great conflagrations, books were published as quickly as possible with some information about the fire, but mainly listing the casualties, to induce the relatives of those killed or injured to buy the book. It is not uncommon to find books with pages bound upside down, due to the haste with which the books were printed.

Catalogs

Fire equipment catalogs are highly collectible and are excellent reference material. They describe, price, and date an item clearly. This provides an important frame of reference for the collector.

Currency

From colonial times to the latter part of the nineteenth century, paper money was printed by a variety of agencies. This, it can be imagined, caused a great deal of confusion in commerce. In February of 1863, the National Bank Act was enacted. It forbade banks, financial institutions, or other agencies from printing their own money.

During the 1860s, prior to this legislation, several notes were imprinted with firematic motifs. These notes are now highly collectible.

Dance Programs

In the early twentieth century, an important social event of many towns was the annual Firemen's Ball. An extravagant atmosphere was a "must" for such events. Banners, caps, trumpets, ladders, and axes were among the decorations, and having a hose cart or engine in the middle of the dance floor was not unusual. Under the management of the Firemen's Committee, the Firemen's Ball was the principal source of revenue for the Widows and Orphans Fund.

At the gala Firemen's Ball an orchestra provided music and the guests danced and sang; firemen wore their parade uniforms and the ladies their ball gowns. The songs and music were dedicated to the firemen, and it was common for a fire company to have music composed in its honor, or in honor of its Chief Engineer.

Beautiful engravings or lithographs in full color enhance the covers of Firemen's Ball programs. It was the custom for young ladies to write the names of their dance partners in the programs. Because it was fashionable to keep a scrapbook in the last half of the nineteenth century, many of these items survived.

Five-Cent Novels

Around the turn of the twentieth century, the five-cent novel, printed on pulp paper, was extremely popular all over the country. At least two five-cent novels focused on the "fire laddies." They were *Pluck and Luck* and *Wide Awake Weekly*. New issues came out every week with endless stories of heroism and adventure. These stories were for the most part fiction and took place in the latter half of the nineteenth century with daring rescues of "fair maidens" as the order of the day. The books averaged thirty pages in length and those dealing with fire had beautifully lithographed fire action covers.

Firehouse Journals

The first written report of fire department activities was recorded in the journal of the New York City Fire Department on November 4, 1791. In the following years, most firehouses kept a daily log of events of the company, with examples of everything from the amount of hay received to information about the major fires they fought. Most sought after are those from early 1800s with illustrations and those from large cities up to the 1920s.

Magazines

Early magazines are desirable due to the advertisements, pictures, and methods of fire fighting illustrated in them. These magazines traced the development of fire equipment and techniques for fighting fires. They also advertised the latest equipment of the period and critiqued major fires of the day.

Movie Items

In the early 1920s, the derring-do of a fireman rescuing a woman or child would bring the audience into the theater. Elaborate displays and colorful posters were designed and sent to theaters to advertise the new movies. This material was made to be displayed and then moved to the next theater showing the film. After the film had made the rounds to all the theaters, the displays were discarded.

Sheet Music

The development of better printing methods and the popularity of the piano caused publishers to increase the production of sheet music. Firemen were the popular romantic heroes of the day. Therefore, many songs were written, illustrated, and published with fire themes. Fire companies were proud of their officers and often had ballads written and dedicated to them. The most sought-after pieces of sheet music date back to the middle of the nineteenth century. Some were beautifully illustrated.

With the advent of the phonograph came Edison Discs, followed by records. These permanently memorialized the sounds and stories surrounding firefighting from the turn of the twentieth century to modern times.

Postcards

The golden age of postcards was between 1898 and 1918. Wherever postcards were sold, there was always a large selection of fire-related cards. Fire postcards are grouped into several categories: real photos, black and white postcards, colored postcards, and drawings. Sending postcards was popular—everyone collected cards and had albums in which to keep and protect them. Thanks to this practice there is a good supply of early cards available today.

This bit of information may help you to date postcards: prior to 1907, the post office insisted that the address be on one side and that the message be on the other side with the picture. After that date both address and message were permitted on the same side.

Trading Cards

During the early 1950s, sets of cards called the "Fire Fighters" were sold at candy stores. They were published by the Bowman Gum Company. These cards depicted nearly all the major apparatus of the period, as well as examples of early hand, horse-drawn, and motorized apparatus.

The total set consisted of sixty-four cards, each with a detailed drawing of a fire-related item. The cards were sold in wax packs with gum, as were all cards of that period. The back of the card had a brief description of the rig shown, and a picture of some type of fireman's tool or early protective clothing. This set was not popular with children and no additional sets were produced until the 1980s. Since then several sets have been published and newer sets have little value.

Trade Cards

In the 1870s to 1890s, advertising or trade cards were given to the public by tradesmen or storekeepers. Cheap color lithography offered a way to use pictures to sell products. The trade cards were either left in a tray on the counter, handed to the customer, or put in the wrapped package. The front of the card usually showed the product and the back had advertising. These cards usually measured 3"x5".

In 1881, a series of six trade cards depicting comic firemen was printed by Cosack and Clark. Other cards were made by a pump manufacturer, thread manufacturer, etc.

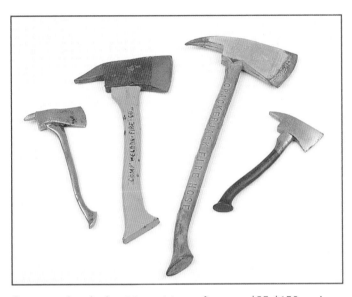

Ornamental and advertising miniature fire axes. $35-$150 each.

American LaFrance advertising calendar, 1948. $375.

Assorted collectible books, fire related. $10-$150 each.

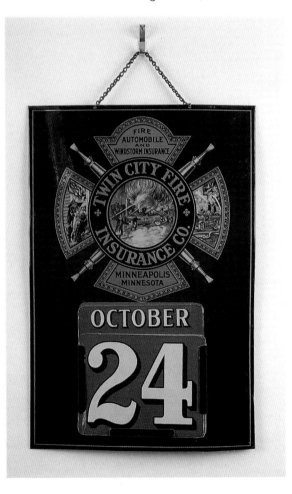

Tin insurance company perpetual advertising calendar, c. 1930. $500.

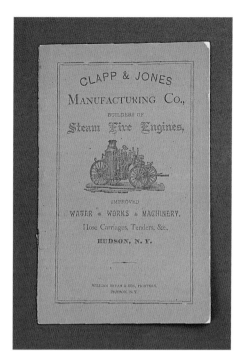

Clapp and Jones steam fire engine
catalogue, c. 1880. $300.

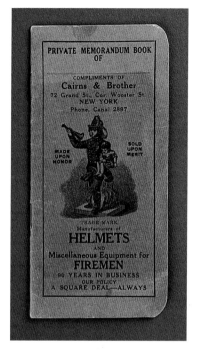

Fire helmet manufacturer's
giveaway memorandum book.
$35.

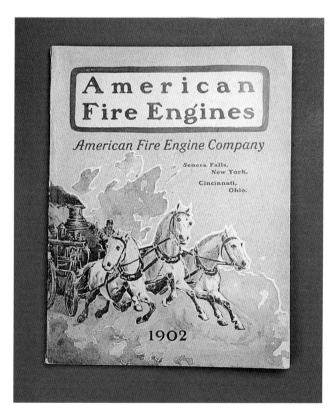

American fire engine advertising catalogue, c. 1902. $400.

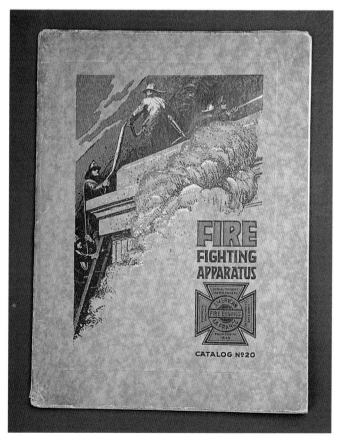

American LaFrance fire fighting apparatus catalogue, c. 1920.
$300.

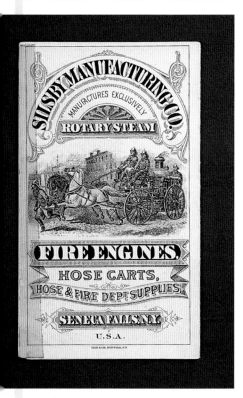

Left: Silsby Company fire engine advertising brochure, c. 1880. $300.

Above: Fold over color lithograph from Silsby Company brochure.

Cereal boxes with firematic interest. Kellogg's Sugar Frosted Flakes. $175; Wheaties. $75.

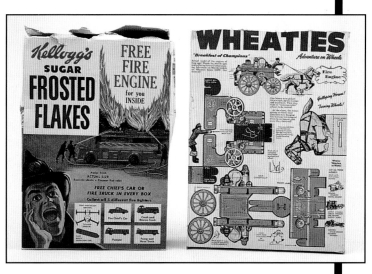

Back of the firematic Frosted Flakes and Wheaties boxes.

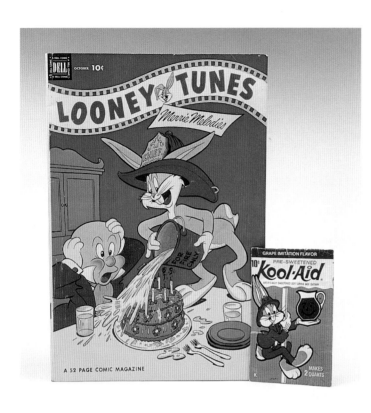

Cartoon character in firematic costume on comic book and on soft drink package. $25 each.

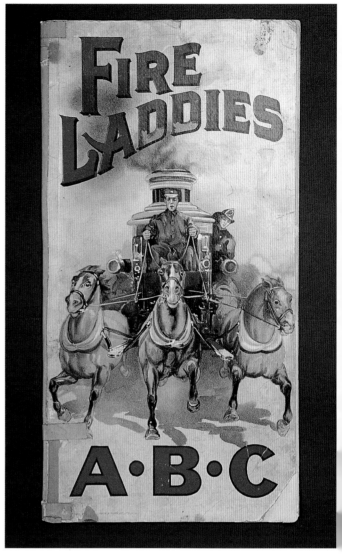

Fire Laddies A.B.C. book. $75.

Assortment, Smokey Stover cartoon books. $25-$35 each.

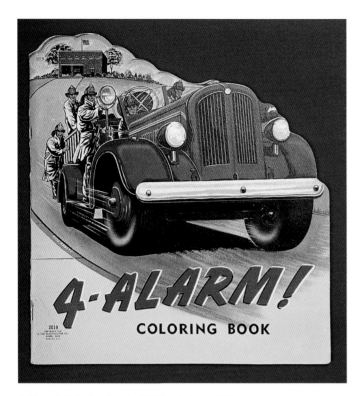

4 Alarm! Coloring book, 1950s vintage. $25.

Fireman die cuts, c. 1880. $75.

Firemen in Action kiddies book, c. 1930. $75.

Fire Engines coloring book, c. 1940. $25.

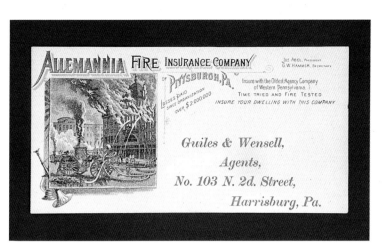

Fire insurance blotter, c. 1900. $35.

Fireman's Insurance Company advertising clock, Newark, New Jersey, c. 1910. $450.

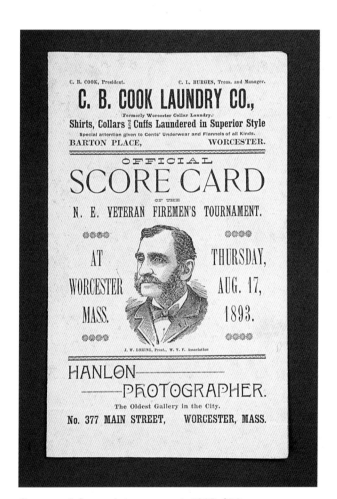

Score card, firemen's tournament, 1893. $50.

New Departure fire bells advertising clock. $250.

Business card, 1850. $75.

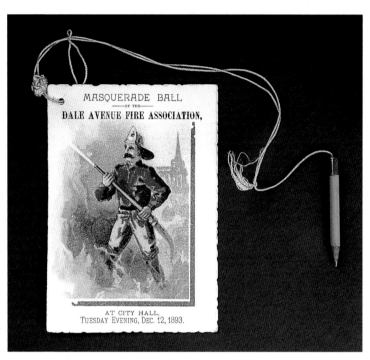

Dance card, firemen masquerade ball, 1893. $35.

Firemen's ball ticket, 1858. $60.

Watch fobs with advertising. Left: New Departure fire bells, c. 1890. $125. Right: Gamewell Co., c. 1890. $450.

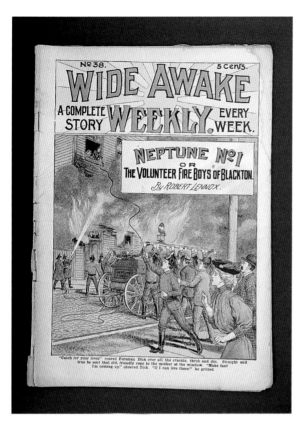

Wide Awake weekly stories, firematic themes, c. 1900.
$25.

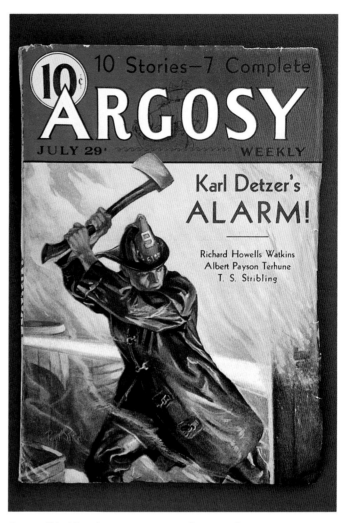

Argosy Weekly adventure magazine for men, firematic cover,
c. 1933. $18.

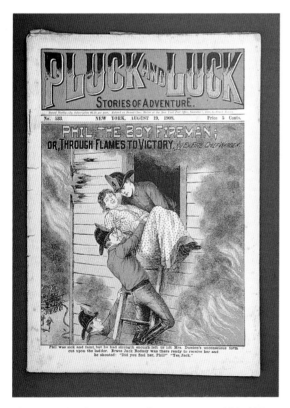

Pluck and Luck magazine, fire stories, c. 1900. $25.

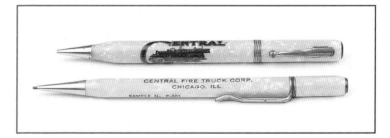

Mechanical pencils, fire engine advertising, c. 1930. $35 each.

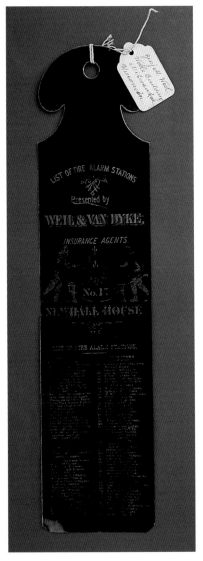

Celluloid advertising piece, c. 1910. $20.

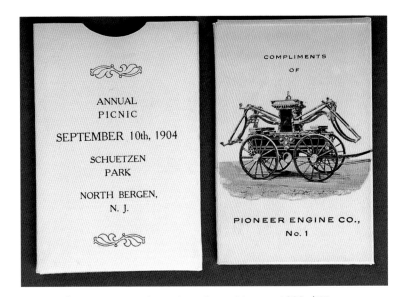

Tin ledger marker, c. 1860. $500.

Firemen's picnic souvenir, pocket mirror with case, 1902. $75.

Door knob, firematic theme, c. 1900. $125.

Lobby card, Charlie Chaplin, c. 1910. $500.

Movie theater lobby screen (front view), *The 3rd Alarm*, c. 1920. $1,500.

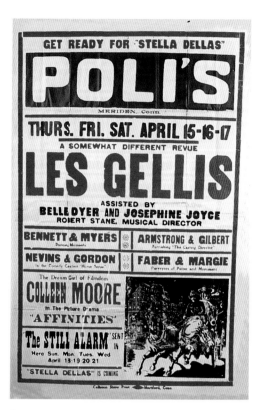

Broadside advertising *The Still Alarm*, c. 1910. $375.

Lobby screen (end view).

One sheet movie poster with Ralph Bellamy, *Wild Brian Kent*, 1936 $250.

Suicide Squad, one sheet movie poster, 1936. $275.

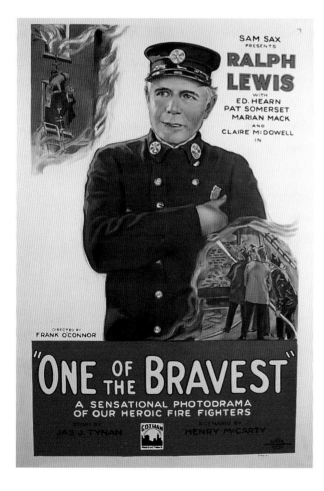

The False Alarm, one sheet movie poster. $750.

One of the Bravest, one sheet movie poster, c. 1930. $750.

Flames lobby card, 1932. $110.

Night Alarm, dramatic one sheet poster with very effective composition, 1934 $800.

She Loved a Fireman lobby card, 1937. $75.

The Towering Inferno, one sheet movie poster, 1974. $50.

The Fire Trap lobby card. $60.

Hoot Gibson lobby card, *Hook and Ladder*. $50.

Heroes of the Night lobby card. $100.

The False Alarm lobby card. $75.

My Dog, Buddy lobby card. $15.

Fireman Save My Child, Joe E. Brown, window card, 1932. $175.

Arson for Hire lobby card. $50.

Advertising paperweights. $100-$250 each.

Metal paperweight. $100.

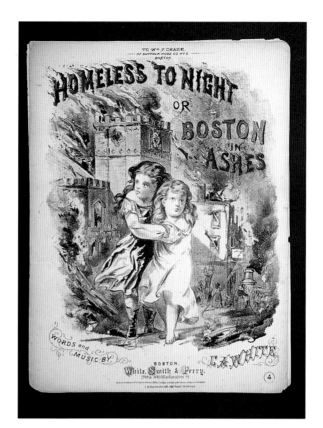

"Homeless Tonight" sheet music. $75.

Glass advertising paperweights. $100-$125 each.

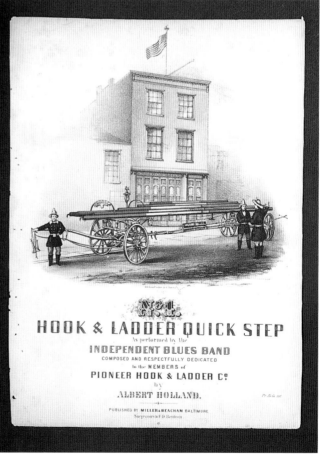

"Hook & Ladder Quick Step" sheet music. $175.

"False Alarm" sheet music. $60.

"My Ragtime Fireman" sheet music. $50.

"It's a Waste of Time to Worry" sheet music. $50.

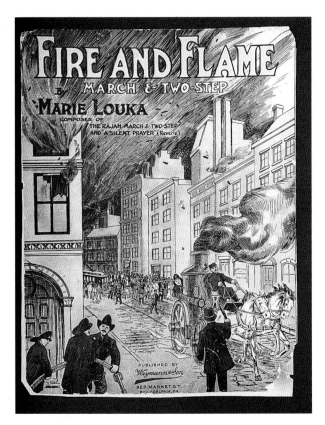

"Fire and Flame" sheet music. $60.

"Emergency" sheet music. $35.

"The Midnight Fire Alarm" sheet music and player piano roll.
Music $15; roll $45.

Photographic postcard. $22.

Postcard, Intaglio steamer. $15.

Postcard, painted fire scene. $8.

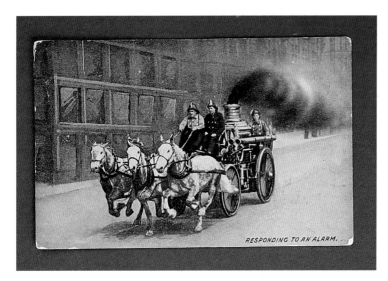

Steamer postcard, photo of "rig" with a running trio of horses. $12.

Advertising postcard, artist's rendering, "Rig" with running horses. $25.

Fireman's Fund match safe, advertising giveaway, c. 1905. $395.

Sterling silver match safe, Home Insurance Company, c. 1910. $475.

Match safes, advertising giveaways, c. 1900. Left: $400; Right: $300.

Sterling silver match safe, Fireman's Fund Insurance Co. $400.

Match safe, c. 1910. Front has a Maltese cross and reads "Baker Fabric Fire Hose." $50.

Sterling silver match safe, Home Insurance Company. $500.

51

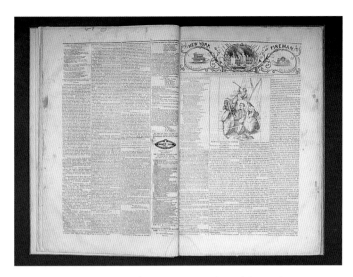

New York Fireman Weekly newspaper, 1841. $75 each.

The New Sensation magazine, 1874. $125.

Connecticut Courant newspaper, c. 1810. $50

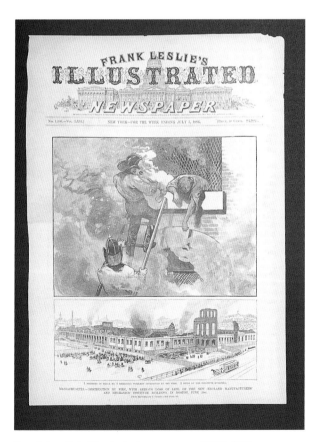

Frank Leslie's Illustrated newspaper, 1886. $50.

The Record, by Fred Miller,
1879. $50.

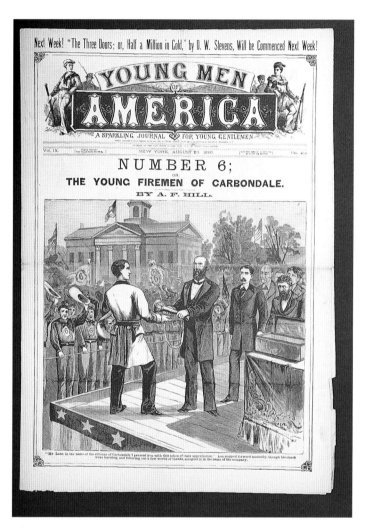

Young Men of America, 1886. $75.

Utica Saturday Globe newspaper,
1884. $50.

The World, Sunday Magazine, newspaper supplement, c. 1898. $85.

Western Mutual Fire Insurance paperweight. $225.

Metal sign, United Fireman's Insurance Co. of Philadelphia. $350.

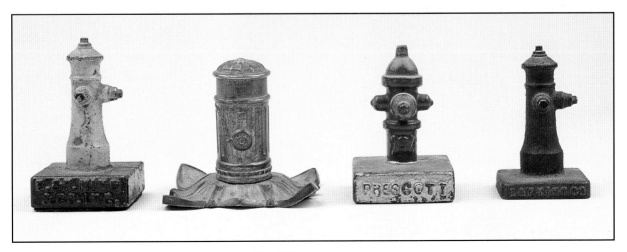

Fire hydrant advertising paperweights, assorted. $75-$150 each.

Pyrene flange sign. $350.

Tub tobacco package. $50; metal flange sign. $450.

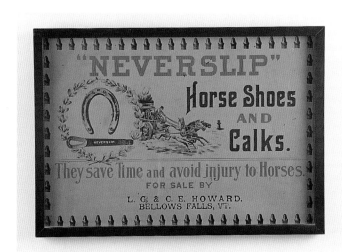

Neverslip Horse Shoes tin sign, c. 1910. $450.

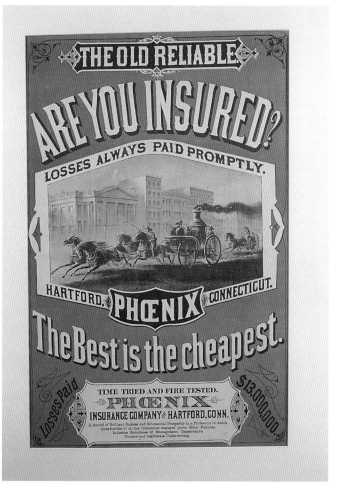

"Are you Insured?" lithograph insurance poster, c. 1890. $1,800.

Fairfax cigar poster, lithograph Fire Laddie, c. 1890. $750.

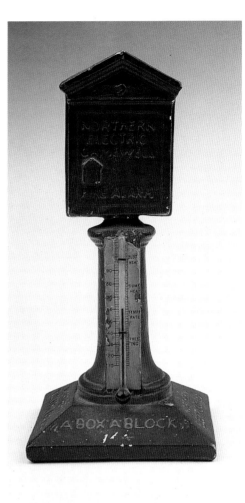

Right: Promotional thermometer, Northern Electric, Gamewell Fire Alarm Company, c. 1900. $750.

Copenhagen Tobacco cardboard subway advertising sign. $125.

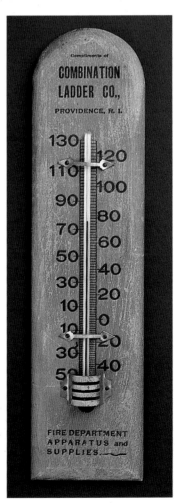

Combination Ladder Company promotional thermometer. $100.

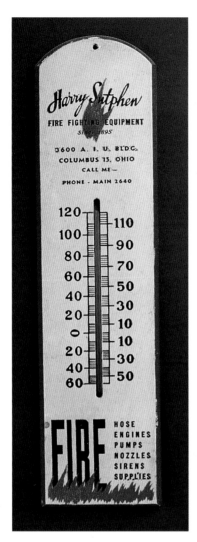

Harry Sutphen Firefighting
Equipment advertising thermometer. $225.

S. F. Hayward advertising thermometer, c. 1900. $250.

General Fire Truck Corporation advertising thermometer,
c. 1930. $125.

Advertising trade card, Automatic Signal Telegraph Company,
c. 1880. $175.

Advertising trade card, German American Insurance Company,
c. 1890. $50.

Comic figure advertising trade card. $45.

Cloth dinner napkin with roster. $100.

Advertising beer tray, c. 1900. $750.

Brass advertising ash tray. $35.

3-D cardboard Easter candy container. $200.

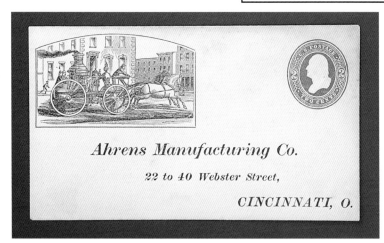

Envelope with fire engine logo design. $45.

Decorative plaster plaque of fire engine. $475.

Fireman motif motion lamp. $300.

Chapter Five
Extinguishers

Soda acid fire extinguishers have been used in factories, schools, and commercial buildings since the late 1800s. In recent years, changes in fire codes have resulted in their replacement with more efficient extinguishers.

In the first half of the twentieth century, the pump-type carbon tetrachloride fire extinguisher was popular. Made of brass, these extinguishers were sold in large quantities for use in homes and automobiles. In recent years, however, carbon tetrachloride has proven to be a health hazard and an environmentally sensitive public has forced its removal from the market.

Grenades

In its catalog of the late 1800s, S.F. Hayward and Company describes its glass grenade fire extinguishers as "glass globes of about four inches in diameter, filled with a chemical fluid which generates enormous volumes of extinguishing gas when brought into contact with fire. As the bottle is hermetically sealed and the fluid itself is not susceptible to the influence of the atmosphere, no fermentation or evaporation can take place. It is in fact a cheap, simple and durable fire extinguisher that will not freeze, and can be used by man, woman, or child."

Sizes ranged from half-pint to two quart, the most common sizes being pints and quarts. The contents contained such simple chemicals as saltwater, bicarbonate of soda, and muriate of ammonia. The addition of salt allowed the grenade to be advertised as nonfreezing. Corks were cemented in to prevent evaporation. The grenade came into existence around 1868 and lost its appeal about 1903.

Unique hand-blown fire grenade, incised with the word "Fire." $750.

Harden Star hand grenade, descriptive brochure, c. 1890. $150.

Selection of blue glass hand grenades. Range $150-$500.

Basket of two Hayward pleated, clear (large size) grenades, c. 1890. $450 for both with basket.

Trio of Hayward glass grenades, green, clear, and blue. $1,000 for all three with basket.

1878 patent model of a fire extinguisher. $550.

Chemical and dry fire extinguishers. Left: $75; Right: $125.

Advertising ash trays for Pyrene extinguishers, c. 1930. $50 each.

Three tin tube fire extinguishers, c. 1910.
Left to right: $125; $85; $75.

Tip tray with fire extinguisher advertising. $85.

Left: glass insulator from fire alarm telegraph line. $125. Right: large size acid bottle for fire apparatus. $125.

Assortment early liquid extinguishers. Left to right: refill can for Exo extinguishers, $75; Harden Star extinguisher glass grenade, $135; tin, dry chemical extinguisher, $50.

Chapter Six
Fine Art and Folk Art

Firematic objects of fine art quality are of course desirable. We must ask ourselves, then, what would define fine art quality? It would be appropriate to say that, in general, fine art objects are objects that reveal a combination of talent and an educated hand. Sophistication of design or composition and a concern for such art elements as drawing, dark and light, color, and texture might be evident. Simply put, the fine art object is produced by the trained hand, in the presence of considerable time and sometimes for its own sake alone. It may be expressed in such forms as oil or watercolor painting, sculpture, or print making. A fine art collection might include portraits, illustration art pieces, fire scenes, firefighter sculptures, and fire scene prints.

Folk art has its own special appeal. Objects of this quality are often seen as beautiful and worthy of acclaim though produced by an untrained person. They are sometimes the fortuitous byproduct of a decorated utilitarian object or are the object itself. In other words, folk art objects are made by the untrained or self-trained person, may be useful objects, sometimes decorated and sometimes not, or are objects that are made to be art themselves. Quaint, charming, primitive, and naive are other descriptive words sometimes used to define folk art. Engine house signs, decorated fire buckets, silhouettes, and scrimshaw are some firematic pieces that are illustrative of folk art.

Buckets

During the mid 1600s, the effort to fight fires with gourds, tubs, and pails proved to be quite futile. The Executive Council of the City of New York felt that leather buckets would be sturdier and would hold more water than anything used up to that date. They called together seven shoemakers on August 1, 1658, and negotiated with them to make fire buckets with a capacity of three gallons each.

In 1686, a law was passed in New York City that required "every person having two chimneys to his house provide one bucket." Buckets occupied a place near the front door where they could easily be thrown into the street upon the cry of "Fire!" Firemen and civilians on their way to the fire would pick up the buckets and carry them to the fire. Once at the fire, bucket brigades were formed and these men threw the water directly on the fire. Later, as hand engines were purchased, buckets were used to fill the reservoirs of the engines. Until the early

1800s buckets were the only means of supplying water to the engines. With the advent of suction-type engines, water could be forced up from cisterns or wells and then buckets were seldom used.

Because of early problems with buckets being lost or stolen, a watchman usually collected the buckets after the fire was out and took them to a central location for retrieval by their owners. Owners were required to have their names on their buckets. This led to the practice of decorating buckets for easy identification, which then led to competitions in decorating them. Many of these fire buckets were beautifully painted with the owner's name and were frequently decorated with colorful paintings of fires and/or mythological scenes. Today, leather buckets are considered examples of folk art and are prized artifacts from Colonial America.

The practice of having private homes provide buckets ultimately did not function very well and many communities began to provide their engine houses with buckets. Every company was provided with two poles long enough to hold twelve buckets each. These poles and buckets were carried on the shoulders of the firemen. The general rule was that the first fireman to reach the engine house after the alarm of fire would have the right to the pipe (nozzle) and would take it with him to the fire; the next four firemen to arrive would bear the bucket pole; and the rest of the company would run off with the engine as best they might, bawling out, *"FIRE!"* and demanding the aid of citizens as they went.

In 1801, New York City had sixteen hundred buckets made, which were to be carried in special bucket wagons. They were distributed to fifteen headquarters. Two men were appointed to draw each wagon of one hundred buckets. The use of these carts continued only a short time.

Calligraphy

Calligraphy is fine or elegant writing or penmanship. When a person had been an active member of a fire company for a certain number of years, it was the custom of certain departments to issue a proclamation or tribute. Many of these were done in calligraphy; some contained a photograph of the person as well as drawings of fire scenes, firemen, and/or landmarks. Other companies gave visiting companies tokens of respect and thanks with fine calligraphy.

Fire Engine Panels

Fire engine panels added a touch of elegance to the fire engine. As early as 1796, Engine Company 15 had a wreath of roses painted on the back and side panels of its engine. In the 1800s, it was not uncommon for engines to be ordered in a primer coat of dull gray. This engine would then be painted according to the particular taste and budget of the engine company.

The panels were usually painted on mahogany with an appropriate symbol or scene, and fitted into the engine. After a parade or special event, they could be removed for safekeeping. Only the ablest painters were employed to exercise their talents on the "machine," and they were paid a handsome fee for their work. Among the nineteenth-century artists who dignified the panels of fire engines and hose carts with their work were H. Inman, J. Quigg, John Woodside, and Thomas Sully.

Fire Marks

Fire marks were metal plates or signs affixed to building structures, indicating that the building was covered by fire insurance. Each insurance company provided its policy holders with a distinctive mark that was displayed on the dwelling.

The fire mark was introduced in the United States by the country's first insurance company in 1752. "The Philadelphia Contributionship For Houses From Loss By Fire" was organized on April 13, 1752. Use of fire marks quickly spread as additional insurance companies were formed. Several reasons were advanced for the use of fire marks. First, the fire mark was used on insured buildings to indicate to volunteer firemen and to advertise to the citizens that a certain company carried the insurance. Second, there was a generally accepted theory that arsonists would not molest insured property. Third, there were incentives on the part of volunteers to receive a reward for successfully extinguishing a fire. The first company to get a stream of water on the fire was entitled to compensation from the insurance company. With the inauguration of paid fire departments, the fire mark lost its usefulness, although insurance companies still issue fire marks as promotional items.

Models

Models of fire apparatus have always been an integral part of fire history. When the first piece of apparatus was purchased by a fire company, a fireman talented in model making would begin work on the model. This practice continues to the present day. Most of these models have intricate detail and take many months to build. They reveal the deep pride each fire company has in its apparatus.

Promotional models, salesmen's samples, and patent models actually worked. These are some of the hardest models to obtain. Since the 1940s, model companies have produced inexpensive plastic model kits. These continue to be very popular, but will be most collectible if left in their original unbuilt condition.

The "Scratch built" and the "cross-kit" procedures are two new areas in model building. These are models made from plastic kits and modified to produce a particular piece of apparatus. Some craftsmen will "build to order" for a particular type of apparatus. The detail and work that goes into these models is fantastic and they will greatly appreciate in value.

Paintings

In a time before photography, men were anxious to preserve their likenesses while dressed in the honorable regalia of their fire company. Thus, we find portraits of fire chiefs and wealthy firefighters preserved for our viewing today. So, too, are we able to find paintings of exciting events of the past and great fires that stimulated the imagination of artists.

Parade Hats

Confusion at early fire scenes led to the need for some way of identifying firemen from different companies: a Philadelphia fireman of the 1800s recommended round hats with the name of the fireman and his company painted in bold letters. Most of these "stovepipes" or "parade hats" were made of pressed felt, but a few were believed to be made of leather, and at least one member of Hope Hose Company of Philadelphia used canvas.

The Charter and Bylaws of 1838 for the United States Fire Company of Philadelphia stated that their hats should be six and one-half inches high with a brim three and one-half inches wide. In 1839, the constitution of the Philadelphia Hose Company specified that their hat be six inches high and the brim three and one-quarter inches wide. By 1849, the hat was still six inches high, but the brim was three inches wide. Many of these hats were decorated with patriotic symbols, mythological figures, or famous people, and painted in bright colors with artistic lettering and glazed with varnish.

Presentation Shields

In the 1800s, it was common for one fire company to visit another on the occasion of a parade or anniversary. Gifts were often exchanged, and today these gifts are valuable collectibles.

Ornate leather presentation shields in the shape of helmet fronts were often the gifts of choice. Such shields would be framed and hung in the firehouse. They varied from eight inches to more than three feet in height. Shields were also presented to fire companies by helmet manufacturers, as tokens of respect to good customers. Scenes, portraits of patriots, landmarks, and apparatus were hand painted in oil while the lettering was carved out of leather. Decorative stitching added to the beauty of the shield.

Scrimshaw

On long whaling voyages, early seamen kept themselves busy during their free time by carving whales' teeth. The tooth was cut from the gums of the lower jaw, dried, soaked in brine, then filed and smoothed with a piece of sharkskin or other abrasive. Following that, the tooth was polished and then engraved with a design. Ink or another coloring agent was rubbed into the incised lines to bring out the art work. Very few pieces of scrimshaw are known to have depicted firefighting activities.

Shaving Mugs

In 1830, barber shops introduced plain shaving mugs. Between 1860-1870, the occupational-type mug was introduced. It became a mark of prestige to have your mug decorated with a painting of something associated with your occupation and to have your name printed on the mug in gold letters.

By 1870, every barber shop had a rack of mugs for its steady customers. Barber supply houses made mugs in a variety of styles, with designs available for virtually all occupations. For an additional fee, your mug would have a customized design or piece of apparatus. In the 1880s, porcelain shaving mugs were imported from Europe and decorated in this country. Among the decorations were steamers, hose carts, hooks and ladders, and so on.

Signs

Signs have become highly prized memorabilia, not only by collectors of firematic items, but also by collectors of folk art. The major drawback with signs is their size: many station house signs are ten to fifteen feet in length and require an enormous display area.

Most firehouses had signs in front of them. As companies moved to modern facilities, most of these signs were destroyed, making them difficult to find. Other collectible signs include office location signs and traffic signs.

Statues

Statues of firemen have always been in great demand. The Staffordshire Company produced a four and a half, a five and a half, and a nine and a half inch statue of a fireman. Wooden statues of firemen have been made as large as twelve feet high. One is located at a firehouse in Butler, New Jersey. C. G. Braxmar, a famous badge manufacturer, made a seventeen inch high statue representing the American fireman. It depicts a fireman with a spanner wrench in one hand and a coat in the other. The statue was produced in pot metal and was available in three finishes: bronze, silver, and gold. Many other examples of firemen statues exist but they are seldom offered for sale and are very expensive.

Hand cut, stained glass door panel, c. 1880, 16" x 36". $5,000.

Paper cut silhouette water color enhancement, early fireman figure by Auguste Edovart, 7-1/2" x 9". $3,500.

Charcoal drawing of fire scene, 1859, 13-1/2" x 17". $750.

Fine oil painting of fireman by F. Stucker, 1858, 15" x 11-1/2". $12,000.

Fine oil portrait of John Damrell, Chief, Boston Fire Department, c. 1870, 9-1/2" x 16". $8,000.

Inlaid wooden plaque depicting a hose cart, fireplug, and pump, c. 1890, 16" x 28". $750.

Early oil painting, New York harbor fire, c. 1890, 6-1/2" x 11-1/2". $1,800.

Hand pumper engine panel, oil painting on wood, classical subject, rare, c. 1840, 16-1/2" x. 31-1/2". $10,000.

Fire bucket with oil painting portrait of R. F. Denver, 1912. $5,000.

R. F. Denver fire bucket, rear view.

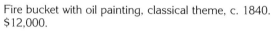

Fire bucket with oil painting, classical theme, c. 1840. $12,000.

Fire bucket, "A. Jenkins," No. 1, c. 1830. $450.

Fire bucket, "Tiger," No. 7 Boston, c. 1850. $4,500.

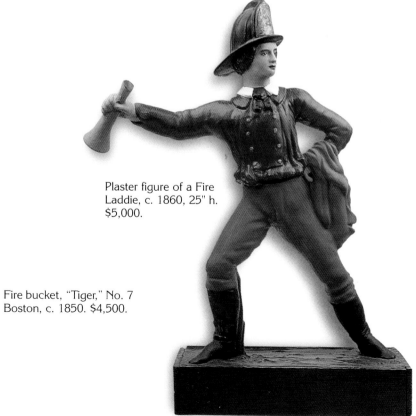

Plaster figure of a Fire Laddie, c. 1860, 25" h. $5,000.

Graduated sizes of Staffordshire figures, c.1850. Left to right: 9",
$900; 5-1/2", $700; 4-1/2", $500.

Fireman, Staffordshire, cigar/match holder, c. 1870, 4-1/2" h.
$2,000.

Metal figure of fireman, early apparatus
ornament, c. 1850. $3,500.

Matching firemen figures, one gilt, one bronze, Braxmar and
Company, c. 1890. $1,500 each.

Brass ornamental fireman figure, 3" h. $350.

Bronze sculpture, pointing fireman, Roman Bronze Works, New York, 16" h. $5,000.

Fine bronze with gilt patina sculptural group, ornamental, desk top size, Roman Bronze Works, New York, c. 1910, 12" x 12". $3,500.

Gaslight figure of fireman, 10" h. $1,500.

Porcelain fireman shaving mugs. $1,000-$1,500 each.

Porcelain mustache cup, c. 1890, front and reverse. $1,000.

 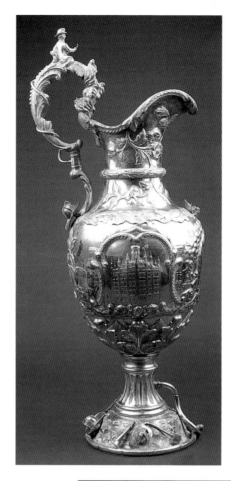

Spectacular silver-plated ewer, heavily ornamented with 3-D figures of a fireman, axes, hoses, etc. and featuring repoussé work of fire scenes on body, 1853, 21-1/2" h. Rare and unique. Presentation: TO MILES GREENWOOD, CHIEF ENGINEER CINCINNATI FIRE DEPARTMENT FROM HIS FELLOW CITIZENS. $15,000.

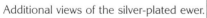

Additional views of the silver-plated ewer.

Hooked rug depicting hose cart, 1880. $1,000.

Zephyr 1875 hook and ladder certificate, completely hand lettered, 22" x 27". $500.

Fine albumen photographic portrait of Chief of Newburgh, New York Fire Department, surrounded by hand-carved, folk art frame, c, 1860, 19" x 22-1/2". $950.

Lady Washington certificate featuring photograph and fine, hand done calligraphy, 34" x 27". $1,500.

Alert Hose Company, No. 1, calligraphy certificate, 1875,
17" x 20". $500.

Dynamic fire scene oil painting, signed John Roderick, dated
1941, 21" x 26". $2,000.

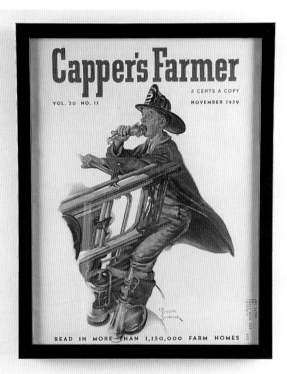

Magazine cover featuring the Sambrook oil painting. $15.

Fine commercial art oil painting, signed by Russell
Sambrook, 1939, 25" x 33-1/2". $9,000.

Wonderful black and white gouache magazine illustration, fire scene, signed by listed artist, P. E. Yohn, dated 1920, 15" x 20". $3,500.

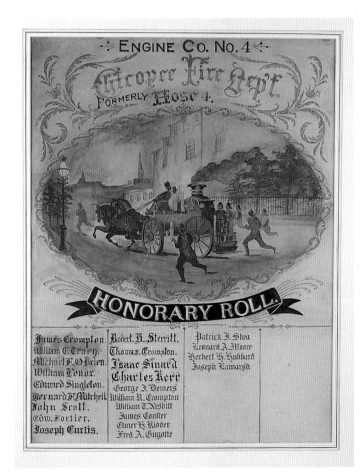

Fine folk art, hand-lettered and painted "Honorary Roll" with water color fire scene, c. 1880, 22" x 29. $3,500.

Oil portrait of fireman, signed John Stites, dated 1890, 15" x 19-1/2". $1,800.

Illustration art, water color sketch and sample of firemen's ball dance card, c. 1890. $1,500.

Water color sketch and sample of firemen's ball dance card, c. 1890. $1,500.

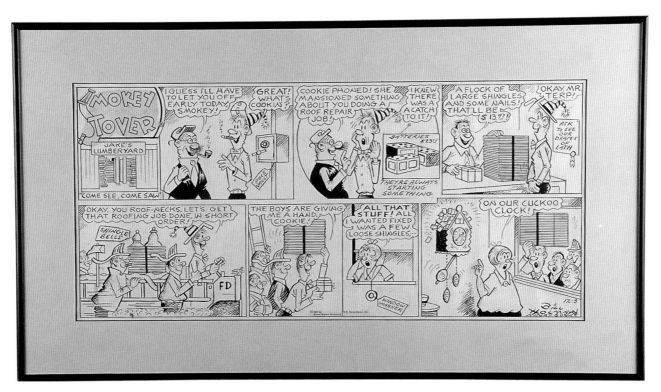

Cartoon art, "Smokey Stover," original strip, c. 1960. $800.

Cartoon art, "Steamer Kelly," original strip, c. 1940. $750.

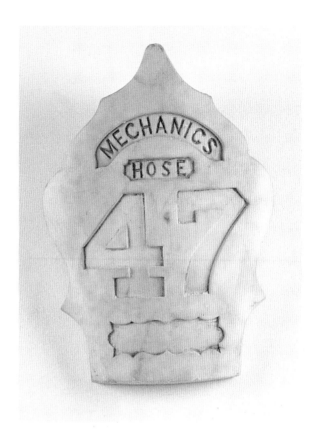

Marble carving depicting helmet front, New York City, c. 1850, 9" h. $2,500.

Folk drawing with water color and colored pencil, Civil War era, Philadelphia, Pennsylvania, 7" x 12-1/2". $750.

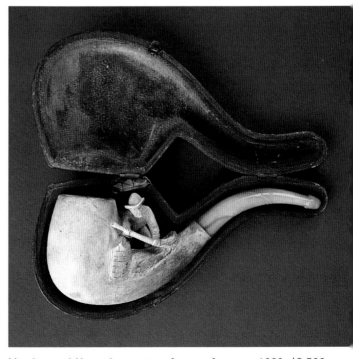

Hand-carved Meerschaum pipe, fireman figure, c. 1880. $2,500.

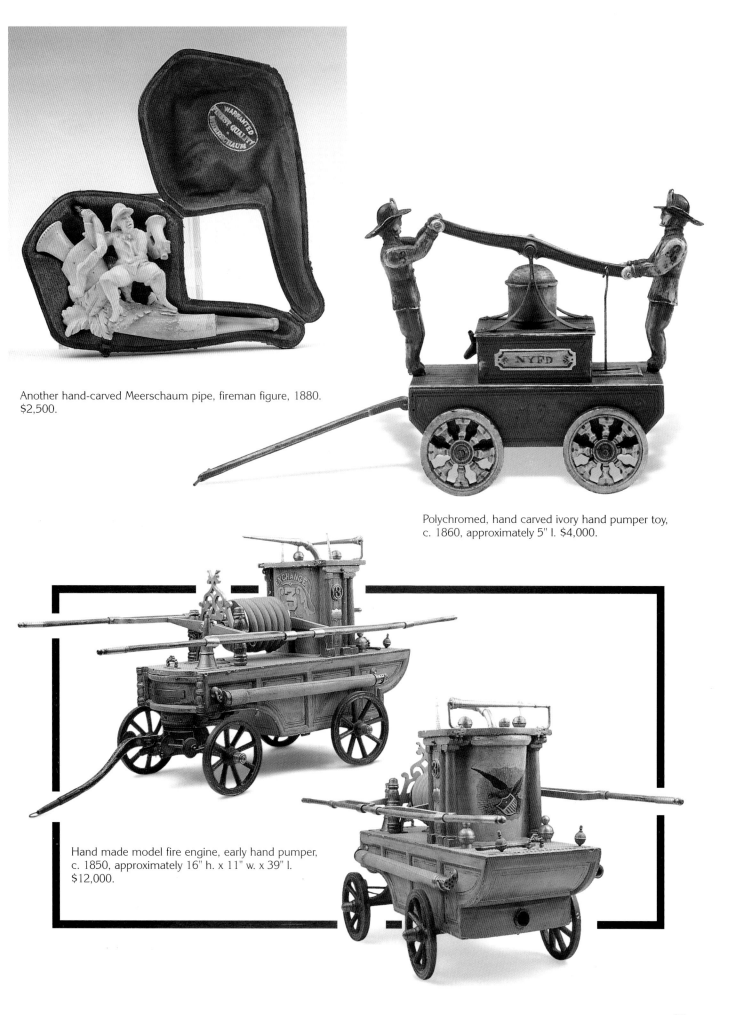

Another hand-carved Meerschaum pipe, fireman figure, 1880. $2,500.

Polychromed, hand carved ivory hand pumper toy, c. 1860, approximately 5" l. $4,000.

Hand made model fire engine, early hand pumper, c. 1850, approximately 16" h. x 11" w. x 39" l. $12,000.

Hand made model fire engine, early goose neck hand pumper, c. 1920, approximately 7-1/2" x 18". $1,200.

Hand made fire engine model showing engine panel paintings, c. 1920, approximately 7-1/2" x 20". $1,200.

Hand made pumper fire engine model, goose-neck style, c. 1870, approximately 9" x 22". $2,500.

Patent model water tower, c. 1870,
approximately 23" x 25-1/2". $4,500 .

Wooden model of an antique, man carried and pumped fire
engine, approximately 9" x 8-1/2". $375.

Hand pumper fire engine model, c. 1950, 4" x 8". $150.

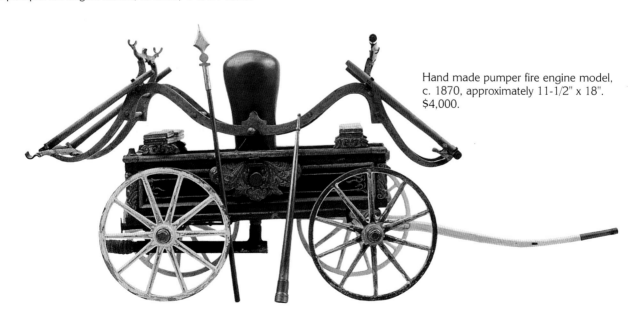

Hand made pumper fire engine model,
c. 1870, approximately 11-1/2" x 18".
$4,000.

Presentation fire helmet shield, outsized, hand made and hand painted, c. 1860, approximately 14" h. $1,900.

Presentation fire helmet shield, hand made and hand painted, c. 1860, approximately 12" h. $2,000.

Presentation fire helmet shield, hand made and hand painted, c. 1860, approximately 22" h. $7,500.

Fire Association of Philadelphia cast iron firemark. $175.

Cast iron fire mark. $250.

Franklin Insurance Co. of St. Louis fire mark. $250.

Cast zinc (green tree) fire mark on replacement board. $500.

Tin fire marks. $75-$150 each.

Carved whale's tooth scrimshaw, two samples.
Left: c. 1870, $2,500; Right: c. 1850, $5,000.

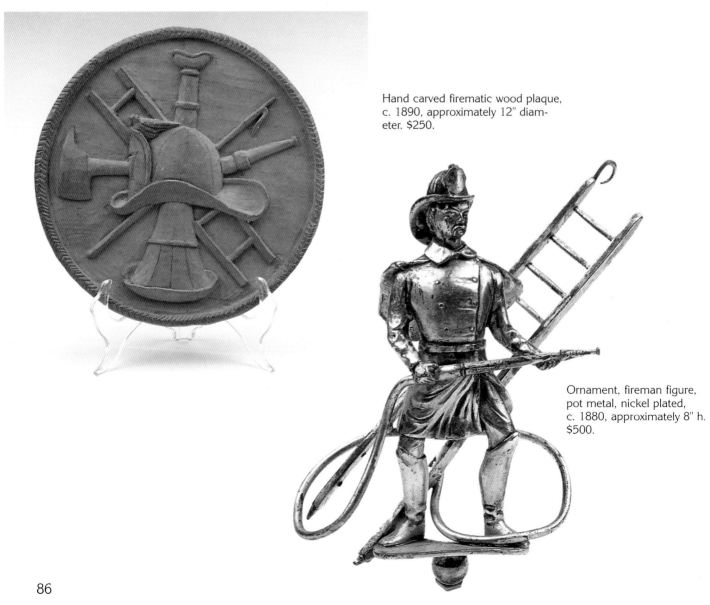

Hand carved firematic wood plaque,
c. 1890, approximately 12" diameter. $250.

Ornament, fireman figure,
pot metal, nickel plated,
c. 1880, approximately 8" h.
$500.

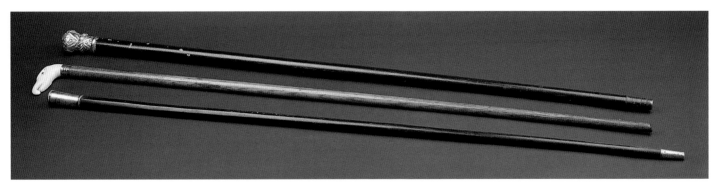

Walking canes with firematic presentations. Top: c. 1880, $750; Middle: ivory eagle's head, c. 1860, Philadelphia, $2,500; Bottom: sterling silver, New York City (Metropolitan Fire Dept.), 1868, $1,800.

Large wooden dedication shield for a fireboat, dated 1913, approximately 24" h. $1,000.

Firehouse roster, metal, c. 1890, approximately 18" h. $750.

Magnificent oil portrait, fine quality, c. 1840, approximately 29-1/2" x. 25". $25,000

Chapter Seven
Helmets

Jacobus Turck of New York City is credited with inventing the first fire cap in approximately 1740. It was round with a high crown and narrow rim and was made of leather. Improvements on this design were made by Matthew DuBois, who sewed iron wire into the edge of the brim to give the helmet shape and provide resistance to heat, moisture, and warping. Other early helmet makers were John and his son William Wilson, William Baudoin, George Henry Ramppen, and Robert Roberts. The most famous helmet maker was Henry Gratacap, who opened his shop in 1836. Most of the helmets used during the next thirty-two years were manufactured by him. Gratacap is noted for raised and stitched front pieces and the eagle shield holder, which was originally leather and later was changed to brass.

The "eight comb" regulation fire hat (a hat design composed of eight segments) was originally adopted by the New York City Fire Department. The following are significant comments found in early catalogs: "The facility with which its stiff, hard leather surface resists the direct force of falling bricks and slate, and its cape-like brim carried off water, prevented the latter from running down the neck of the wearer." In his 1890 catalog, John Olsen described his helmet as "made for firemen in large cities where strength and durability are required. The crown is full, allowing the hat to fit comfortably on the head, and is re-enforced with a 2 inch brass band firmly riveted, which keeps the hat in shape and prevents it from shrinking. A ring is provided on the back of the brim to hang the hat from the apparatus. An ear/neck protector was added to keep firemen warm in winter and folded on the inside when not in use."

Helmets were made with the following numbers of combs: 8, 12, 16, 24, 32, 40, 48, 56, 64, 72, 80, 88, 96, 104, 120, 136, 148, and 164; as the number of combs increased, so did the cost. A wide variety of shield holders was available, including a fireman, a serpent, a fox, a beaver, a seahorse, a greyhound, a lion, and the extremely rare rooster. Special lightweight helmets were also available for parade use.

Aluminum helmets were introduced in the last quarter of the nineteenth century but only a small number were made due to the high cost of the metal.

Upon a firefighter's retirement or promotion, presentation helmets were sometimes the order of the day. These helmets were "special order" with embossed firematic scrollwork on the back of the brim and a brass or silver plaque commemorating the event. Today they are some of the most sought-after helmets.

The color of the helmet identifies rank and apparatus assignment. Chief Engineers normally wore helmets painted white. Fire Wardens wore helmets with black brims and white crowns. In many cities, Hook & Ladder companies wore red helmets and members of engine companies wore helmets painted black. Helmets made strictly for parade use varied in color.

It was a tradition in some departments to paint a date on the rear brim of a fire helmet. It should be noted that this date represents the organization date of the company, not the date the helmet was manufactured.

During the 1930s, Cairns and Brother introduced a new "low front helmet." The eagle shield holder was removed and the result was a saving of two inches in height.

Modern helmets are often made of materials other than leather. However, many fire departments still insist on leather fire helmets. Helmets made of material other than leather are becoming collectible due to their reasonable prices.

Front Pieces

The use of helmet fronts for company identification possibly originated with the military and was adapted to fire service during the Revolutionary War. The first fronts used on fire caps were made of a single thickness of heavy sole leather, with the number of the fire company painted on the smooth side.

In the 1830s, Henry T. Gratacap introduced the first stitched front. Chief Engineers often had their helmet fronts illuminated with gilding and paintings of their best fire engines. Foremen and Assistant Foremen wore fronts painted white with black letters; regular firemen wore black fronts with white lettering. Hook & Ladder company members had fronts with painted or cut-out hook and ladder symbols and were often painted red. Hose companies had black helmet fronts depicting a coiled hose.

Metal fronts were quite popular for parade use. They made a very grand appearance, and added greatly to the "attractiveness of the uniform," as described by an old Olsen catalogue. Metal fronts are in great demand today and are more difficult to obtain than leather fronts.

During the 1930s, helmet fronts changed in size from eight inches to six inches due to a new style of helmet that did not have an eagle holder. Six-inch fronts retained the same color coding as earlier fronts: chief officers wore white, truck companies red, and engine companies black. Hand-painted fronts were still available for chief officers and are eagerly collected.

Early parade hat, hand painted, Philadelphia, c. 1850. $6,000.

All leather helmet with hand painted front, c. 1850. $1,500.

All leather fire helmet, painted, with unique molded dog front piece, c. 1840. $5,000.

All leather helmet with leather eagle front holder, c. 1850. $1,000.

Close-up of helmet, "Hero No. 6" rear brim.

Gratacap helmet with leather eagle, c. 1850. $1,250. Shown with two salesmen sample helmets, c. 1880. $875 each.

Hand painted parade hat, Good Intent Fire Company, Philadelphia, c. 1850. $4,000.

Leather helmet featuring gold leaf front depicting hose cart (former Andy Warhol collection piece), c. 1890. $5,000.

Close-up of rear brim showing brass insert with presentation.

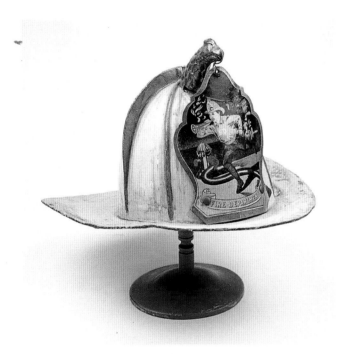

Cardboard children's helmet by Shohut, c. 1910. $450.

White leather helmet, Chief, Jamaica, N.Y. Fire Department, c. 1890. $1,500.

White, extremely rare, leather helmet featuring rooster helmet front holder, c. 1870. $3,800.

Close-up of rear brim, featuring brass insert with presentation.

White leather "District Chief" helmet, Newtown, N.Y. Fire Department, c. 1900. $650.

Black leather helmet featuring serpent front holder, c. 1890. $1,200.

Jockey style parade helmet with fireman holder, c. 1900. $1,200.

Red leather helmet, featuring "Fire Patrol" front, c. 1910. $700.

Close-up of rear, showing presentation.

Jockey style helmet, Brookline, Massachusetts, c. 1890. $750.

Hook 'n ladder, nickel-plated, metal parade helmet with horse hair plume, c. 1900. $650.

White leather chief's helmet; hand painted and gilt front fireman figure shield holder, c. 1890. $1,250.

Unusual black ribbed Cairns helmet with metal shield, c. 1900. $500.

Parade hat, Diligent Fire Company, Philadelphia, c. 1850. $6,000.

Very rare, white leather helmet, hand painted and gilded front showing sea horse front holder, c. 1890. $3,800.

Yellow jockey-style helmet with South American style helmet holder and metal front, c. 1890. $750.

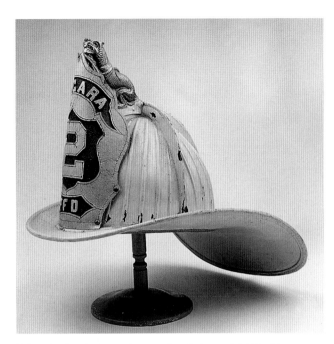

White leather helmet showing lion helmet shield holder, c. 1890. $950.

White jockey-style helmet with South American style helmet holder and metal front, c. 1890. $750.

Leather parade hat, c. 1890. $550.

White leather high eagle helmet with painted and gilded front, c. 1880. $2,500.

Parade hat, hand painted with polychrome portrait of Thomas Jefferson, Independence Fire Company, Philadelphia, Pennsylvania, c. 1850. $7,000.

Close-up of rear, showing presentation.

Black helmet, jockey style with eagle holder, c. 1880. $750.

White, soft cap-type parade hat, c. 1880. $500.

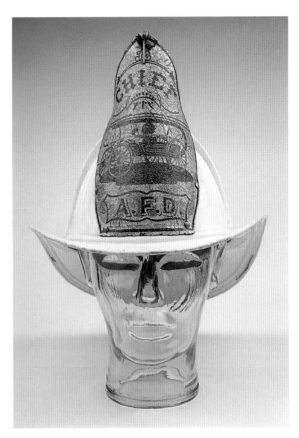

White high eagle aluminum helmet, showing hand painted and gilded front. $950.

White high eagle helmet with hand painted front, c. 1880. $1,800.

Chief engineer helmet, Jamaica Fire Department, c. 1880. $2,000.

Jockey-style helmet, South American holder, c. 1880. $950.

Parade hat, Goodwill, Philadelphia, Pennsylvania, c. 1850. $4,500.

Unusual, captain fire patrol, leather helmet with painting of patrol wagon, c. 1880. $2,500.

High eagle helmet, c. 1870. $750.

Parade helmet with rare Cairns parade torch, c. 1880. $2,200.

Jockey style helmet with rare greyhound holder, c. 1880. $1,250.

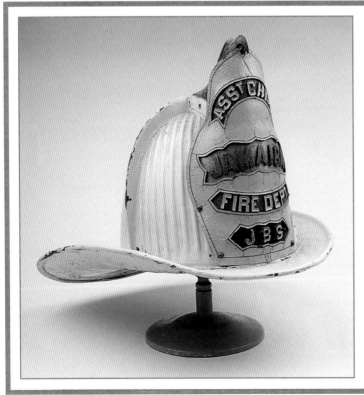

Close-up of insert.

Presentation leather helmet, c. 1900. $1,250.

Presentation helmet, New York, c. 1900. $1,200.

Three helmet shield holders: fox, $375; serpent, $450; eagle, $250.

Parade helmet, c. 1880. $750.

Three more helmet shield holders: beaver, $400; sea horse, $500; lion, $275.

Helmet shield from leather parade cap, c. 1890. $200.

"Northern Liberty" hose helmet shield featuring polychromed, hand-painted figure of liberty with flag and shield of U.S., c. 1860. $1,000.

White Cairns New Yorker style leather helmet with gilded and painted front, c. 1970. $300. Shown with Cairns miniature leather helmet, c. 1970. $175.

Three 8" metal helmet fronts. $350-$500 each.

Weccacoe Hose polychromed helmet front showing Indian figure, c. 1870. $1,000.

Shiffler Hose polychromed
helmet front, c. 1860. $1,000.

Ringgold Hose polychromed helmet front, c. 1860. $1,000.

Fire insurance patrol helmet shield,
New York City, c. 1870. $350.

Two hand painted, polychromed fronts.
Left: c. 1850, $850; Right: c. 1880, $375.

Jefferson 26 shield, New
York City, c. 1860. $450.

Two gold helmet shields. Left: c. 1880,
$500; Right: c. 1880, $650. Shown in
foreground is a black leather shield.
$250.

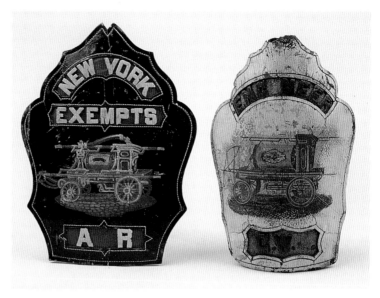

Two helmet fronts. Left: c. 1870, $500; Right: c. 1860, $850.

Chief, Bradford, Pennsylvania Fire Department helmet shield, c. 1880. $500.

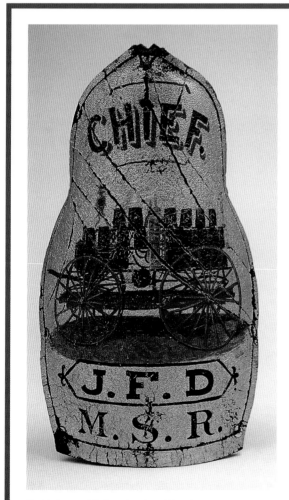

Gold front with hand painted bucket wagon, Jamaica, New York, c. 1870. $750.

Hand painted bucket from the same company, c. 1870. $750.

Three metal fronts, c. 1880.
$350-$500 each.

Molded leather helmet with hand made silver medallion. London, England, c. 1810. $3,000.

Hand painted front with hand pumper, c. 1870. $750.

Chapter Eight
Lighting Devices

Firemen spared no expense when outfitting their engines. An example of this was the brass or silverplate engine lamps found on the engines of the 1800s and of the early 1900s. The main lamps as advertised in an early catalog were "ornamental in design and heavy in weight." Lamps were screwed on to the apparatus and removed after a parade to avoid damage when the engine was fighting fires. Most apparatus also had side lamps, smaller in size and usually not as ornate.

The finials on the engine lamps were shaped— sometimes as a fireman, King Neptune, or, most commonly, an eagle. Main lamps usually featured a scene, apparatus, patriotic symbol, company name, and number on one piece of glass, while the other pieces had stock designs.

The kerosene lantern was a necessity in the days before the electric hand lamp. Lanterns were commonly carried on fire apparatus for utilitarian purposes, although some were ornamented in order to decorate the apparatus. These lanterns were engraved with the name and number of the fire company. The most highly prized are those with engraved globes.

Around the turn of the twentieth century a more prosaic lantern, the Dietz Fire King, was commonly used. These were supplied on motorized apparatus until the 1930s. The most prized of the Fire Kings are those with the apparatus manufacturer's name stamped on the top portion of the cage, and in the case of the Peter Pirsch Company, on top of the round water shield.

There are several varieties of Dietz fire lanterns: an early style with pull-off cage, the common model with swing-out cage; and two rare models, the Dietz Queen and the Fire Wizard, a short globe lantern resembling a barn lantern, manufactured briefly in 1917. Dietz Fire King lanterns were made in tin, brass, and nickel plate, the brass being the most desirable.

Dietz was not the only manufacturer of fire lanterns. Other famous manufacturers (examples of which may be hard to find) include Adams and Westlake, De Voursney, C. T. Ham, William Porter, and White Manufacturing Company. The Eclipse, considered to be the Cadillac of lanterns, was made in tin and brass and is difficult to find.

Another important type of lantern is the presentation lantern, which was given to officers in the department for various accomplishments. These had globes etched with the officer's name, rank, and company

Engine light from Amoskeag Steamer. $3,500.

name. A variation of the presentation lantern had the presentation etched on the metal part of the lantern and may or may not have had an engraved globe.

The globes used for lanterns are another major field of collecting associated with these items. Globes came in various colors, including clear, green, blue, ruby, bull's-eye clear and colors, and the rare half clear/half red and half clear/half blue.

In the days before street lights, torches were needed to light the way to night fires. As the firemen left their engine houses, these torches were lit and held high above their heads. The common torches were made of tin; the more expensive ones were made of brass. A small number of the early ceremonial parade torches were made of tin with mica panels and were finely painted. Others were very ornate, and were made of silver or pewter. These were primarily presentation pieces. Presentation torches had a variety of engravings, including figurative plaques, company names and numbers, or inscriptions. Today these examples are the most valuable.

Engine light, red and blue glass, Hose 7, with unusual finial. $1,500.

Engine light from a hose company, with replacement finial. $1,800.

Engine light, Bradford, Pennsylvania. $2,000.

Engine light, Jackson 4, Paterson, New Jersey, replacement finial, c. 1860. $4,500.

Side light from hook and ladder. $750.

Engine lights, side marker lamps. Left: "Passaic 2," $500; Right: "Neptune 7," $750.

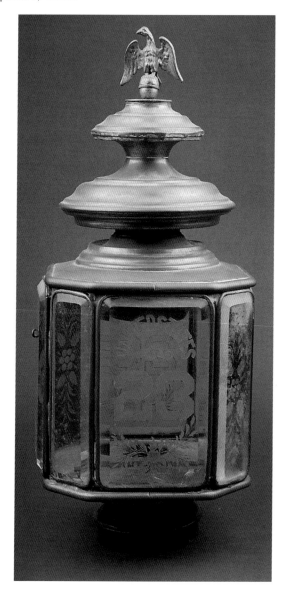

Side light from Metropolitan 39, New York City. $1,500.

Engine light, engraved "United States 23," New York City, c. 1860. $3,500.

Pair of side lights "Phoenix 3 Hose." Pair $1,800.

Lantern, engraved "Goodwill 3." $1,000.

Side light, engraved "Alert 41," New York City, replacement finial, c. 1860. $1,500.

Side light, engraved "Goodwill 1." $850.

Glass from engine light "Weccacoe 19," Philadelphia, c. 1860. $750.

Engine glass, "M. T. Brennan 60," New York City. $500.

Rare piece of engine glass from Lady Washington Engine Co., New York City, c. 1850. $1,800.

Engine light glass, Long Island City, New York, c. 1880. $375.

Liberty, clear engine light, glass
panel with deer, c. 1880. $300.

Gas street light, c. 1870.
$1,500.

Detail of engine light catalogue.

Catalogue from engine light manufacturer, c. 1880.
$300.

Engraved lantern globes. Left: $400; Right: two-tone, $1,000.

Whale oil lantern inscribed "David M. Lyle: Chief Engineer Philadelphia Fire Dept.," c. 1860. $5,000.

Wall lamp, Vigilant Fire Company, Philadelphia, Pennsylvania, c. 1879. $500.

Dietz King fire lanterns. Left: embossed "White" with aqua globe, $1,200; Right: embossed "Seagrave" with deep blue globe, $850.

Left: Dietz King lantern with amber globe, $300; Right: with slide off cage, embossed "Gleason and Bailey," $1,200.

Left: early fire lantern with slide off cage, $750; Right: Dietz King lantern with slide off cage, $375.

Left: Dietz King lantern with slide off cage, $750; Right: "Hams" lantern with split clear/red globe, $1,200.

Left: Dietz tubular lantern with slide off cage, $425; Right: Dietz Queen lantern, $1,100.

Early brass lantern, globe engraved "C 1" (chemical one). $900.

Pair of Eclipse lanterns with half red, half clear globes. Pair $3,000.

Dietz "Squatty" Fire Department lantern. $850.

Early fire lantern with red globe, engraved "A. Sayler Hook and Ladder #1 Second Assistant." $1,500.

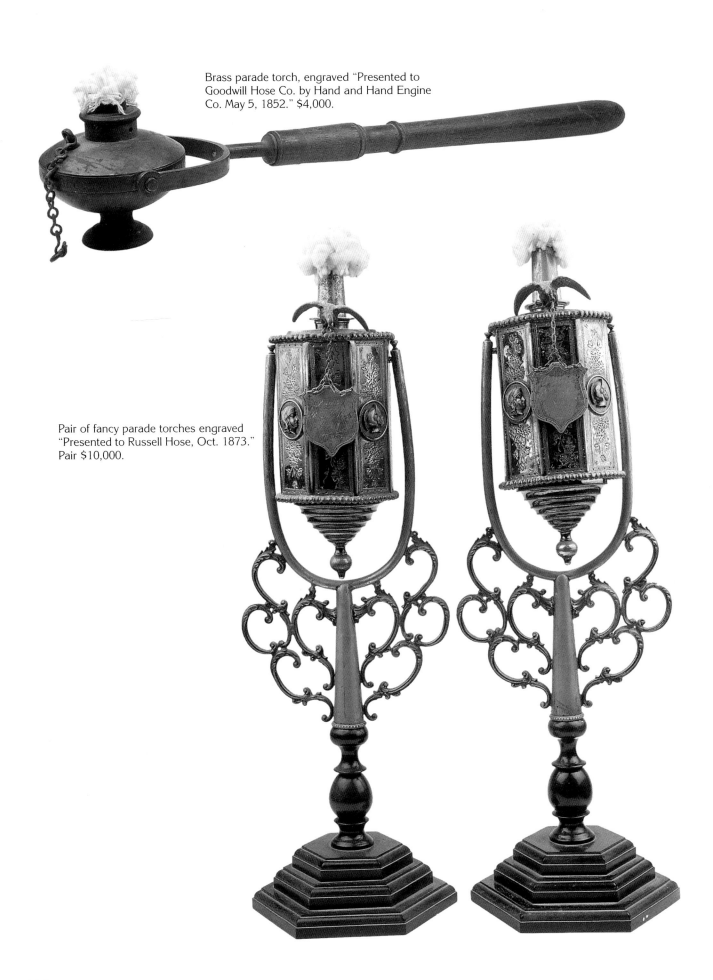

Brass parade torch, engraved "Presented to Goodwill Hose Co. by Hand and Hand Engine Co. May 5, 1852." $4,000.

Pair of fancy parade torches engraved "Presented to Russell Hose, Oct. 1873." Pair $10,000.

Chapter Nine
Miscellaneous Items

Candy Containers

In the early 1900s, candy manufacturers began to package their wares in plain, colored, and molded glass containers shaped as toys. Most containers had metal cap closures, but some were fitted with cardboard labels as sealers, which were pressed into the opening. The manufacturer's name and trademark were sometimes printed in the cap or closure, offering the only means of identification. Several containers depicting fire engines were produced.

Mugs

Mugs with firematic themes have been popular collectibles since the turn of the century. A good example of an early mug—one of the first produced—is the one made for the Montgomery Firemen's Association Convention in 1909. Since the early 1970s, mugs have seen a resurgence in popularity and are now available in many shapes and sizes, reflecting several firematic designs. Modern fire companies issue mugs for all major events. They seem to compete with each other for novelty of design and shape.

Molds

In the 1860s, an ingenious businessman developed candy molds in the shape of firemen and steam fire engines to attract youthful new customers. These molds were made of lead. They were large, heavy, and made of two sections that fitted together. As their exterior appearance was smooth, they gave no clue as to their contents' designs.

Around the turn of the century—during the height of the ice-cream-parlor era—molds were developed to shape ice cream. Children visiting an ice cream parlor could select the shape of their ice cream. Two ice cream molds with firematic themes were made: one depicted a fireman, the other, a steamer. Both were hinged molds made of pewter.

Patent Models

In 1836 the Patent Office was elevated to the status of a bureau in the State Department. Expert examiners were appointed to evaluate each application. Novelty, originality, and utility were factors they considered. The law required each applicant to "furnish a model of his invention . . . of a convenient size to exhibit advantageously its several parts."

The first of the Patent Office's four wings was completed in 1840. Within forty years, the building was totally filled with models. In 1880, requirements for submitting models were dropped. By this time, nearly 250,000 had been cataloged and stored. Later, because space was needed for other purposes, many of these models were sold to private collectors.

Plates

Over the years, several plates were produced related to fire fighting. There were early plates with paintings of fire apparatus, Staffordshire plates, and private issue plates illustrating firehouses, ruins, and a winning team of fire horses. Lenox produced a plate in sepia tone depicting a Currier and Ives fire scene. It is highly collectible as it was taken off the market due to copyright problems. In the 1960s, fire departments started issuing commemorative plates in large quantities for anniversaries. These are readily available and reasonably priced.

Rattles

The following is one version of the significance of rattles in early American history. In 1658, a "rattle watch" was begun: it was composed of eight men who patrolled the city of New Amsterdam with rattles. When a fire was sighted they would sound the alarm. These men became New York's first fire alarm system and police force.

Householders often kept hand rattles of wood available, which made a distinctive noise, providing the alarm of fire. It was a simple way of waking the neighborhood to the danger of fire. The rounded body of the rattle was carved from one piece of wood. A flat tongue fit into the rounded toe at one end and intersected with a wooden cog attached to a carved wooden handle. Swinging it moved the cog so that the tongue clacked against each edge, producing a sound loud enough to be heard for several blocks.

Muffin Bells

Muffin bells came into use after the rattle, and were a second attempt at fire alarms. Muffin bells were comprised of two saucer-shaped brass bells enclosing a clapper that were connected to a turned wooden handle. If a fire was seen, the person carrying the muffin bell would activate it by swinging the bell back and forth. Upon hearing the muffin bell, the watchtower attendant would sound the alarm bells to alert the townspeople and firemen.

Fire Ward or Warden Staffs

During colonial times, the position of fire warden was created in order to protect the community against fires and to quell outbreaks of rowdiness at fires. Boston created a fire warden board of ten leading citizens in 1711. They were organized to direct operations at fires, order citizens to bucket brigades, and arrest looters or troublesome persons. These fire wardens were required by law to carry a large staff, five feet long with a six-inch brass or wooden spire at the top, as an emblem of their authority. Many large cities followed Boston's example and created fire warden positions. Most required the warden to carry a staff of authority.

Metal "Fire Laddie" match holder, 4" h., c. 1870. $375.

Ink wells. Left: "Chief of Dept. 1908," $750; Right: "Fire Assn. of Phila.," $500.

Whimsical baby "Fire Laddie" atomizer, pot metal, cold painted. $350.

Bass drum from firemen's marching band. $500.

118

Comic black fireman teapot, sugar bowl, salt and pepper set. Teapot: $350; Sugar bowl: $150; Salt and pepper set: $100.

Firemen's band music pouch, New York City. $125.

Selection of miniature firematic accouterments. $20-$100 each.

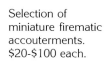

Silver plated toothpick holder, fire hat and barrel, c. 1890. $475.

Rough cotton salvage bag with owner's ID and 4" muffin bell. Salvage bag: $200; Muffin bell: $325.

Bucket, hat, or coat hanger, cold painted metal showing fireman profile. $500 pair.

Selection of firematic glass paperweights with scenes and advertising. $75-$100 each.

Paper imprint devices, firematic seal, c. 1890. $125 each.

Early glass paperweight. $300.

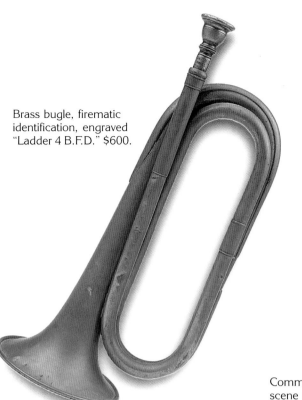

Brass bugle, firematic identification, engraved "Ladder 4 B.F.D." $600.

Two Staffordshire dishes from "great fire" series, transfer design, 1835. $350 each.

Commemorative dish, firehouse scene photo, Philadelphia, Pennsylvania, 1901. $175.

Porcelain dish showing hand pumper, Baltimore, Maryland. $350.

Blue transfer china plate, "Fred" and "Frank" horses. $275.

Large china charger, hand painted ladder truck, 14" diameter, c. 1880. $500.

China plate, Baltimore fire souvenir, 1904. $175.

Reverse of Baltimore plate.

Blue china plate, fire souvenir of "Chelsea Fire" Chelsea, Massachusetts, c. 1900. $125.

Firehouse china, Fire Patrol #3, Philadelphia, Pennsylvania. $90.

Firehouse china, Defiance Hose. Co. #1. $75.

Children's Mickey Mouse china, "Fireman Mickey," c. 1930. Dish: $175; Cup: $200; Divided plate: $225.

Insurance company china. $50.

Mickey Mouse cereal bowl and Post Toasties box featuring Mickey Mouse firematic scene. Bowl: $200; Box: $250.

Fire house china, hook and ladder #1. $20 each .

Selection of firematic china figures, c. 1940-1980. $8-$20 each.

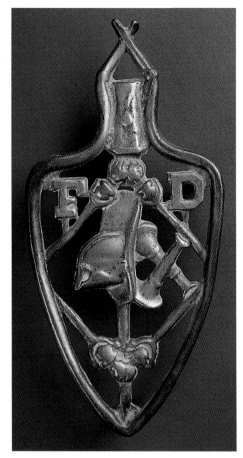

Fire trivet. $175.

Steamer candy mold, c. 1870. $175.

Close-up of rifle stock showing the words "City of Boston. Fire Dept. Ladder 8."

Fireline gun. $250.

Steamer shaped items. Left to right: lighter, c. 1950, $25; pin cushion, c. 1900, $100; ice cream mold, c. 1920, $125.

Turn-of-the-century convention mugs. $35-$60 each.

Candy mold, fireman figure, c. 1870. $175.

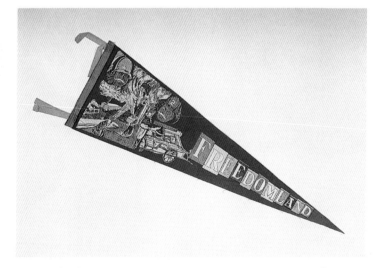

Freedomland banner, showing fire drama, New York, c. 1960. $20.

Large candy mold, steamer, c. 1870. $375.

Banner advertising a four county fireman convention, c. 1915. $50.

China firematic souvenirs. $35-$70 each.

Chicago World's Fair souvenirs, cold storage house fire 1893. Left to right: $125; $100; $150.

Glass souvenirs. Left: $35; Right: $45.

Dog collar for "Rex," the firehouse mascot, brass studded, c. 1900. $750.

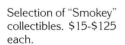

Selection of "Smokey" collectibles. $15-$125 each.

Brass soap container, firematic design, c. 1860. $125.

Selection of firematic tobacciana and fireman figure tin sign. Boxes: $250-$350 each; Sign: $2,000.

Comic pipe, plastic, "Smokey Stover." $150.

Selection of tobacciana. Left to right: tobacco pail, tin, $200; match holder, $250; cigar box (alarm), $275; Tub Tobacco/Tiptop Cigar packages, $50 each; tobacco pail with paper label, $125.

Cigar box, Darktown firematic scene. $350.

Wine bottle from 1906 Worcester Fire Society dinner, featuring picture of fire buckets on label. $125.

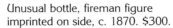

Tobacciana, boxes and label. Left box: $200; Label: $75; Right box, $250.

Unusual bottle, fireman figure imprinted on side, c. 1870. $300.

Glass candy containers in various fire engine shapes. $50- $175 each.

Selection of firematic mugs, patches, and medals. $2-$25 each.

Glass candy containers. Left to right: $175; $75; $95.

National Association of Firefighters emblem liquor bottles. Large: $35; Miniature set of three: $50.

Chapter Ten
Photography

A photo of a fireman is classified as an occupational photograph by photography collectors and is therefore highly collectible. As with other vintage occupational photographs, the more elaborate and unusual the subject's accouterments, the higher the value.

Daguerreotypes, Ambrotypes, and Albumen Photographs

In 1839, the French photographer Louis J. M. Daguerre invented the daguerreotype, a photograph made on a silver-coated cuplate. It is called a "mirror image" because of its highly reflective, mirror like surface. The most common sizes were 2-1/4 x 3-1/4 inches and 3-1/4 x 4-1/4 inches. The daguerreotype was housed in a case to preserve the delicate image.

Since daguerreotypes were the first form of photography, examples are extremely rare and are eagerly sought by collectors. Among the most sought after is an outdoor scene of a fireman and/or apparatus. Daguerreotypes of this sort are considered unique and especially valuable.

The ambrotype was invented in 1851 by Frederick Archer. Ambrotypes are thin collodion negatives on glass plates, coated with a light-sensitive emulsion. The glass negative was purposely underexposed, leaving a transparent image with light and dark areas. When this glass plate was given a black backing of paper, velvet, or mat, or was coated with a dark varnish, it became a positive photographic image. After 1856, the ambrotype gradually replaced the daguerreotype because its image was more natural than the mirror image of the daguerreotype. Disadvantages of the ambrotype include the possibility of surface cracks and peels as well as poorer quality in the photographic image as compared to the daguerreotype.

Photographers of the period took many pictures of Americans at work. Firemen could be seen rushing to the scene on fire engines, fighting fires, etc. Great fires, along with floods and other disasters, were covered in detail.

Albumen photographs circa 1860 were taken from wet plate negatives. The colors range in shades of light brown and are nearly always mounted on paperboard. This is the earliest form of paperbacked photography and for the first time many copies of an image could be produced.

Gutta Percha Cases

Samuel Perch wanted to design a case to protect the daguerreotype and ambrotype. On October 3, 1854, he obtained a patent for his plastic compound "composed of gum shellac and woody fibers and dyed brown or black." When heated and pressed into a mold it would reproduce the image of the mold.

Designs for the cases reflected themes that appealed to the public's taste. Two cases depicted firemen. One showed a hand pumper and firemen fighting a fire; the other, which is more difficult to obtain, shows a fireman with a trumpet, leaning against a hydrant.

Cartes de visite

A Carte de visite (the French phrase for "visiting card" or "calling card") or C.dV., c. 1855-1868, is a 2-1/2 x 4 inch cardboard-backed portrait originally used as a substitute for a calling card. These photographs were produced from glass negatives, allowing for unlimited copies.

Usually, a C.dV. will illustrate a single, stern-faced person posed inside a studio, either standing or seated erect. The most unusual C.dV.s are of groups, outdoor scenes, or include animals. The photographer's name and address were usually printed on the back of the card, providing information that helps in identification.

Tintypes

Cheap, popular, and readily available, tintypes are the easiest to find specimens of early photography. Tintypes were photographs made on black, brown, or gray japanned metal, and were of poor quality when compared to other examples of vintage photography. They came in several sizes, from a small size similar to a playing card to a whole plate measuring 6-1/2 to 8-1/2 inches. As in other photographica, size is important. The larger the size of the tintype, the more difficult it becomes to obtain.

Stereographs

The stereo view or stereograph provides a pictorial history of this country and the world from 1860-1920. Any significant events were recorded by the stereo camera and photographer. The basic type of stereo view has a pair of photographs pasted on a piece of cardboard. When observed with a stereo viewer, the two photographs appear as one three dimensional picture.

Cabinet Photographs

Cabinet photographs are the most common type of early fireman pictures found today. Introduced in the late 1860s, the cabinet photograph measured 4 x 5 inches and flourished until shortly after the turn of the century. The pictures were pasted to cardboard measuring 4-1/2 x 6-1/2 inches, with the photographer's name and address printed on the bottom border or back. They were usually found unframed. Some of the more difficult cabinets to obtain depict firemen with unusual helmets or equipment, or apparatus in front of firehouses or on parade.

Modern Photography

The late nineteenth and early twentieth century brought drastic improvements in the photographic process. When hand held cameras and affordably priced film became available, photographs of every aspect of life became reasonably abundant. As a result, the firematic collector should be very discerning. Photos of high quality and those that show firemen in firefighting gear, fire engines, and firemen with fire equipment at fire scenes should bring the highest prices.

Daguerreotype, engineer from United States Hose Co. of Philadelphia, Pennsylvania, c. 1850. $5,000.

One-quarter plate daguerreotype photo showing fireman with speaking trumpet. $4,500.

One-half plate ambrotype, hand pumper, c. 1858. $3,500.

Ambrotype, young boy in fireman clothes with trumpet and toy fire engine, c. 1860. $850.

One-quarter plate ambrotype, man with underside of fire helmet showing presentations. $750.

One-quarter plate ambrotype fireman, c. 1855. $500.

Hand tinted, one-quarter plate ambrotype, c. 1855. $1,000.

Gutta percha photo case, fireman figure, c. 1850. $400.

Carte de visite, fireman. $150.

Gutta percha photo case showing fireman and hand pumper. $275.

Carte de visite, chief with helmet and trumpet. $135.

Carte de visite, fireman with helmet and parade shirt. $125.

Carte de visite, fireman with hat and coat. $100.

Carte de visite, early steam fire engine, c. 1860. $175.

Early hand pumper, Paterson, New Jersey. $175.

Carte de visite, fire brigade fantasy with a female mascot, hand colored. $150.

Carte de visite, hose cart. $175.

Tintype, fireman in leather cap. $125.

Tintype, full figure fireman. $125.

Tintype, two fireman in running outfits. $100.

Tintype, female in firefighter outfit. $200.

Tintype of fireman and wife. $100.

One-half plate tintype fireman in full slicker. $350.

Tintype, fireman in uniform. $100.

Tintype, three firemen in uniform. $100.

Tintype, fireman in slicker with nozzle. $150.

Tintype, full gathering of firemen. $100.

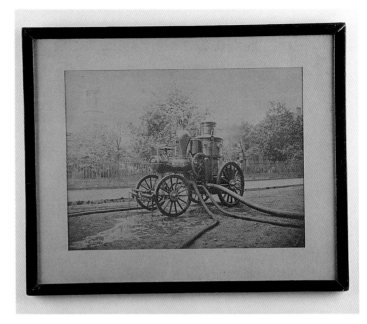

Albumen photo of steamer. $200.

Cabinet photo of steamer. $100.

Chicago fire department photo montage, 18" x 36". $500.

Cabinet photo, fire chief. $125.

Stereo card, hose cart with horses. $75.

Cabinet photo, young boy in fire hat with axe.
$125.

Stereo card, steamer and hose cart. $100.

Cabinet photo, "Fire Patrol" wagon with
children being pulled by goat. $150.

Stereo card, fireman saving child. $75.

Photo affixed to large metal button. $50.

Fireman photos in Maltese cross frames. $225 each.

Daguerreotype, one-half plate, outdoor scene of firemen and fire engine, c. 1850. $20,000.

141

Chapter Eleven
Presentation Items

Gavels

Formal meetings held by early volunteer fire companies usually followed Robert's Rules of Order. The president used a gavel to call the meeting to order—in some cases by striking a marble block. Many of these gavels were presented to presidents and ex-presidents as tokens of esteem and were suitably engraved. Many of the marble blocks were carved with the name of the company and its organization date.

Trophies

The spirit of competition has always been foremost in the fireman's mind. In recognition for winning various events associated with firemen's outings, tournaments, sporting events, and parades, many varieties of trophies were presented as prizes. The trophies ranged from plain to highly ornate, some with ladders, trumpets, helmets, etc. attached. Some were sterling silver, others were silver plate.

Watches

Since the time of the Civil War it has been traditional to give watches to retirees or to people who were promoted to important positions. Following this tradition, firemen were given pocket watches—many with inscriptions. Especially sought after are cases with snap-open covers. Early watches had the inscription on the inside of the back cover. Most valuable are solid gold cases with precious stones, followed by gold alone, then by silver, gold-filled, and finally, nickel plated. Toward the end of the nineteenth century, the backs of the watches were engraved with fire apparatus or badge likenesses. Pocket watches with fire motifs were given as late as the 1940s. Wristwatches were also given, with presentations on the face or back of the case.

Pearl handled S & W revolver with firematic presentation, c. 1869. $3,500.

Presentation gavel, c 1905. $350.

Presentation gavel with presentation box, c. 1900. $400.

Marble gavel plate, c. 1870. $275.

Presentation gavel, c. 1890. $400.

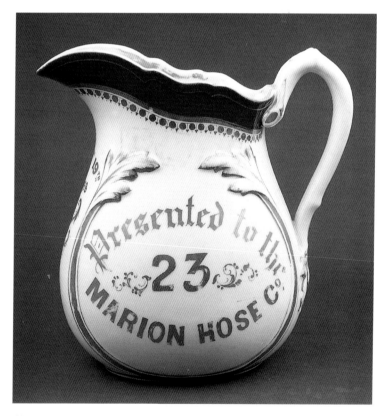

China pitcher with presentation, Philadelphia, c. 1860. $3,000.

Close-up of sword grip from Civil War sword with presentation, Paterson, New Jersey, c. 1860. $3,500.

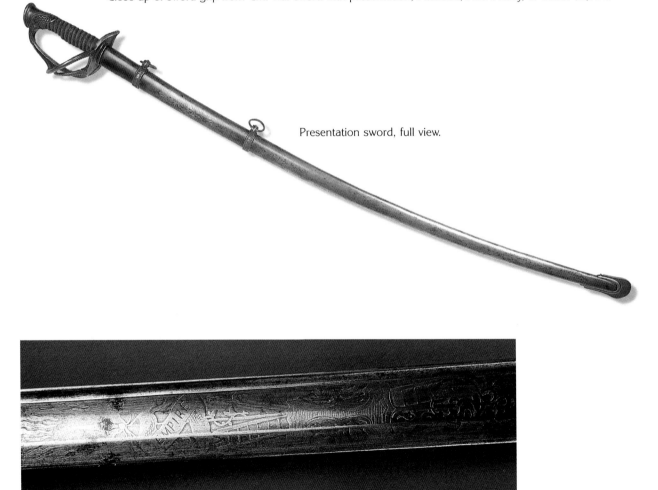

Presentation sword, full view.

Another Civil War sword, showing close-up of firematic design on blade. $4,500.

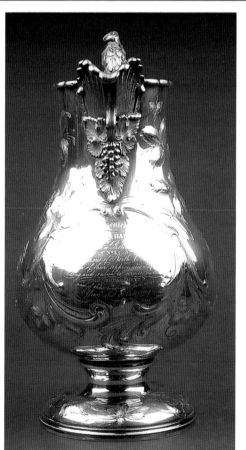

Fine coin silver presentation ewer, chased, repoussé work, incised and applied design, 16", c. 1850. $6,000.

Vase with handle, silver plated, "Presented at the Continental Fair 1893 to Union Hose Co.," 6". $350.

Presentation trophy, silver plated unique design, 14", c. 1907. $375.

Presentation trophy, silver plated, stag horn handles, "Long Island City, NY," 12", c. 1909. $350.

Gold plated art deco trophy, 18", c. 1910. $225.

Pewter trophy with antlers, "Whitestone, NY 1904," 10". $300.

Silver plated presentation water pitcher with cups, c. 1900. $950.

Presentation urn, Trenton, New Jersey, c. 1860. $1,500.

Silver plated water container, Bradford, Pennsylvania, c. 1880. $650.

Sterling ewer and cup with repoussé and applied design work, c. 1852. Ewer: $1,500; Cup: $650.

Silver plated presentation basket, c. 1890. $375.

Silver pitcher with presentation, "Chief Webber, Boston Fire Dept.," 10", c. 1888. $400.

Gold medallion with hair strands reputed to be those of America's first president George Washington encapsulated in the small glass center, 1-1/2". $20,000.

Presentation from reverse of gold medallion, "Presented to John Wees by Washington Engine Co. of Philadelphia...," c. 1833.

Presentation sterling silver fountain pen, Chicago, c. 1950. $65.

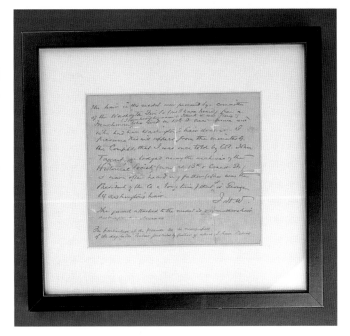

Provenance for gold medallion by receiver's son.

14k gold presentation medallion, Tiffany and Co. makers, "In Recognition of Bravery and Duty as a Fireman", F.D.N.Y., 2-1/2" , c. 1930. $1,500.

Sulfide watch fob for "Northern Liberty Fire Co., Phila.." $750.

Reverse of fob, showing presentation.

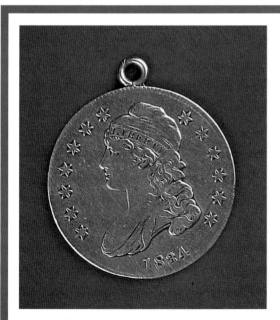

Sterling silver, coin sized charm presented to Chief of the Philadelphia Fire Dept. $250.

Reverse of coin sized charm.

Firematic wrist watch,
"Chief F.D.N.Y.," 14k
Waltham, c. 1915.
$400.

Gold presentation pocket watch, "20 Years Service F.D.N.Y.,"
c. 1915. $1,200.

Presentation pocket watch, gold with engraved New York
City fire captain badge, c. 1930. $1,000.

Chapter Twelve
Prints

Prints were one of the earliest methods of duplicating pictorial matters. Most famous among those who made prints in the mid to late nineteenth century was the printmaking house of Currier and Ives. Nathaniel Currier opened a printmaking shop in New York City at One Wall Street in 1835. He was joined in that business by his general manager, James Merritt Ives. Artists were hired and prints were produced which, one might imagine, were very popular at a time when newspapers and many magazines did not contain pictures. Fires and firefighting scenes, especially, were some of their most popular scenes.

Lithography is the art or process of printing from a flat stone (or metal plate) by a method based on the repulsion between grease and water. The design is applied to the surface with a greasy material and then water and printing ink are successively applied; the greasy part, which repels water, absorbs the ink, but the wet parts do not.

Currier and Ives issued two sets of highly sought-after, fire-related prints—a large folio, "The Life of a Fireman," and a medium folio, "The American Fireman."

Most of the Currier and Ives prints were watercolored by hand. Many other print makers issued prints with fire-related themes as well; today all are difficult to find.

Certificates

The fire certificate was presented to an active fireman after he had attended fires for a certain number of years. Others who received certificates were exempt members who had served the required time; contributing members, those who had given monetary donations; and honorary members, those who had performed some service for the company.

Most fire certificates were ornate and colorful. They were either hand painted, lithographed, or done in calligraphy. Most illustrated fire scenes of the time and thus are significant for their historical value.

Federal era engraved certificate dated 1799, New York, showing firemen fighting fire, hand pumpers, and bucket brigade, 9" x 11". $750.

New York Fire Department certificate, lithograph, c. 1810, drawing of King Neptune on top, early fire scene on bottom, 13" x 16". $450.

Certificate of exemption, lithograph, c. 1840, Hoboken, New Jersey, 14-1/2" x 19". $175.

Hand colored lithograph, fire department membership certificate, by Currier and Ives, 19" x 24". $475.

Printing plate for the certificate of exemption, 14-1/2" x 19". $300.

Hand colored insurance lithograph, c. 1860, 20" x 25". $1,500.

Fireman membership certificate, Michigan, dated 1865, 6" x 9". $65.

Color advertising lithograph, Rumsey and Company, c. 1870, 25" x 33". $1,500.

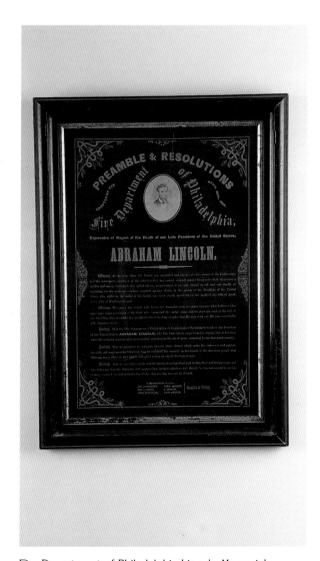

Fire Department of Philadelphia Lincoln Memorial certificate, 15" x 20", 1865. $1,000.

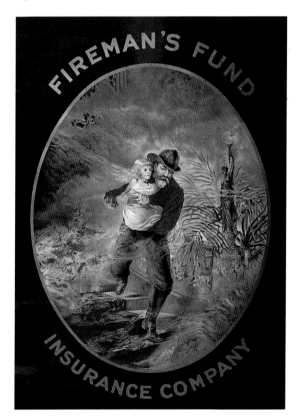

Colored lithograph advertising Fireman's Fund Insurance Co., c. 1900, 22" x 28". $750.

Fire laddie child, colored lithograph, c. 1880, 15" x 29". $500.

Large pictorial cloth showing female Fire Laddie and whimsical sayings, 31" x 31". $500.

Large folio Currier and Ives hand colored lithograph, cut margins, c. 1870. $750.

Large folio Currier and Ives hand colored lithograph, c. 1870. $500.

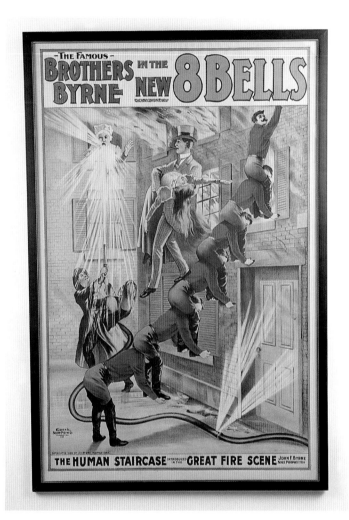

Large colored broadside advertising firematic circus act, c. 1890, 29" x 43". $750.

Large, two color printed broadside, c. 1911, 29" x 42". $600.

Chapter Thirteen
Toys

Toys have historically been objects from adult life which were made child sized. With these, children would emulate adult behavior or "play." Fire toys produced in the middle of the last century were made of painted tin and were good representations of actual fire apparatus. Due to their high cost, the material used in their manufacture, and the limited amount produced, few survived. In the 1880s, cast iron toys became popular and brought much joy to the children whose parents could afford to buy such toys. Bright colors, movable parts, and galloping horses contributed to the excitement.

As motorized equipment replaced horses, toy manufacturers changed the design of their toys to include motorized cast iron equipment. Cast iron was mostly replaced with large pressed steel toys in the 1920s and 1930s and pot metal replaced cast iron in many small toys.

During World War II, toys were made of wood; after the war, the toy industry went back to traditional materials. In the 1950s, Japan entered the market with cheap tin lithographed toys. Today toys are made of a wide variety of materials, especially plastic.

Games and Puzzles

In times past, boys often occupied their idle hours not only playing with fire toys, but also sharing a few fun-filled hours with a friend playing a fire game. Prior to 1890, games were packaged in wooden boxes; after that, they were found in lithographed cardboard boxes.

Today finding a game with all its parts in good condition is no easy task. Most sought after are those with color lithographed boxes.

Sand toy with moving "jiggle" figure, c. 1870. $750.

Early tin toy hand pumper, c. 1860. $2,500.

Early tin horse drawn
steamer, c. 1870. $250.

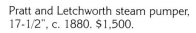

Pratt and Letchworth steam pumper,
17-1/2", c. 1880. $1,500.

Ives firehouse, c. 1890, shown with cast
iron fire pumper toy. Firehouse: $4,000.
Pumper: $375.

Hubley steam fire engine,
c. 1900, 24". $1,750.

Cast iron fire patrol wagon. $350.

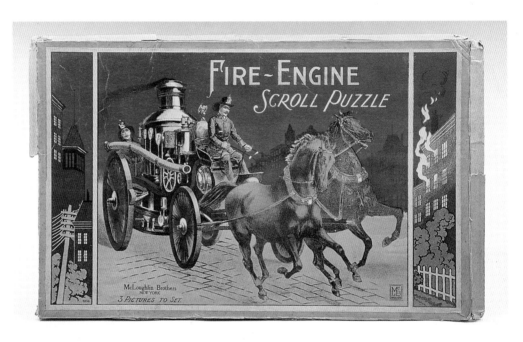

McLoughlin fire engine scroll puzzle, c. 1890. $375.

Children's blocks, c. 1890. Set $200.

Cast iron fire engine toy, 12" long. $400.

Cast iron hook and
ladder, 8" long. $275.

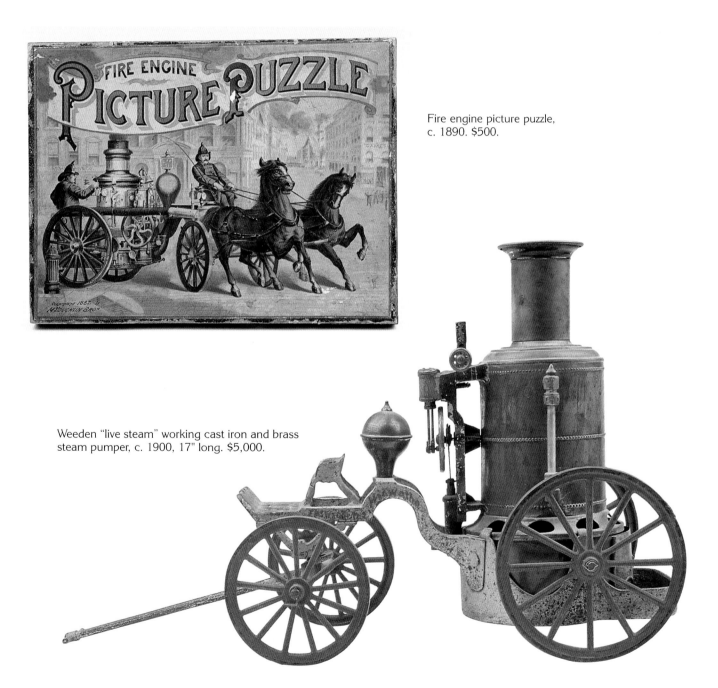

Fire engine picture puzzle,
c. 1890. $500.

Weeden "live steam" working cast iron and brass
steam pumper, c. 1900, 17" long. $5,000.

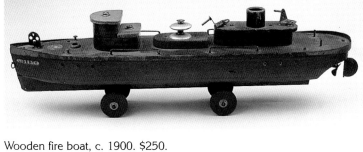

Wooden fire boat, c. 1900. $250.

Darktown Fire Brigade picture puzzle, box and puzzle, c. 1890. $200.

Fireman doll with bisque head, made in Germany, c. 1900. $75.

Tin hose cart, c. 1900. $300.

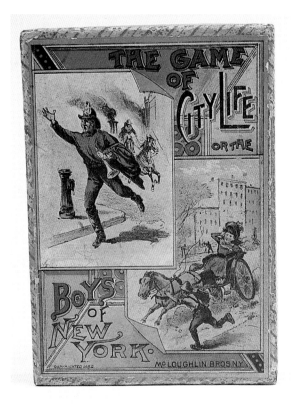

The Game of City Life, c. 1890. $200.

Left to right: Going to the Fire game, $125; Fire Department puzzle, $200; Steamer puzzle, $275.

Left to right: Fire Department puzzle, $75; Fire Fighter's Game, $100; cut and fold toy, $175.

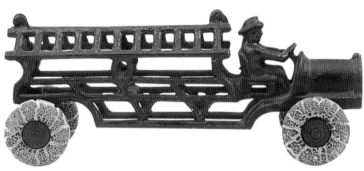

Hill climber friction tin toy, c. 1910. $400.

Cast iron ladder truck, 4" long. $175.

Tin fire toy, c. 1910. $200.

8" Hubley ladder truck. $350.

8" Hubley cast iron pumper. $350.

Kenton cast iron pumper, c. 1920, 10" long.. $500.

Left: Dent fire chief's car, $650; Right: cast iron motorcycle policeman, $125.

Left to right: cast iron ladder truck, 3" long, $150; cast iron pumper, $350; slush toy fire engine, $60.

Cast iron fire truck (replacement driver), 3-1/2". $125.

Three cast iron fire pumpers. Bottom left: $150; Bottom right: $300; Top: $325.

Kenton hook and ladder truck,
c. 1920, 11-1/2" long. $750.

Left: cast iron ladder truck, $150;
Right: ladder truck, $175.

Kenton fire pumper, c. 1920,
18" long. $850.

Hubley cast iron Ahrens Fox pumper, c. 1920, 11¼" long. $8,000.

"Oh Boy" steel aerial ladder, c. 1920, 18-1/2" long. $475.

Buddy "L" pumper, c. 1930, 24" long. $2,000.

Keystone "ride on" pumper, c. 1920, 26" long. $1,200.

Marx siren fire chief's car, c. 1920, 14" long. $350.

Kingsbury tin fire station, c. 1920. $500. Shown with fire chief's car, c. 1920, 14" long. $375.

Marx siren sparkling fire engine, c. 1920. $250.

Fire chief's car, c. 1920, 14" long. $375.

Marx tin fire chief's car, c. 1920. $350.

Pair of fire chief's cars, 14" long. $350 each.

165

Two section Kingsbury fire station, c. 1920. $550. Shown with Kingsbury ladder truck, c. 1920. $300.

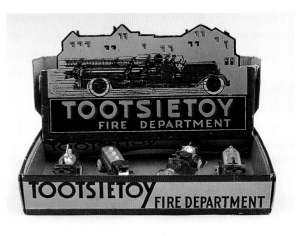

Tootsietoy fire department boxed set, c. 1930. $450.

Wooden fire house with three wooden fire toys, c. 1930. $350.

Cardboard Fanny Farmer Candies fire engine container, c. 1930. $150. Shown with two Marx tin firemen. $25 each.

Child's pair Mickey Mouse fire boots, $250; Shohutt child's fire helmet, $350; wooden child's toy fire axe, $75.

Mickey Mouse cut-outs from cereal box, c. 1930. $350.

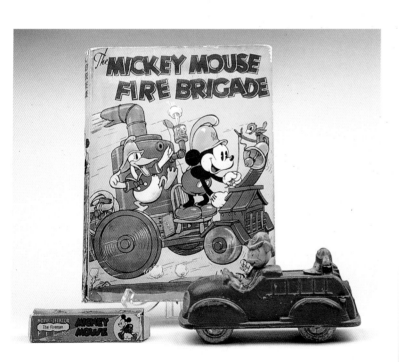

Mickey Mouse toy projector film *The Fireman*, c. 1930, $20; *Mickey Mouse Fire Brigade* book, c. 1930, $250; Mickey Mouse rubber fire engine, $75.

Ed Wynn's wooden jointed toy, c. 1930. $75.

Ed Wynn's siren pipe, c. 1930. $75.

Left: Marx climbing fireman, c. 1940, $275;
Right: Japanese tin climbing fireman, c.
1950, $150.

Left: Ed Wynn puzzle, $150; Right: Ed Wynn booklet, $35.

Left: Hubley Ahrens Fox toy, c. 1930, $150; Right: Hubley Ahrens Fox toy, c. 1950, $100.

Marx climbing fireman with box,
c. 1940. $350.

Alburn Rubber Company
Ahrens Fox toy, c. 1940. $150.

Three Hubley ladder trucks. Left:
c. 1930, $50; Center: c. 1950,
$45; Right: c. 1940, $85.

Wooden fire boat, 3" long. $35.

F. A. O. Schwartz fire house, c. 1950. $375. Shown with plastic fire
truck, c. 1950. $20.

Left: fire chief's car, c. 1940,
$65; Right: Marx fire chief's
car, c. 1930, $50.

Left: Marx fire chief's car, c. 1950, $350; Right: tin fire chief's car, c. 1950, $100.

Hubley fire engine, c. 1950. $275.

Tonka fire pumper, c. 1955. $375.

Tonka fire pumper, c. 1957. $300.

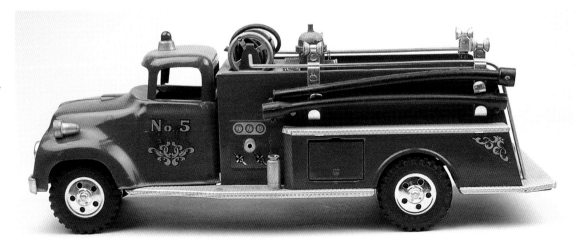

Saunders plastic
fire chief's car
with box. $225.

Structo fire engine,
c. 1950. $225.

Four plastic fire engine toys,
c. 1950. $35 each.

Two plastic ladder
trucks. $15 each.

Doepke "model toys" ladder truck, c. 1950. $300.

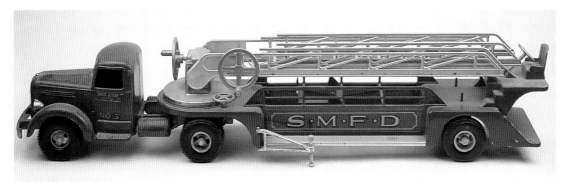

Smith Miller ladder truck, c. 1950. $750.

Left: hot papa fireman, $125; Center and right: fireman with axe and fireman with hose, $20 ea.

Plastic Santa Claus on fire engine, c. 1950. $35.

Central station firehouse lunch box, c. 1950. $175.

G.I. Joe Crash Crew Fire Truck in box. $2,500. Shown with G.I. Joe in fireman outfit. $250.

"Old Smoky" Japanese tin fire engine with box, c. 1950. $175.

Madame Alexander's firefighter doll, c. 1990. $85.

Chapter Fourteen
Trumpets

Kenneth Dunshee, in *Enjine, Enjine* (a classic firematic reference), states that the earliest mention of a fireman's speaking trumpet was in 1752 in New York, when Jacobus Turck was authorized to purchase six small speaking trumpets for use by the Chief Engineer and other officers. In the early days of fire fighting, an officer ran ahead of the pumper in order to determine the location of the fire and would shout orders to his men through his trumpet. The trumpet enabled his voice to be heard blocks away from the fire scene.

The trumpet had other uses besides that of shouting orders at a fire, however. The mouthpiece would be removed and, it is rumored, replaced with a stopper—whereupon the trumpet became a vessel that could be filled with a beverage. During a fight, it became a weapon. During a parade, the Chief could carry flowers in his trumpet.

Trumpets were of two varieties: the work horn and the handsome presentation horn. Working horns were used at actual fires; they were produced in brass, nickel, or silver-plated brass and painted tin (toleware). An unusual variety of brass working trumpet was the Cairns and Brothers' "octagonal," patented in 1877. It was an eight-sided horn that had its own distinct beauty.

Presentation horns were usually sterling silver or heavily silver plated. A message of esteem along with the owner's name and date of presentation were sometimes inscribed on the horn. The best-appearing apparatus in a parade could be awarded a trumpet. Winners of muster competitions could also receive a presentation trumpet as a prize. Trumpets were also given by one fire company to another as a token of appreciation during a visit. When ordering a trumpet from various equipment supply companies, one had a choice of standard or ornate engraving—the latter included an engraving of a steamer, hose cart, hook and ladder, or other designs.

The tassel was a decorative rather than functional addition to a trumpet. It was held on the trumpet via metal rings on the side of the horn. These metal rings were in turn held by mounts either in the shape of an eagle (with the metal loop held in his beak), a fire helmet (with the loop between the eagle's head and the face plate), or plain circular mounts. On early trumpets of brass and toleware, sash mounts were not evident.

Trumpets can range in size from 12 to 25 inches in length. They may be decorated with lozenge-shaped metal additions bearing the likenesses of Greek or Roman gods or goddesses, etc. Some are ornamented with miniature metallic ladders and hoses extending from the body of the trumpet. Others were elaborately engraved with designs, equipment, and, in rare cases, a photograph of the presentee.

Tole speaking trumpet, c. 1840, 18" high. $500.

Sterling silver trumpet, c. 1830.
$8,000.

Octagonal trumpet, Newburgh,
New York, c. 1845, 18" h. $1,000.

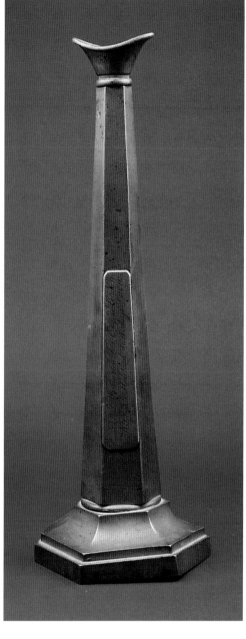

Tole speaking trumpet, "3ʳᵈ Ward
A.B.," c. 1830, 17" high. $750.

Trumpet (21-1/2"), helmet, and trophy belonging to George Arnot, c. 1908. Trumpet: $1,200; helmet: $850; trophy: $300.

Photo, Chief of the Rockville Center Fire Dept., c. 1910. $35.

Rare glass presentation speaking trumpet, Harrisburg, Pennsylvania, c. 1885, 24". $12,000.

Spectacular sterling trumpet, Washington portrait, special Roman-headed sterling cartouches, figural tassel holders, c. 1880, 24". $4,500.

Interesting full-headed, ornate speaking trumpet, plated repoussé silver leaf design, c. 1909, 18". $2,800.

Fire trumpet (21-1/2") with advertising postcard, c. 1905. Trumpet: $1,000. Postcard: $50.

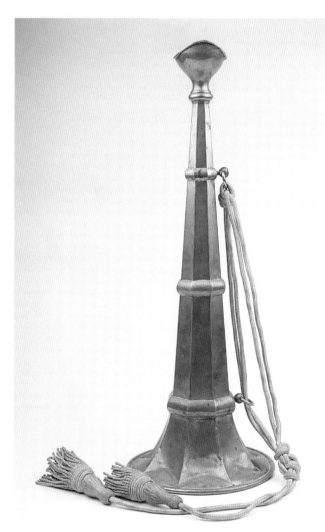

Cairns octagonal trumpet, c. 1875, 19". $900.

Two silver presentation trumpets with incised design, c. 1900. Left: 20" with lion ring holders, $1,500; Right: 18" with helmet sash holders, by Fred Miller, $1,500.

Brass working trumpet, "Jefferson Engine 26," New York City, c. 1860, 20". $1,000.

Fireman's presentation trumpet with Hunneman hand pumper engraving, c. 1870, 18". $1,500.

Fluted bell speaking trumpet, plated, c. 1890, 21-1/2". $1, 000.

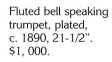

Silver trumpet with incised design, c. 1900, 18". $950.

179

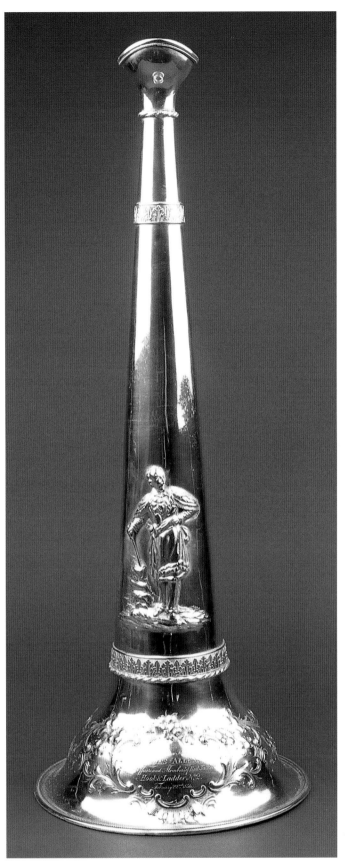 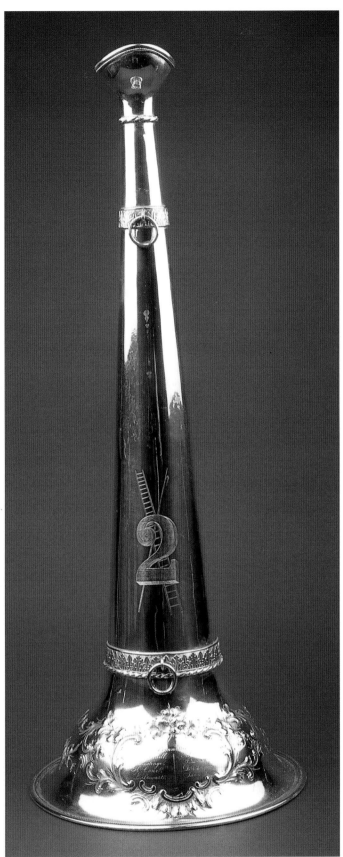

Sterling trumpet, incised and with repoussé figure of the Indian Chief "Red Jacket," c. 1850, 22". $7,000.

Rear view of Indian Chief trumpet.

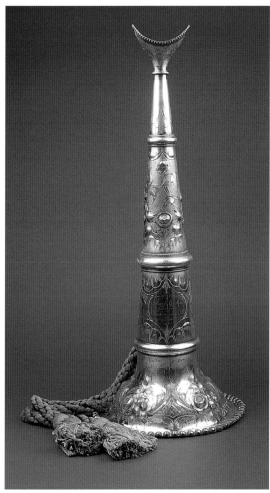

Silver trumpet incised, etched and repoussé, "Presented to David Lyle Chief Engineer Philadelphia Fire Dept. 1860," 23". $3,000.

Silver plated trumpet, shield presentation with dolphin tassel holders, c. 1880, 18". $1,200.

Rare amber glass speaking trumpet, c. 1870, 18". $8,000.

181

Ornate plated speaking trumpet with design of applied floral swag, c. 1912, 21-1/2". $1,800.

Delicately incised speaking trumpet, "Young America Hook and Ladder, Newburyport," c. 1867, 18". $2,000.

Two brass speaking trumpets.
Left: 18", 1880, $500; Right: 22",
presented in 1860, $1,500.

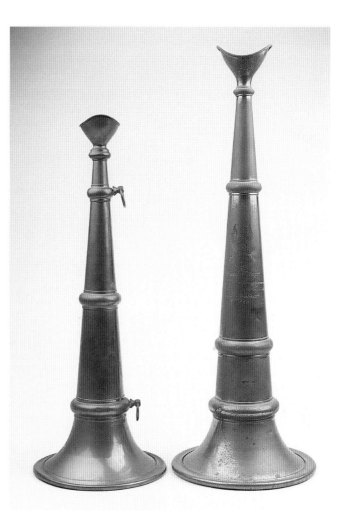

Lovely coin silver trumpet with repoussé floral design, c. 1853,
20". $4,000.

Pewter speaking trumpet with helmet
ring holder, c. 1910, 18". $1,200.

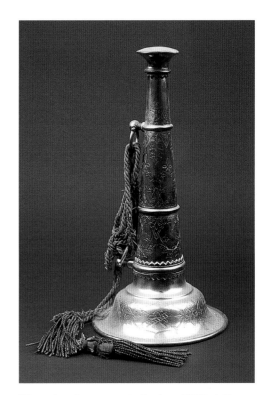

Silver plated trumpet, incised, c. 1880, 14".
$750.

Incised, silver plated trumpet with unusual Indian motif on rim, c. 1880, 18-1/2". $2,000.

Silver plated trumpet, incised design, engraved "Fore-man, West Hartford, Conn.," c. 1900, 20". $1,000.

Silver plated presentation trumpet from Newtown, New York, c. 1908. $1,200.

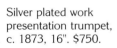
Silver plated work presentation trumpet, c. 1873, 16". $750.

Plated trumpet with incised design, c. 1880, 23-1/2". $1,100.

Brass working trumpet, c. 1880, 16". $450.

Silver plated trumpet, c. 1900, 18". $750.

Chapter Fifteen
Uniforms

Firemen were conscious not only of the appearance of their engines, but of their own appearance as well. A distinctive clothing feature was the unique parade uniform worn by each company. These uniforms ranged from everyday garb to "fatigue," or traveling clothes, to elaborate parade dress.

Early firemen wore a distinctive bib-front shirt with a large company number sewn in the center, along with the first letter of the name of their company. Today bib-front shirts are extremely rare. Colors of firemen's shirts were not always the traditional red. According to the Woodhouse Catalogue of 1888, "these shirts are available in any color."

Many people are beginning to collect early uniforms. They are relatively inexpensive and easy to find. An interesting way to display them is by acquiring a store mannequin and dressing it in an early uniform.

A pair of "gallowses," or fancy suspenders, was easily seen over a fireman's shirt. Many of these gallowses were decorated with the number of the company and a fancy design. Today they are a rare find in any condition.

An unusual item sometimes worn by firemen was the neckerchief ring. These were usually front-piece shaped, 2 inches high, with a company number on the front and a ring in the center of the back.

The earliest use of leather belts in fire service was to carry spanner wrenches. As the fireman's dress uniform gradually became more elaborate, the belts, which were made of patent leather and finished by japanning, became strictly ornamental and were decorated with contrasting letters and bright colors. Some belts showed the company name, others the rank of line office, such as "Chief," "Foreman," etc., while still others showed elected offices such as "President," "Trustee," or "Secretary." Presentation and metal prize belts are known to exist. They are very rare and command high prices when found.

To accompany the fancy parade uniforms of the firemen, many departments adopted metal buckles for their parade belts, instead of the usual leather slides. There were several varieties, including a rectangle with an embossed shield and a coiled leather hose with a company number in the center. One of the most sought-after types shows a Hunneman fire engine and was worn by Boston firemen in the 1860s.

To this day, most fire department parade and dress uniforms have elaborate uniform buttons. These buttons include either the city seal, fire equipment, the company emblem, or the letters "F.D." in their design. They are made with a gold or silver finish, and are flat or dome shaped. Coat buttons are larger than sleeve buttons. Many bib-type parade shirts are also decorated with fancy buttons. Some buttons date back to the last half of the nineteenth century and are rare.

The first record of oilcloth coats worn by members of a fire department appeared in the minutes of the Assistance Fire Company of Philadelphia, February 3, 1794, when it was noted that the company would provide its engineers with oilcloth coats and capes. Capes were worn by firemen for protection against water and embers. Early capes were made of "oyl cloth," but later they were made of canvas and treated with heavy layers of paint.

The cape was usually painted in the company's colors and often bore the date of the company's founding. Many capes were decorated with symbolic illustrations by local artists, who also painted engine panels and parade hats.

The use of capes began to decline around 1845. Many companies switched to New York style helmets, and capes and frock coats gave way to tapered, close-fitting jackets and coats.

Capes are prized additions to any collection. Due to the fragility of the material they were made of, few survived. Dates painted on capes are organizational dates, not the dates the capes were painted.

Patch collecting is an area that has grown substantially during the past five years. Patches don't require much storage space, they are reasonably priced, and many varieties are available. Shoulder patches are found in two to six different colors and in a variety of sizes. Plain styles depict a Maltese cross with the name and number of the fire company. More elaborate patches illustrate apparatus, cartoon characters, landmarks, etc.

Belts, duck bill style cap, and tie slide.
Belts: $125 each; helmet holder belt
slide: $50; cap: $50; necktie slide: $90.

"Bib" style shirt with convention
ribbons. Shirt: $125; left ribbon:
$35; right ribbon: $45.

Very rare Civil War style belt buckle with
Hunneman hand pumper, c. 1860. $400.

Duck bill style cap with leather shield. $500.

Uniform button, c. 1870. $35.

Belt with metal name plate. $250.

Prize belt with presentation buckle, c. 1890. $1,500.

Belt buckle, c. 1850. $500.

Duck bill cap with leather front shield. $1,000.

Belt buckle, Philadelphia, c. 1850. $500.

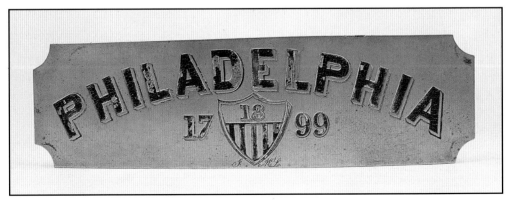

Decorative horse collar: $175;
rosettes with number "8", $35 each;
driver's badges: $125 each.

Belt with brass engraved
plate, "Good Intent,"
Philadelphia, c. 1850. $650.

Left: cap-shaped party favor, $50;
Right: salesman's sample cap,
$150.

Interior of party favor cap.

Bibliography

Costello, Augustine E. *Our Firemen, A History of the New York Fire Department Volunteer and Paid.* New York: Knickerbocker Press. 1977 (first published in 1877).

Cannon, Donald J. Ed. *Heritage of Flames.* Pound Ridge, New York: Artisan Books, 1977.

Cannon, Donald J. "Firefighting in America." © 1980 University of Pennsylvania Hospital Antiques Shows Brochure.

Ditzel, Paul C. *Fire Engines, Firefighters.* New York, New York: Crown Publishers., Inc., 1976.

Dunshee, Kenneth Holcomb. *Enjine, Enjine.* New York, New York: Harold Vincent Smith for the Home Insurance Company, 1939.

Holzman, Robert S. *The Romance of Firefighting.* New York: Bonanza Books, 1976.

Ingrain, Arthur. *A History of Firefighting and Equipment.* Secaucus, New Jersey: Chartwell Books Inc., 1978.

Piatti, James and Mary Jane. "Firefighting Equipment, Momentos of the Smoke Eaters." *The Encyclopedia of Collectibles*, Time Life Books. Inc., 1978.

Smith, Dennis. *Dennis Smith's History of Firefighting in America. 300 Years of Courage.* New York: The Dial Press, 1978.

VISUAL GLOSSARY

Clients often share their frustrations in trying to fully picture what their home will look like based on the floor plans. Use this visual glossary for your reference as you envision your future home, and decide which Sater Design Collection plan will suit your tastes, needs and preferences. Ceiling details are illustrated here.

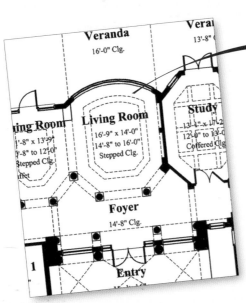

Stepped Ceiling

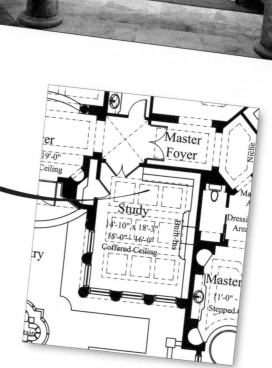

Coffered Ceiling

Barrel Ceiling

Groin Ceiling

Vaulted Ceiling

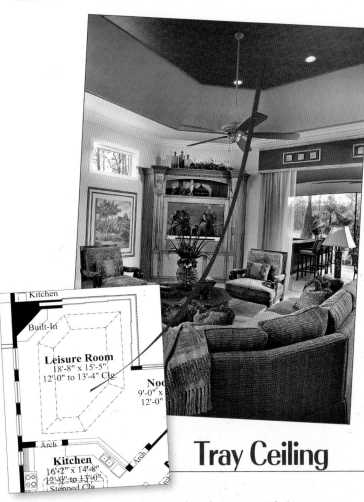

Tray Ceiling

VISUAL GLOSSARY

A luxurious atmosphere is found in each Sater Design Collection home courtesy of elegant and astute detailing throughout each plan. These details are indicated on floorplans as shown here.

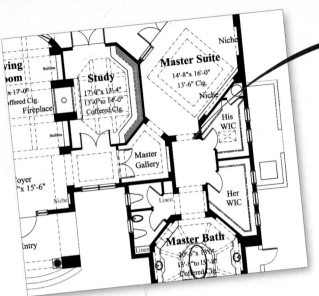

Arches

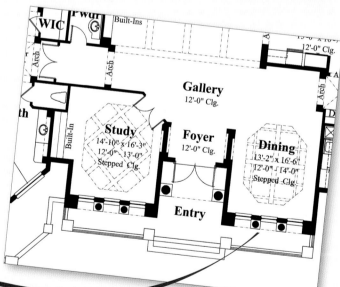

Columns

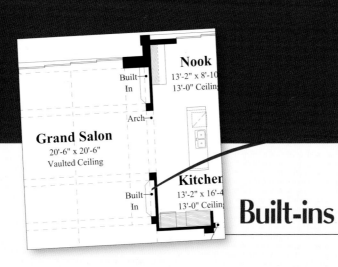

Nook
13'-2" x 8'-10
13'-0" Ceiling

Built
In

Arch

Grand Salon
20'-6" x 20'-6"
Vaulted Ceiling

Built
In

Kitchen
13'-2" x 16'-4
13'-0" Ceiling

Built-ins

wet bar

island
17'

arch

Pantry

arch

built-ins

WIC

arch

Dining
" x 14'-6"
" to 14'-0"
ped Clg.

Art Niche

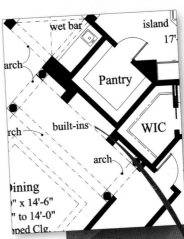

Pwdr

la
ove

Dining Room
17'-2" x 15'-11"
Barrel Vault

Built-In

ult

Gallery
18'-0" to 18'-8"
Stepped Clg.

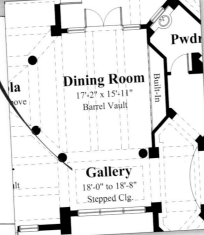

Gallery Hall

Benichini

FRONT ELEVATION

Intoxicating
Waterfront Views

Rich in detail, the exterior of Benichini features spiral pilasters, carved eave brackets and clerestory windows. Every room in this home was oriented to take in as much of the wide, rear waterfront as possible. The result is a home that embraces the tranquil views that surround it.

Despite the grand and luxurious aspects of the overall design, ceiling treatments, warm finishes and thoughtful details foster an intimate and inviting feeling throughout the home. Formal dining and living rooms, served by a gourmet kitchen and stylish wet bar, as well as a spectacular outdoor kitchen, were designed around the frequent entertaining of the homeowners.

PHOTO ABOVE, BELOW: Spectacular stair towers are a Sater Design specialty, and this home is no exception. Small windows light the space, which is topped by a unique ceiling treatment.

PHOTO ABOVE: A striking, curved balcony overlooks the foyer, where stone columns and a custom designed marble floor greet guests.

PHOTO TOP: This dedicated outdoor living space features a firepit that became a fast favorite for the owners because both sunsets and sunrises are visible from this space.

PHOTO ABOVE: The home's master suite enjoys a connection to the outdoors via a large, second-story balcony and commanding views through the floor-to-ceiling windows.

PHOTO ABOVE: The master bath features a prominent tub set off by detailed woodwork and stately columns.

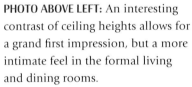

PHOTO ABOVE LEFT: An interesting contrast of ceiling heights allows for a grand first impression, but a more intimate feel in the formal living and dining rooms.

PHOTO BELOW: The waterfront views are embraced along the rear of the home, and outdoor living spaces are present on both floors to maximize enjoyment for the owners.

PHOTO ABOVE RIGHT: The high, beamed coffered ceiling and striking built-in entertainment center serve as superb design details in this centerpiece room.

Ferretti | Plan 6786

A secret oasis awaits within

With its terracotta-hued barrel roof tiles, limestone sheathed walls, stone accents and golden-hued stucco façade this is a quintessential Tuscan-inspired home. After entering the courtyard through a pair of wrought iron gates, a loggia of stone-covered pillars and arched openings travels the length of the home. Myriad windows and glass doors grace the interior walls resulting in an instant and irrevocable synergy that connects the interior and exterior spaces.

To the left of the foyer, the master suite faces the pool and seemingly draws the outdoors inward. The library is located near the foyer and adjacent to the airy kitchen, dining

and great room, which naturally transition outward onto the covered loggia and ensuing pool area. Facing the enclosed courtyard, two second-story guest suites share a common loft that opens up onto a covered balcony and pergola-shaded deck. Anchored on one side by a private guesthouse, a privacy wall encloses the courtyard, enhancing the home's oasis-like ambiance.

PHOTO ABOVE: A balcony accessed from the second-floor loft and third guest suite provides a quiet respite from a harried day to enjoy wide views of lush scenery.

PHOTO LEFT: This home features a warming outdoor fireplace adjacent to the built-in grille and outdoor kitchen, all oriented to accommodate a swim-up eating bar for swimmers enjoying the refreshing pool.

PHOTO LEFT: The spacious kitchen and dining area, with its large center island and extended breakfast bar, transitions easily into the great room, which opens out onto the covered lanai and subsequent pool deck. Modern amenities will delight aspiring chefs; conveniences like the pot-filling spigot above the range and prep sink on the center island anticipate needs.

PHOTO FAR LEFT: Adjacent to the dining room and kitchen, the great room, with its repeating arches, beamed coffered ceiling and carved mantel, ties together like a perfectly accessorized outfit.

PHOTO BELOW: Dark wood and wrought-iron accents continue the elements found at the entry of this courtyard home.

PHOTO ABOVE: An expansive wall of glass-fronted doors connects the master suite, with its softly hued walls and elegantly tiered ceiling, to the stunningly designed pool and spa area.

PHOTO RIGHT: The master retreat begins with an elegant foyer and boasts a spacious walk-in closet, but the crowning jewel is this luxurious master bath, spaciously designed to enhance functionality.

PHOTO RIGHT: Essential to the home's design are the visual and physical associations that connect each interior space, including those in the detached guesthouse and second-story guest wing, to the outdoors.

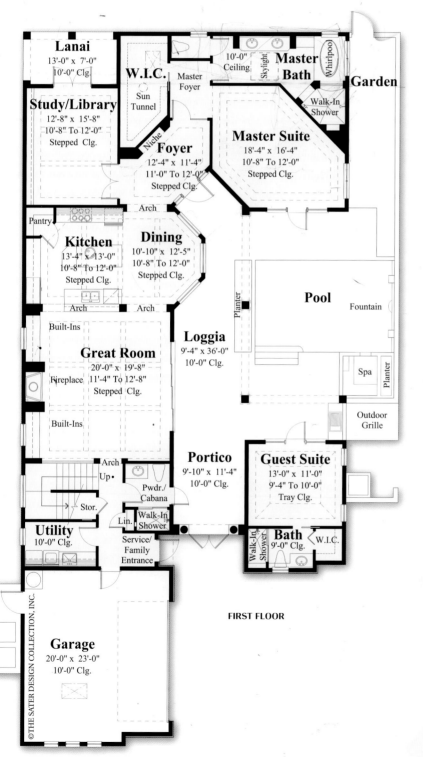

FIRST FLOOR

Lanai
13'-0" x 7'-0"
10'-0" Clg.

W.I.C.

Study/Library
12'-8" x 15'-8"
10'-8" To 12'-0"
Stepped Clg.

Master Foyer

Sun Tunnel

Niche

Foyer
12'-4" x 11'-4"
11'-0" To 12'-0"
Stepped Clg.

10'-0" Ceiling

Skylight

Master Bath

Whirlpool

Garden

Walk-In Shower

Master Suite
18'-4" x 16'-4"
10'-8" To 12'-0"
Stepped Clg.

Pantry

Kitchen
13'-4" x 13'-0"
10'-8" To 12'-0"
Stepped Clg.

Arch

Dining
10'-10" x 12'-5"
10'-8" To 12'-0"
Stepped Clg.

Arch

Pool

Fountain

Planter

Built-Ins

Great Room
20'-0" x 19'-8"
11'-4" To 12'-8"
Stepped Clg.

Fireplace

Built-Ins

Arch

Loggia
9'-4" x 36'-0"
10'-0" Clg.

Spa

Planter

Portico
9'-10" x 11'-4"
10'-0" Clg.

Up

Stor.

Pwdr./Cabana

Lin.

Walk-In Shower

Guest Suite
13'-0" x 11'-0"
9'-4" To 10'-0"
Tray Clg.

Outdoor Grille

Utility
10'-0" Clg.

Service/Family Entrance

Walk-In Shower

Bath
9'-0" Clg.

W.I.C.

Garage
20'-0" x 23'-0"
10'-0" Clg.

©THE SATER DESIGN COLLECTION, INC.

SECOND FLOOR

Deck
10'-4" x 11'-10"

A/C **Mech.** **A/C**
20'-0" x 8'-4"
7'-0" Clg.

©THE SATER DESIGN COLLECTION, INC.

Skylights

Loft
10'-2" x 16'-10"
9'-4" To 10'-0"
Stepped Clg.

Balcony
18'-0" x 6'-0"

Guest Suite 3
13'-0" x 11'-0"
9'-4" To 10'-0"
Stepped Clg.

Dn.

Bath
9'-4" Clg.

Shower

Balconette

Shower

Bath
9'-4" Clg.

W.I.C.

Guest Suite 2
13'-7" x 13'-4"
9'-4" To 10'-0"
Stepped Clg.

Ferretti

Plan No. **6786**

Bedrooms: **4**	Width: **45' 0"** / 52' w/gaster
Baths: **5**	Depth: **95' 8"**
1st Floor: **2011 sq. ft.**	2nd Floor: **777 sq. ft.**
Guest Suite: **243 sq. ft.**	
Total Living: **3031 sq. ft.**	
Foundation: **Slab**	

PDF **$1517**   Vellum **$1517**   CAD **$2728**

Fiorentino | Plan 6910

Traditional Tuscan Style

The graceful curves of rotundas, dramatically changing roof pitches and architectural enhancements like half columns, corbels, and an arbor delight the eye with their gentle movement. Guests know they've arrived as they step up to the entry terrace and are embraced by the home's elegant entry. The gentle curve of the elegant staircase that sweeps upward in a rotunda, the curved windows in the living room and breakfast nook, and the graceful arc of a wet bar and wine room heighten the visual appeal of this plan.

A media room is the ultimate retreat for the owners of the home and the guests enjoying the privacy of two second floor guest suites. Seclusion is found in the loft overlooking the dining room and the deck above the loggia-an ideal vantage point for stargazing.

The master suite sets the stage for serene interlude, beginning with the elevated garden tub that looks through three arched windows onto a privacy garden and culminating in the bedroom's sitting area overlooking the loggia-meant to be enjoyed with a refreshing beverage from the suite's morning kitchen.

PHOTO ABOVE: Despite its spacious 600 square feet, the leisure room is still one of the coziest rooms in the home, featuring a corner fireplace, built-in entertainment center, exposed beam ceiling and retreating glass walls that open to the loggia.

PHOTO LEFT: Rich accents in wood bring an aura of old-world grace and sophistication to a private study adjacent to the formal living room.

PHOTO LEFT: The emphasis might appear to be more on "form" than "function", but this picture-perfect kitchen is deceptively hard-working. Enjoying ample space for a professional-grade hooded range, double sinks and spacious dual pantries, the chef of this home could easily manage a dinner party for twelve.

PHOTO FAR LEFT: The loft above the dining area – its boundaries defined by an ornate, wrought-iron railing – provides access to two spacious, second-story guest suites and an observation deck, in addition to a picturesque view of the beautifully appointed first floor.

PHOTO BELOW: Casual dining is at its finest when enjoying a meal in the dining nook where mitered glass windows showcase the resort-like rear view.

PHOTO ABOVE: Classic architectural design meets contemporary convenience in the pampering master suite bath. An elevated garden tub in the master suite overlooks the privacy garden.

PHOTO RIGHT: The master suite is truly a haven, replete with a morning kitchen and his-and-hers walk-in closets. The sitting area opens to the loggia via French doors. For pure enjoyment, simply add an evening cocktail or morning coffee.

PHOTO RIGHT: A breezy, rambling loggia wraps the rear elevation. Decorative columns and pillars gracefully bear a beautiful burden – the weight of a second-story observation deck that opens to the starry sky above.

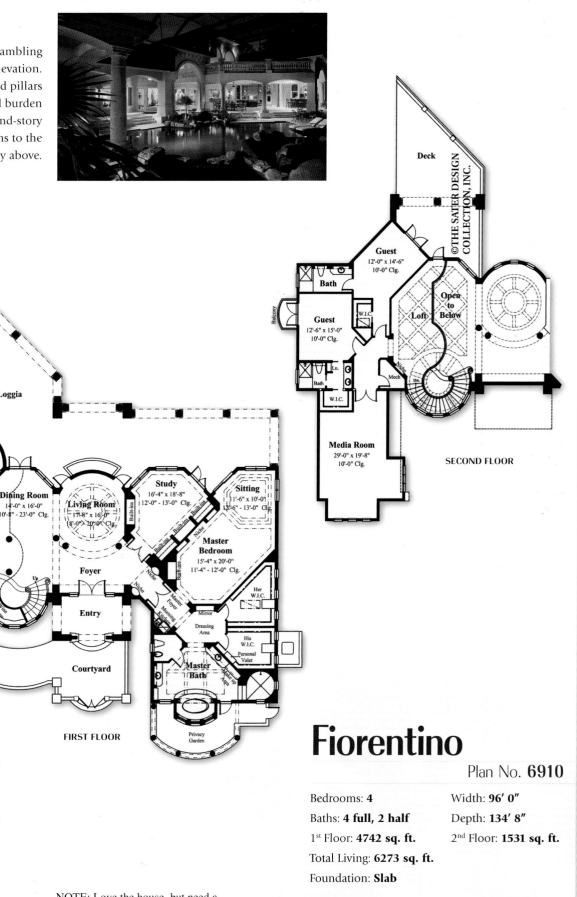

SECOND FLOOR

Deck

Guest
12'-0" x 14'-6"
10'-0" Clg.

Bath

Balcony

Guest
12'-6" x 15'-0"
10'-0" Clg.

W.I.C.

Loft

Open to Below

Bath

W.I.C.

Mech.

Media Room
29'-0" x 19'-8"
10'-0" Clg.

©THE SATER DESIGN COLLECTION, INC.

FIRST FLOOR

Outdoor Kitchen

Pool Bath

Fireplace

Loggia

Built-ins

Leisure
21'-4" x 28'-8"
14'-6" - 15'-6" Clg.

Breakfast
12'-8" x 12'-0"
10'-0" - 10'-8" Clg.

Kitchen
16'-8" x 18'-8"
10'-0" Clg.

Dining Room
14'-0" x 16'-0"
10'-8" - 23'-0" Clg.

Living Room
17'-8" x 16'-0"
18'-0" x 20'-0" Clg.

Study
16'-4" x 18'-8"
12'-0" - 13'-0" Clg.

Sitting
11'-6" x 10'-0"
12'-6" - 13'-0" Clg.

Pantry

Foyer

Master Bedroom
15'-4" x 20'-0"
11'-4" - 12'-0" Clg.

Bath

W.I.C.

Guest
14'-0" x 13'-0"
9'-4" Clg.

Linen

Wine Room

Up

Entry

Courtyard

Niche

Mstr. Foyer

Her W.I.C.

Mirror

Dressing Area

His W.I.C.

Pwdr Bath

Impress Iron Center

Studio

Stor.

SinkSpa

Duet DryAire Washer Cabinet & Dryer

Master Bath

Make up Area

Personal Valet

Privacy Garden

Garage
23'-4" x 37'-4"
9'-4" Clg.

©THE SATER DESIGN COLLECTION, INC.

Fiorentino

Plan No. 6910

Bedrooms: **4**	Width: **96' 0"**
Baths: **4 full, 2 half**	Depth: **134' 8"**
1st Floor: **4742 sq. ft.**	2nd Floor: **1531 sq. ft.**
Total Living: **6273 sq. ft.**	
Foundation: **Slab**	

PDF **$6273**	Vellum **$6273**	CAD **$10664**

NOTE: Love the house, but need a little less space? Check out plan 6960, *Vienetta*, for a highly similar but slightly smaller version.

Classic Craftsmanship

Clearly Mediterranean-inspired, with a barrel-tile roof in terracotta hues, lancet arches and Tuscan columns, the sun-drenched façade of this home extends a formal welcome. Crisp, white trim speaks of Spanish influence, and iron detailing adds a hint of non-conformity.

Past the foyer, an open floor plan emphasizes outdoor living with a seamless transition of indoor and outdoor spaces. Columns, built-ins and ceiling treatments define rooms, while a flowing floor plan creates natural movement.

The formal living room is punctuated by natural light welcomed in by floor-to-ceiling windows. The openness of the leisure room, nook and kitchen create casual gathering areas extended by ample outdoor spaces.

Spacious guest accommodations on both floors assure that visitors stay in comfort. Guests enjoy private or semi-private full baths and private spaces – a garden on the first floor and a loft upstairs.

PHOTO ABOVE: The handcrafted built-in entertainment center and molded ceiling details provide drama to the spacious leisure room, which opens seamlessly onto the veranda's outdoor kitchen.

PHOTO LEFT: Elegant arches and stunning wood columns define the dining space while giving it a unique connection to the diamond-shaped living room.

PHOTO LEFT: This extra-large study has it all: a wall of custom cabinetry, another of windows overlooking a front garden, a stepped ceiling and lots of floor space for working and relaxing.

PHOTO FAR LEFT: Well-appointed and well-planned, this kitchen boasts ample storage for tools of the trade and two large islands that add workspace. Ornate woodwork on the cabinetry and soffits adds an exotic flair.

PHOTO LEFT: Wood adds drama to a stepped ceiling, and three dramatic windows provide natural light and an effortless connection to the veranda.

PHOTO ABOVE: A stepped ceiling with molding details and elegant lighting crowns a generous master suite. An art niche separates two walk-in closets and provides a visually appealing entry to a fully appointed master bedroom.

PHOTO RIGHT: A whirlpool tub in the master bath is anything but ordinary, nestled between dark wood columns and overlooking a private garden.

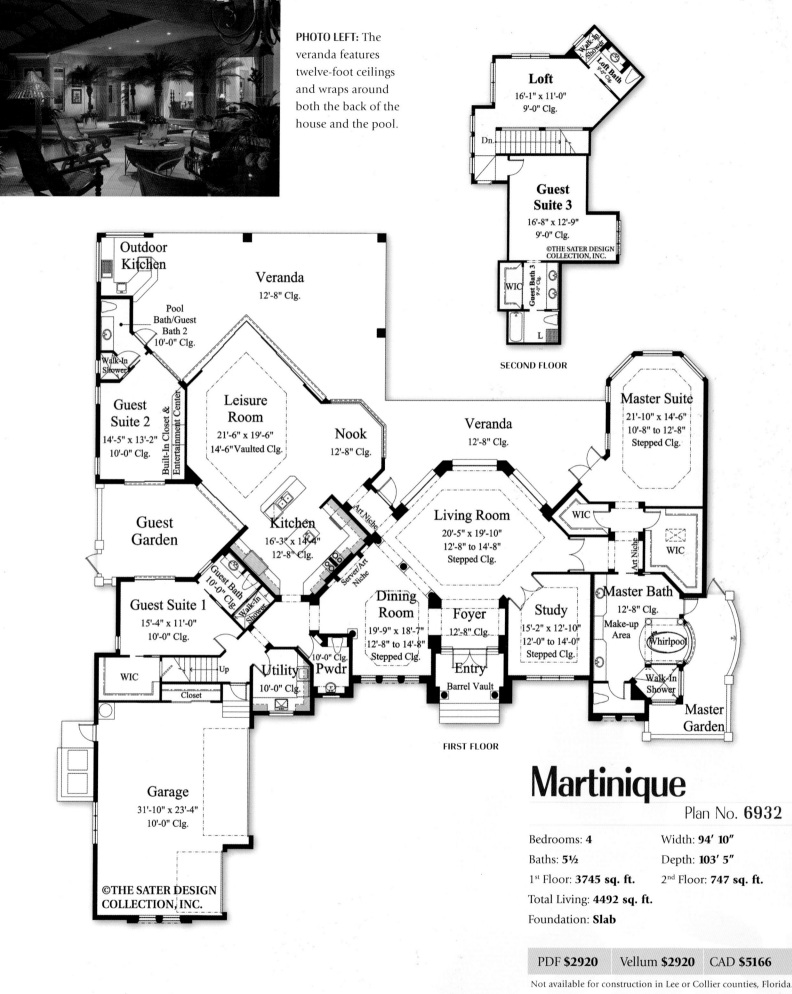

PHOTO LEFT: The veranda features twelve-foot ceilings and wraps around both the back of the house and the pool.

Loft
16'-1" x 11'-0"
9'-0" Clg.

Walk-In Shower

Loft Bath
9'-0" Clg.

Dn.

Guest Suite 3
16'-8" x 12'-9"
9'-0" Clg.

©THE SATER DESIGN COLLECTION, INC.

WIC

Guest Bath 3
9'-0" Clg.

L

SECOND FLOOR

Outdoor Kitchen

Veranda
12'-8" Clg.

Pool Bath/Guest Bath 2
10'-0" Clg.

Walk-In Shower

Guest Suite 2
14'-5" x 13'-2"
10'-0" Clg.

Built-In Closet & Entertainment Center

Leisure Room
21'-6" x 19'-6"
14'-6" Vaulted Clg.

Nook
12'-8" Clg.

Veranda
12'-8" Clg.

Master Suite
21'-10" x 14'-6"
10'-8" to 12'-8"
Stepped Clg.

WIC

Guest Garden

Kitchen
16'-3" x 14'-4"
12'-8" Clg.

Art Niche

Living Room
20'-5" x 19'-10"
12'-8" to 14'-8"
Stepped Clg.

WIC

Art Niche

WIC

Guest Bath
10'-0" Clg.

Walk-In Shower

Server/Art Niche

Master Bath
12'-8" Clg.

Make-up Area

Whirlpool

Guest Suite 1
15'-4" x 11'-0"
10'-0" Clg.

Dining Room
19'-9" x 18'-7"
12'-8" to 14'-8"
Stepped Clg.

Foyer
12'-8" Clg.

Study
15'-2" x 12'-10"
12'-0" to 14'-0"
Stepped Clg.

Walk-In Shower

WIC

Utility
10'-0" Clg.

10'-0" Clg.

Pwdr

Entry
Barrel Vault

Master Garden

Up

Closet

Garage
31'-10" x 23'-4"
10'-0" Clg.

©THE SATER DESIGN COLLECTION, INC.

FIRST FLOOR

Martinique

Plan No. **6932**

Bedrooms: **4**	Width: **94' 10"**
Baths: **5½**	Depth: **103' 5"**
1st Floor: **3745 sq. ft.**	2nd Floor: **747 sq. ft.**
Total Living: **4492 sq. ft.**	
Foundation: **Slab**	

Alamosa | Plan 6940

A Spectacular Retreat

Dramatic rooflines, ornamented windows and a boldly articulated entry combine to create a striking façade. Inside, a barrel-vaulted foyer opens to spectacular views through the cupola area to the Grand Solana. Soaring coffered and curved beamed ceilings and pre-classical marble columns define the varied spaces of the public realm. A two-sided fireplace warms the formal rooms as well as the secluded study.

A view-oriented design, windows line the rear perimeter of the home creating a seamless connection with the outdoors. Retreating glass walls open the leisure room to the solana and lanai, creating a flexible space for every occasion. The gourmet-caliber kitchen enjoys wide-open views of the casual living areas, defined not by walls, but stone floors and coffered ceilings.

Away from the public rooms, the entire left wing of the home is dedicated to the private master retreat. A private garden, spacious walk-in closet, morning kitchen and access to the lanai create a spa-like retreat. On the upper level, a winding balcony hall connects a loft, wet bar, exercise room and media room with a spacious guest suite.

PHOTO ABOVE: A two-story stepped-ceiling soars over the generous leisure room while retreating glass walls further expand the space to the lanai and solana.

PHOTO LEFT: Laden in stone, the plein air solana extends the livability of the leisure room and includes a corner fireplace and an alfresco kitchen.

PHOTO LEFT: Stone floors and coffered ceilings define the wide-open spaces of the casual living area. An arching doorway secludes a convenient butler's pantry that links the food-preparation area to the wet bar.

PHOTO FAR LEFT: A sky-high barrel vaulted ceiling in the formal dining room will surely elevate fine dining occasions. A unique built-in server eases entertaining.

PHOTO LEFT: A stunning home theatre will delight movie lovers and sports fans alike.

PHOTO ABOVE: A series of square transoms and a stunning mitered-glass window set off the sitting bay of the owners' suite, permitting views and light to enhance the retreat.

PHOTO RIGHT: Decorative pillars and columns demonstrate the influence of the ancient Greeks in this magnificent master bath, while a luxurious whirlpool tub offers a very modern indulgence.

PHOTO ABOVE: Open rooms engage the rear perimeter of the home with wide views and a sense of the outdoors.

Alamosa

Plan No. **6940**

Bedrooms: **5**

Baths: **5 full, 2 half**

1st Floor: **6122 sq. ft.**

Total Living: **8088 sq. ft.**

Foundation: **Slab**

Width: **118' 0"**

Depth: **147' 10"**

2nd Floor: **1966 sq. ft.**

PDF **$10110**   Vellum **$10110**   CAD **$16176**

Truly An Exotic Estate

This grand villa displays an affinity for the native terrain, with natural materials and large expanses of glass that permit earthen-hued walls to absorb the scenery. Rough-hewn timbers contradict a highly refined palette of textures in the living room, and a two-sided fireplace links this formal space with a private study. Sculpted forms and elaborate arches articulate the ornate vocabulary of the revival style, offset by naïve elements, such as rugged trusses and masonry walls.

An open arrangement of the formal living and dining rooms creates an entertainment area that is completed by a wine cellar. Paneled cabinetry enhances the wet bar and pantry positioned between the dining room and kitchen to facilitate planned events. Retreating glass walls permit a fluid boundary between the casual living zone and the outdoor spaces, which include an alfresco kitchen and a rambling terrace with a pool and spa.

Two über-luxe guest suites frame a spacious solana with a beamed ceiling and a massive fireplace. On the opposite side of the plan, the master wing features a secluded sitting bay and a compartmented bath with a bumped-out bay that harbors an oversized walk-in shower.

PHOTO LEFT: Pointed arch windows with delicate framework make for elegant outdoor viewing from a comfortable dining room. A mirrored buffet boasts dramatic carvings and corbels, and softly hued walls emit all the warmth needed for memorable meals.

PHOTO FAR LEFT: This kitchen has it all: a furniture-style, butcher-block island, gleaming commercial range and angled walls of countertops and cabinetry. The beamed coffered ceiling and dramatic lighting add flair.

PHOTO LEFT: Lanai profiles mimic and draw attention to the pointed-arch living room window, while a secluded nook created by angled walls of glass offers an ideal spot for morning lattes.

PHOTO ABOVE: A spectacular master suite occupies one side of the home. An angled bedroom with a tray ceiling features headboard and art niches along with a magnificent sitting room embraced by a quadruple bay window.

PHOTO RIGHT: A freestanding whirlpool tub encased in natural stone and marble takes center stage in this award winning and truly dramatic master bath.

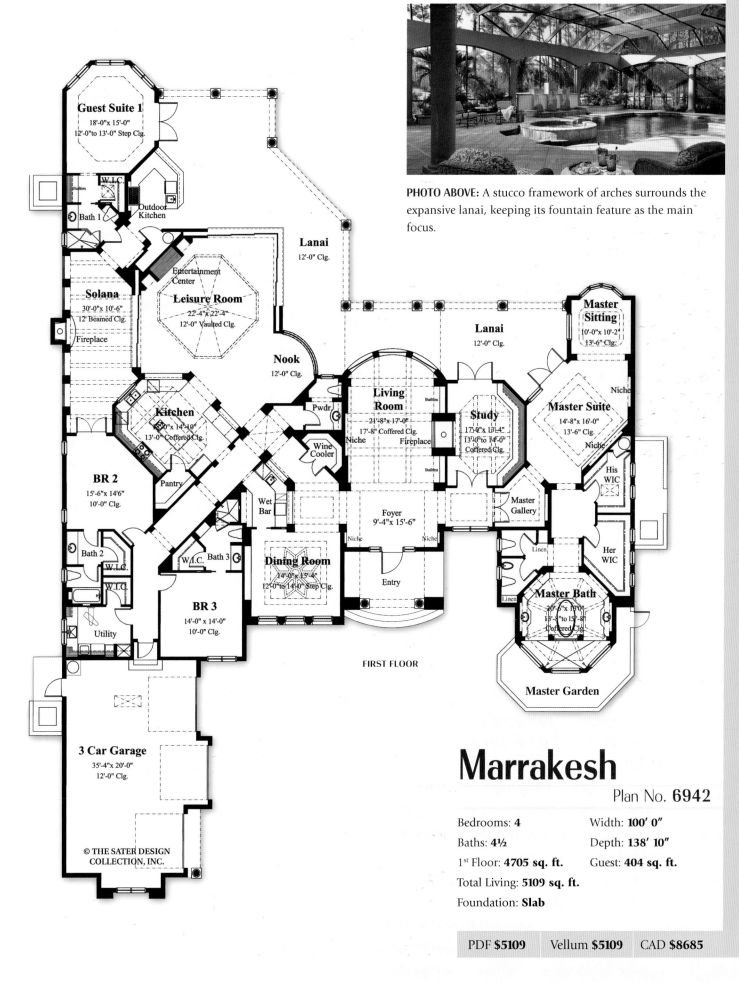

PHOTO ABOVE: A stucco framework of arches surrounds the expansive lanai, keeping its fountain feature as the main focus.

Guest Suite 1
18'-0"x 15'-0"
12'-0"to 13'-0" Step Clg.

W.I.C.

Builtins

Bath 1

Outdoor Kitchen

Lanai
12'-0" Clg.

Entertainment Center

Solana
30'-0"x 10'-6"
12' Beamed Clg.

Fireplace

Leisure Room
22'-4"x 22'-4"
12'-0" Vaulted Clg.

Nook
12'-0" Clg.

Lanai
12'-0" Clg.

Master Sitting
10'-0"x 10'-2"
13'-6" Clg.

Master Suite
14'-8"x 16'-0"
13'-6" Clg.

Niche

Niche

Kitchen
15'-0"x 14'-10"
13'-0" Coffered Clg.

Pwdr.

Living Room
21'-8"x 17'-0"
17'-8" Coffered Clg.

Builtins

Niche

Study
17'-0"x 13'-4"
13'-0" to 14'-0"
Coffered Clg.

Fireplace

Builtins

His WIC

Wine Cooler

BR 2
15'-6"x 14'6"
10'-0" Clg.

Pantry

Wet Bar

Master Gallery

Her WIC

Bath 2

W.I.C.

W.I.C.

W.I.C.

Bath 3

Dining Room
14'-0"x 15'-4"
12'-0"to 14'-0" Step Clg.

Foyer
9'-4"x 15'-6"

Niche

Niche

Linen

Linen

BR 3
14'-0"x 14'-0"
10'-0" Clg.

Entry

Master Bath
20'-0"x 13'-0"
13'-3" to 15'-8"
Coffered Clg.

Utility

FIRST FLOOR

Master Garden

3 Car Garage
35'-4"x 20'-0"
12'-0" Clg.

© THE SATER DESIGN COLLECTION, INC.

Marrakesh

Plan No. 6942

Bedrooms: **4**	Width: **100' 0"**
Baths: **4½**	Depth: **138' 10"**
1st Floor: **4705 sq. ft.**	Guest: **404 sq. ft.**
Total Living: **5109 sq. ft.**	
Foundation: **Slab**	

PDF **$5109**	Vellum **$5109**	CAD **$8685**

Porto Velho | Plan 6950

Airy and Engaging

Spectacular design creates balance and harmony in this outstanding Mediterranean manor. From private guest suites to a wide-open floor plan that melds with a wrapping verandah, *Porto Velho* offers infinite charm and function without sacrificing the ultimate in luxury living appointments. The façade invites, with a dramatic, recessed and turreted entry enhanced by multiple arched windows framed with balusters.

Inside, the foyer opens to a vaulted great room with views stretching well beyond the retreating glass wall. The master suite is allotted an entire wing and a forward dining room and study, both with octagonal stepped ceilings, provide first-class

environments for entertaining and private studies.

A spacious, centralized great room anchors the 4,500 square foot plan. A wall of built-ins is perfect for media components, books and treasures. Another wall is lined with pocketing glass doors, throwing the room open to the verandah and pool area. The gourmet kitchen is accessed through three archways that mimic the Mediterranean windows gracing the front of the home. A breakfast nook, walk-in pantry and powder bath complete the core of the home.

Every amenity for fabulous family living and memorable entertaining is accentuated inside this highly crafted European flavored home.

PHOTO ABOVE: Rustic beams lend texture to the vaulted ceiling of the wide open great room, where glass doors pocket into the walls to extend the room outdoors and elegant arches grant access to the kitchen and its gracious serving counter.

PHOTO LEFT: Tall Tuscan columns and a wooden pergola frame a stunning courtyard. Located near the outdoor kitchen, this plein air living room is idyllic for a lazy Sunday brunch.

PHOTO LEFT: An elaborately carved center island, hand-rubbed cabinetry and a stunning carved-stone hood add drama to this has-it-all gourmet kitchen. There's even a desk nook through the arched doorway.

PHOTO FAR LEFT: The elegant dining room boasts an impressive, dramatic ceiling and forward views to enjoy during fine meals.

PHOTO BELOW: Perfect for airy entertaining, the glass walls to the verandah fully pocket, opening the kitchen and great room to the outdoor area seamlessly.

PHOTO ABOVE: The molded, stepped ceiling is a dramatic canopy to this regal master bedroom, where floor-to-ceiling windows frame a cozy sitting nook and glass doors disappear to access a private corner of the verandah.

PHOTO RIGHT: A center spa tub rests inside gleaming wood and granite, offering an opulent focal point for the master bath. A window-framed, walk-in shower is tucked beneath the curved and wrought-iron adorned wall behind the tub.

PHOTO RIGHT: A beautiful pool with sun shelf and elevated spa glows with reflected light from the striking rear rooms that wrap the verandah.

Verandah
20'-6" x 35'-8"
12'-0" Clg.

Outdoor Kitchen

Nook
13'-2" x 13'-2"
Vaulted Clg.

Verandah
9'-3" x 40'-7"
12'-0" Clg.

Guest Suite 2
13'-4" x 16'-0"
12'-0" Clg.

Bath 2
10'-0"

Master Suite
18'-4" x 19'-4"
12'-0"-13'-0"
Stepped Clg.

Stor.

Great Room
23'-3" x 22'-0"
Vaulted Clg.

Built-In

Kitchen
16'-0" x 16'-0"
12'-0" Clg.

Bath 1
10'-0" Clg.

WIC

Pantry

Linen

WIC

Pwdr.

WIC

Arch

Arch
Art Niche

WIC

Gallery

Guest Suite 1
14'-0" x 13'-2"
12'-0" Clg.

Arch

Desk

Dri/Dry

Foyer
12'-0" Clg.

Master Bath
12'-0" Clg.
Whirlpool Tub

Study
14'-9" x 16'-3"
12'-0"-13'-0"
Stepped Clg.

Built-In

Utility
10'-0" Clg.

Spa Sink

Dining Room
15'-2" x 13'-10"
12'-0"-16'-6"
Stepped Clg.

Walk-In Shower

Storage

Gladiator Workbench

Gallery

Up

Arch

Arch

Entry

Privacy Garden

Gladiator Freezerator

Garage
24'-8" x 30'-8"
8'-8" Clg.

FIRST FLOOR

© THE SATER DESIGN COLLECTION, INC.

Down

Guest Room
17'-6" x 18'-6"
Vaulted Clg.

TV Niche

© THE SATER DESIGN COLLECTION, INC.

Guest Bath

WIC

SECOND FLOOR

Porto Velho

Plan No. **6950**

Bedrooms: **4**	Width: **97' 2"**
Baths: **4½**	Depth: **100' 9"**
1st Floor: **3947 sq. ft.**	2nd Floor: **545 sq. ft.**
Total Living: **4492 sq. ft.**	
Foundation: **Slab**	

PDF $2920	Vellum $2920	CAD $5166

Not available for construction in Lee or Collier counties, Florida.

Absolutely Award-Winning

A desire to create a home that paid homage to Palm Beach's great Spanish-influenced villas while at the same time embracing contemporary design ideas and technologies was the inspiration behind Dan Sater's award-winning design *Cordillera*. The recipient of both a 2006 Aurora and AIBD award, *Cordillera* incorporates modern amenities and elements such as corner-less disappearing sliding-glass walls, clubrooms, outdoor living spaces and full-house automation.

This villa-style plan opens traditionally boxed spaces to satisfying views of the landscape. The vaulted foyer opens through the front gallery to the formal core of the home: a series of three view-oriented rooms designed to encourage intimate gatherings.

To the right of the home, the casual living zone incorporates a spacious leisure room that links with a nook and kitchen. Upstairs, a balcony bridge connects a game room, pub and home theater with two guest suites.

PHOTO ABOVE: The outdoor retreat wraps the leisure room, nook and kitchen with a perfect space for entertaining. Interior and exterior living areas mix seamlessly via retreating glass doors.

PHOTO LEFT: Shapely columns and arches create a fluid boundary between the pool deck and solana, and shelter the outside living area from the midday sun.

PHOTO LEFT: Connected to the living room at the center of the plan, the dining room takes in views of the pool and lakefront. A stunning stepped ceiling adds a touch of drama to its formality.

PHOTO FAR LEFT: Straight ahead of the main entry, a series of three French doors open to a spectacular pool setting, offering brilliant views both day and night.

PHOTO BELOW: The ultimate entertainment room—a wet bar, home theater and French doors opening to a private deck round out the media room's many amenities.

PHOTO ABOVE: Floor-to-ceiling windows permit natural light to permeate the master bedroom. Curved moldings, a coffered ceiling and a flattened arch lend dimension, depth and texture to the room, which leads outside to the sun terrace, pool and spa.

PHOTO RIGHT: Framed by twin Tuscan columns, a sculpted Persian-red marble tub surround subdues the grand scale of the master bath. Past the tall muntin window and fanlight is a glimpse of the private garden.

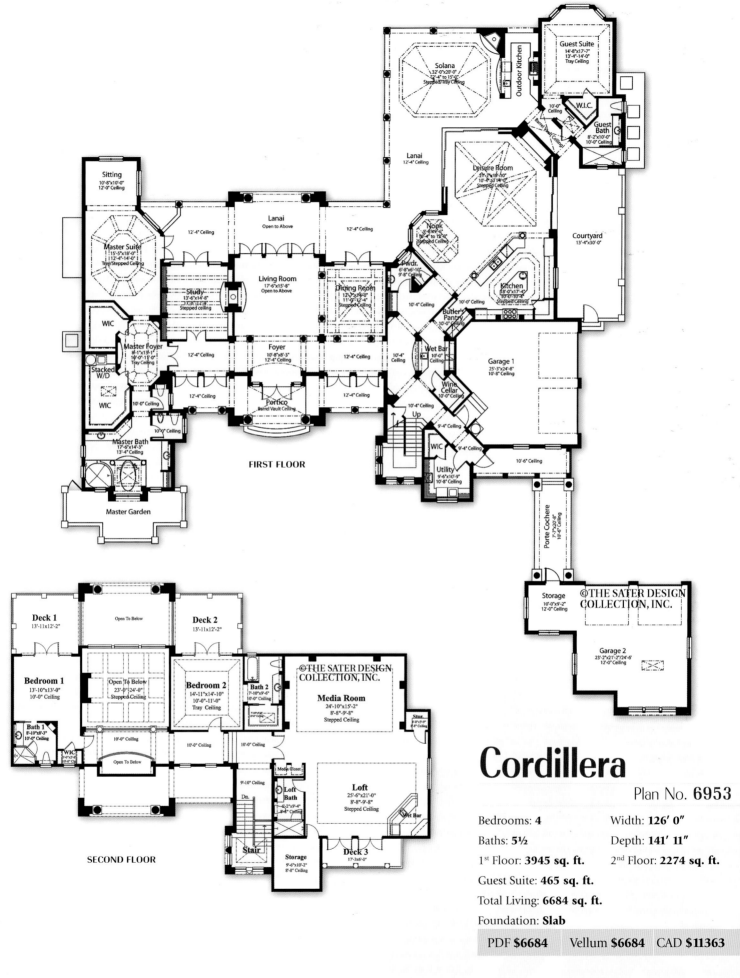

FIRST FLOOR

Sitting
10'-8"x10'-0"
12'-0" Ceiling

Master Suite
15'-5"x18'-0"
12'-4"-14'-0"
Tray/Stepped Ceiling

WIC

Master Foyer
8'-1"x13'-1"
10'-0"-11'-0"
Tray Ceiling

Stacked W/D

WIC

Master Bath
17'-6"x14'-3"
13'-4" Ceiling

Master Garden

Study
13'-6"x14'-8"
Stepped ceiling

12'-4" Ceiling

Lanai
Open to Above

Living Room
17'-6"x15'-8"
Open to Above

12'-4" Ceiling

Foyer
10'-8"x8'-3"
12'-4" Ceiling

12'-4" Ceiling

Portico
Barrel Vault Ceiling

Dining Room
12'-3"x14'-0"
11'-9"-12'-4"
Stepped Ceiling

12'-4" Ceiling

10'-4" Ceiling

10'-0" Ceiling

Solana
32'-0"x20'-0"
12'-4" to 15'-0"
Stepped tray Ceiling

Lanai
12'-4" Ceiling

Leisure Room
21'-2"x16'-10"
14'-0"-32'-0"
Stepped Ceiling

Nook
9'-8"x9'-0"
10'-4" to 13'-0"
Stepped Ceiling

Pwdr.
6'-8"x6'-10"
9'-8" Ceiling

Outdoor Kitchen

Guest Suite
14'-8"x17'-7"
13'-4"-14'-0"
Tray Ceiling

W.I.C.

Guest Bath
8'-2"x10'-0"
10'-0" Ceiling

Courtyard
13'-4"x30'-0"

Kitchen
18'-0"x17'-5"
10'-0"-10'-4"
Stepped Ceiling

Butler's Pantry
10'-0" Ceiling

Wet Bar
10'-0" Ceiling

Wine Cellar
10'-0" Ceiling

Garage 1
25'-3"x24'-8"
10'-8" Ceiling

WIC
9'-4" Ceiling

Utility
9'-6"x10'-9"
10'-8" Ceiling

Up

10'-4" Ceiling

9'-4" Ceiling

10'-6" Ceiling

Porte Cochere
7'-7"x20'-0"
10'-6" Ceiling

Storage
10'-0"x9'-2"
12'-0" Ceiling

©THE SATER DESIGN COLLECTION, INC.

Garage 2
23'-2"x21'-2"/24'-6"
12'-0" Ceiling

SECOND FLOOR

Deck 1
13'-11"x12'-2"

Open To Below

Deck 2
13'-11"x12'-2"

Bedroom 1
13'-10"x13'-0"
10'-0" Ceiling

Open To Below
23'-0"x24'-0"
Stepped Ceiling

Bedroom 2
14'-11"x14'-10"
10'-0"-11'-0"
Tray Ceiling

Bath 2
7'-10"x9'-6"
10'-0" Ceiling

Bath 1
8'-10"x8'-3"
10'-0" Ceiling

WIC

Open To Below

10'-0" Ceiling

10'-0" Ceiling

10'-0" Ceiling

©THE SATER DESIGN COLLECTION, INC.

Media Room
24'-10"x15'-2"
8'-8"-9'-8"
Stepped Ceiling

Stor.

9'-10" Ceiling

Media Closet

Loft Bath

Dn.

Loft
25'-6"x21'-0"
8'-8"-9'-8"
Stepped Ceiling

Wet Bar

Stair

Storage
9'-6"x10'-2"
8'-8" Ceiling

Deck 3
17'-3x6'-0"

Cordillera

Plan No. **6953**

Bedrooms: **4**	Width: **126' 0"**
Baths: **5½**	Depth: **141' 11"**
1st Floor: **3945 sq. ft.**	2nd Floor: **2274 sq. ft.**
Guest Suite: **465 sq. ft.**	
Total Living: **6684 sq. ft.**	
Foundation: **Slab**	

PDF **$6684** Vellum **$6684** CAD **$11363**

Majestic Façade

Prima Porta is a true Italianate charmer. Mediterranean elements of pastoral wood and wrought iron create an old-world atmosphere that is juxtaposed with state-of-the-art appliances and new-world amenities.

The entry portico is the first expression of the Mediterranean atmosphere that infuses the interior, with a quoin surround of the main entry and repeating arches throughout. Once inside, in addition to recurring arches, stepped ceilings accented with wood beams are also found in many rooms.

Entertaining on any scale is accomplished with minimal effort in *Prima Porta*, with a spacious, gourmet kitchen, an additional outdoor kitchen, luxurious dining room, convenient butler's pantry, two fireplaces and an elegant wet bar. Outdoor spaces coax inhabitants and guests alike, out to enjoy the solana and expansive covered lanai. Guests invited to spend the night will be perfectly at home in three guest suites complete with full baths and walk-in closets.

An opulent master retreat begins with a magnificent foyer and continues with a spacious bedroom and walk-in closet with a built-in island. The owners' lavish bath features dual vanities, a curved walk-in shower, makeup counter, bench and a centrally located tub. ❖

PHOTO ABOVE: The leisure room is open to the kitchen with a convenient eating bar dividing the space. This arrangement allows interaction and both rooms to enjoy breezes from the lanai. The deep, wood-beamed ceiling detail is also above the kitchen.

PHOTO LEFT: The leisure room accesses the lanai through retreating glass walls, fusing the two spaces into one. The al fresco dining area easily serves family dinners and reunions with old friends next to the warming outdoor fireplace.

PHOTO LEFT: Rustic elements of rough-hewn wood and wrought iron enhance the organic atmosphere of the outdoor kitchen and sitting area.

PHOTO FAR LEFT: Culinary aficionados of all skill levels will find themselves at home in *Prima Porta's* gourmet kitchen, awash in elegant appointments and state-of-the-art amenities.

PHOTO BELOW: The dining room is open, yet enclosed, by a series of arches. Rustic French doors topped with arched transoms open to the loggia, while an art niche highlights a favorite work.

PHOTO ABOVE: Elegance abounds in this spacious, elongated master suite, reflected in an arched bed niche, built-in shelves, a stepped ceiling and French doors to the lanai.

PHOTO RIGHT: Geometric simplicity plays counterpoint to luxurious details, such as the curved wall surrounding the walk-in shower. Nearby, a makeup vanity and sitting bench round out the amenities.

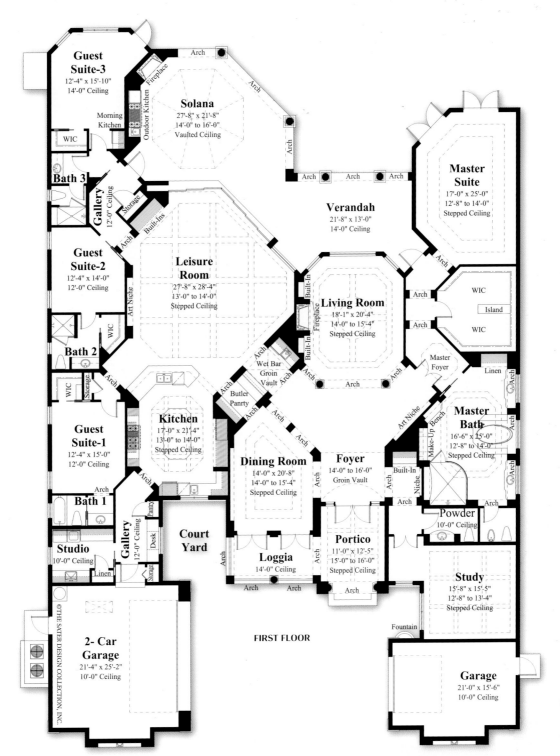

FIRST FLOOR

Guest Suite-3
12'-4" x 15'-10"
14'-0" Ceiling

Solana
27'-8" x 21'-8"
14'-0" to 16'-0"
Vaulted Ceiling

Master Suite
17'-0" x 25'-0"
12'-8" to 14'-0"
Stepped Ceiling

Verandah
21'-8" x 13'-0"
14'-0" Ceiling

Morning Kitchen

Outdoor Kitchen

WIC

Bath 3

Gallery 12'-0" Ceiling

Storage

Built-Ins

Leisure Room
27'-8" x 28'-4"
13'-0" to 14'-0"
Stepped Ceiling

WIC

Island

WIC

Guest Suite-2
12'-4" x 14'-0"
12'-0" Ceiling

Art Niche

Living Room
18'-1" x 20'-4"
14'-0" to 15'-4"
Stepped Ceiling

Built-In

WIC

Bath 2

Storage

Master Foyer

Linen

WIC

Wet Bar
Groin Vault

Master Bath
16'-6" x 25'-0"
12'-8" to 14'-0"
Stepped Ceiling

Butler Panrty

Kitchen
17'-0" x 21'-4"
13'-0" to 14'-0"
Stepped Ceiling

Guest Suite-1
12'-4" x 15'-0"
12'-0" Ceiling

Dining Room
14'-0" x 20'-8"
14'-0" to 15'-4"
Stepped Ceiling

Foyer
14'-0" to 16'-0"
Groin Vault

Make-Up Bench

Niche

Built-In

Powder
10'-0" Ceiling

Bath 1

Arch

Gallery 12'-0" Ceiling

Desk

Pantry

Court Yard

Loggia
14'-0" Ceiling

Portico
11'-0" x 12'-5"
15'-0" to 16'-0"
Stepped Ceiling

Study
15'-8" x 15'-5"
12'-8" to 13'-4"
Stepped Ceiling

Studio
10'-0" Ceiling

Linen

Storage

Fountain

©THE SATER DESIGN COLLECTION, INC.

2- Car Garage
21'-4" x 25'-2"
10'-0" Ceiling

Garage
21'-0" x 15'-6"
10'-0" Ceiling

Prima Porta

Plan No. 6955

PHOTO LEFT: Serene tranquility calls from every room of the house, beckoning for enjoyment of the covered lanai, cozy sitting areas, outdoor fireplace, pool and spa.

Bedrooms: **4**	Width: **80' 0"**
Baths: **4½**	Depth: **118' 0"**
1st Floor: **5224 sq. ft.**	
Total Living: **5224 sq. ft.**	
Foundation: **Slab**	

| PDF **$5224** | Vellum **$5224** | CAD **$8881** |

Valdivia | Plan 6959

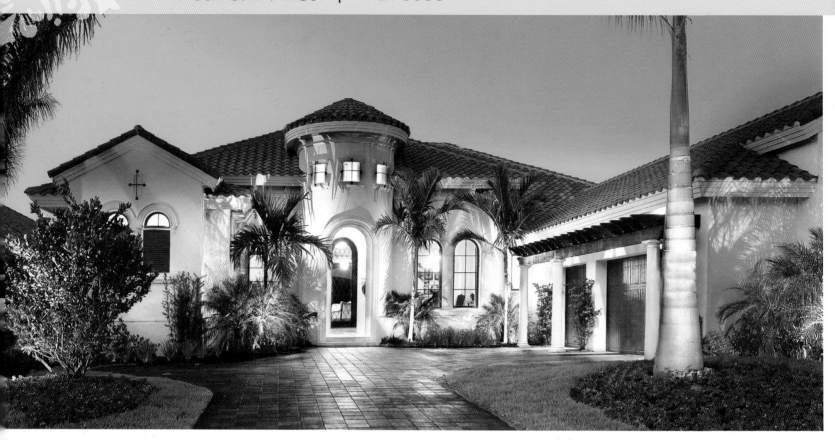

Perfect for Friends & Family

This elegantly detailed façade features a pergola, tiled roof, wrought-iron accents, arch-top windows and a majestic entry turret. A blended influence of Andalusian and Spanish Colonial architectural styles creates a stately ambiance.

Inside, this functional plan boasts a multitude of practicable amenities throughout the casually elegant living spaces. The result is a plan that lives larger than its square footage.

Most suitable for temperate climates, *Valdivia* offers a host of outdoor living space accessible from many public and private places throughout the home. Two outdoor fireplaces and an outdoor kitchen create natural gathering areas under a beautifully crafted wooden ceiling that provides an organic feeling atmosphere.

The central grand salon has a wet bar and is open to the kitchen, where a spacious eating bar invites casual entertaining, though a formal dining space is dedicated to fine meals in style. Perfect for hosting friends and family, the home offers three complete guest suites with private baths and walk-in closets, including one secluded suite fully detached from the main home, but connected by the outdoor living room.

PHOTO ABOVE: The home's entry is open to both the formal dining and great rooms with space delineated by elongated arches, supportive columns and unique ceiling treatments.

PHOTO LEFT: One of the two outdoor fireplaces warms an outdoor dining area adjacent to an outdoor kitchen and the entry of the secluded guest cabana.

PHOTO LEFT: The kitchen, at the heart of the home, offers easy access to the rear lanai, great room, and formal dining room. A breakfast nook augments the eating bar space for casual dining.

PHOTO FAR LEFT: The formal dining room rests beneath a ceiling crafted of pastoral beams configured in an elegant pattern and offers diners forward views through a duo of arch-top windows.

PHOTO BELOW: The great room offers a centralized social area with refreshments available from the wet bar with brick-look tiling, and rear views of the pool through a wall of retreating glass.

PHOTO ABOVE: An amenity-rich master bath hosts his-and-hers matching vanities, which frame the walls of the spacious bath. A center tub and shower with multiple luxury showerheads reside beneath a stepped ceiling.

PHOTO RIGHT: Secluded in the rear corner of the plan is the master retreat. With plentiful storage space, an elegant ceiling treatment and access to the covered gazebo just outside, this suite is sure to delight the owners.

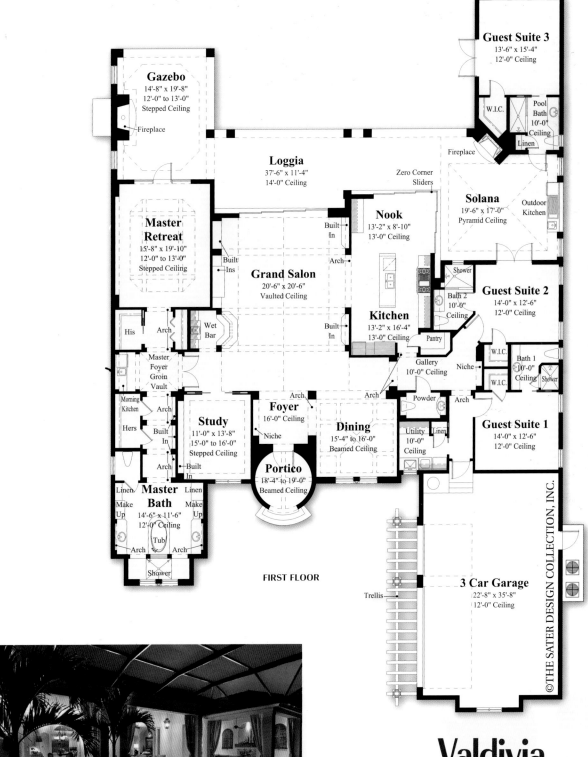

Gazebo
14'-8" x 19'-8"
12'-0" to 13'-0"
Stepped Ceiling

Fireplace

Loggia
37'-6" x 11'-4"
14'-0" Ceiling

Guest Suite 3
13'-6" x 15'-4"
12'-0" Ceiling

W.I.C.

Pool
Bath
10'-0"
Ceiling

Linen

Fireplace

Zero Corner
Sliders

**Master
Retreat**
15'-8" x 19'-10"
12'-0" to 13'-0"
Stepped Ceiling

Built
Ins

Built
In

Nook
13'-2" x 8'-10"
13'-0" Ceiling

Solana
19'-6" x 17'-0"
Pyramid Ceiling

Outdoor
Kitchen

Arch

Grand Salon
20'-6" x 20'-6"
Vaulted Ceiling

Shower

Bath 2
10'-0"
Ceiling

Guest Suite 2
14'-0" x 12'-6"
12'-0" Ceiling

His

Arch

Wet
Bar

Kitchen
13'-2" x 16'-4"
13'-0" Ceiling

Built
In

Pantry

Master
Foyer
Groin
Vault

W.I.C.

Bath 1
10'-0"
Ceiling

Shower

Gallery
10'-0" Ceiling

Niche

W.I.C.

Morning
Kitchen

Arch

Hers

Built
In

Study
11'-0" x 13'-8"
15'-0" to 16'-0"
Stepped Ceiling

Foyer
16'-0" Ceiling

Niche

Arch

Dining
15'-4" to 16'-0"
Beamed Ceiling

Powder

Arch

Guest Suite 1
14'-0" x 12'-6"
12'-0" Ceiling

Arch

Built
In

Arch

Portico
18'-4" to 19'-0"
Beamed Ceiling

Utility
10'-0"
Ceiling

Linen

Linen

**Master
Bath**
14'-6" x 11'-6"
12'-0" Ceiling

Make
Up

Make
Up

Tub

FIRST FLOOR

Arch

Arch

Shower

©THE SATER DESIGN COLLECTION, INC.

Trellis

3 Car Garage
22'-8" x 35'-8"
12'-0" Ceiling

PHOTO ABOVE: The dramatic loggia features 14-foot ceilings and wraps along the entire back of the house and around the pool for first-class outdoor living and entertaining.

Valdivia

Plan No. **6959**

Bedrooms: **4**   Width: **75' 0"**

Baths: **4½**   Depth: **115' 0"**

1st Floor: **3790 sq. ft.**

Total Living: **3790 sq. ft.**

Foundation: **Slab**

PDF **$2465**   Vellum **$2465**   CAD **$4359**

La Reina | Plan 8046

Outdoor Living Abounds

Derived from a blend of cultural influences—including Moorish and Renaissance—this clearly Mediterranean elevation creates an impressive, yet not imposing, street presence. Trios of windows bring light to interior spaces, and accentuate rows of decorative tile vents that line the façade. Carved balusters enhance a side balcony that's spacious enough to serve as an outdoor room. The paneled portal opens to a portico and courtyard, which creates a procession to the formal entry of the home.

To the front of the courtyard, a casita, or guesthouse, offers space that easily converts to a workshop or home office. The foyer opens directly to the grand room and through an arched opening, to the formal dining room. Glass bayed walls in the central living area and in the study help meld inside and outside spaces, and the dining room leads to a loggia—for open-air meals.

PHOTO: Not only visually stunning, the courtyard is a Zen-like retreat for family and friends to relax and unwind.

PHOTO LEFT: Light streams in to the bayed breakfast nook through multi-paned windows. A built-in window seat offers storage and a cozy place to sit.

PHOTO FAR LEFT: Soaring two-story ceilings allow for voluminous views and plentiful light through numerous windows that encircle the room. A grand fireplace provides a central gathering area, and a flowing design offers an open avenue to the dining room nearby.

PHOTO BELOW: Centrally located between the formal and informal rooms, the gourmet-caliber kitchen serves both realms with ease.

PHOTO ABOVE: This master bath opens to the impressive courtyard area and features a whirlpool tub soaked in light from the outdoors, a beautifully stepped ceiling and arches setting off the suite's vanities.

PHOTO RIGHT: Designed for privacy and appointed in elegance, the master suite features a high stepped ceiling and generous views through the suite's multi-paned windows and transoms. French doors provide access to the loggia.

PHOTO ABOVE: Past the door of the groin-vaulted portico, an expansive courtyard includes two loggias, an outdoor kitchen, fireplace, pool and a detached guest suite that flexes as a private retreat.

FIRST FLOOR

©THE SATER DESIGN COLLECTION, INC.

Loggia — 26'-10" x 11'-8" — Open to Above
Loggia — 15'-6" x 10'-0" — 10'-0" Clg.
Master Suite — 14'-8" x 22'-4" — 12'-0" to 14'-0" — Stepped Clg.
Grand Room — 19'-0" x 19'-5" — 21'-0" to 22'-4" — Open to Above
Dining Room — 10'-6" x 13'-4" — 10'-0" Clg.
Built-In
Whirlpool
WIC
M. Bath — 12'-0" to 14'-0" — Stepped Clg.
WIC
Pwdr. — 9'-4" Clg.
Foyer
Up
Built-In Server
Utility — 6'-8" x 9'- — 10'-0" Clg.
Linen
Walk-In Shower
Study — 14'-4" x 15'-0" — 12'-0" to 13'-0" — Stepped Clg.
Loggia — 10'-0" Clg.
Desk
Kitchen — 13'-8" x 15'-4" — 10'-0" Clg.
Nook — 10'-0" Clg.
Pantry
Fountain
Spa
Optional Pool
Courtyard
Loggia — 16'-8" Clg.
Leisure Room — 18'-6" x 17'-10" — 10'-0" to 14'-6" — Stepped Clg.
Garage — 11'-6" x 16'-10" — 10'-0" Clg.
Fireplace
Built-In Entertainment
Outdoor Kitchen
WIC
Loggia — 10'-0" Clg.
Portico — 14'-8" x 14'-4" — Groin Vault
Garage — 22'-4" x 25'-6" — 10'-0" Clg.
Guest Suite — 14'-4" x 13'-5" — 10'-0" Clg.
Pool Bath — 10'-0" Clg.
©THE SATER DESIGN COLLECTION, INC.

SECOND FLOOR

Balcony — 10'-12" x 9'-4"
Grand Room — Beamed Clg.
Open to Below
Bedroom 2 — 10'-11" x 13'-4" — 10'-0" Clg.
©THE SATER DESIGN COLLECTION, INC.
Open to Below
WIC
Bath 2 — 10'-0" Clg.
Linen
Dn.
Bath 3 — 10'-0" Clg. — Walk-In Shower
Balcony — 10'-7" x 14'-4"
Bedroom 3 — 15'-0" x 11'-6" — 10'-0" Clg.
WIC
WIC
Bedroom 4 — 11'-6" x 16'-8" — 10'-0" Clg.
Balcony

La Reina

Plan No. 8046

Bedrooms: **5**	Width: **80' 0"**
Baths: **4½**	Depth: **96' 0"**
1st Floor: **2852 sq. ft.**	2nd Floor: **969 sq. ft.**
Guest Suite: **330 sq. ft.**	
Total Living: **4151 sq. ft.**	
Foundation: **Slab**	

| PDF **$2698** | Vellum **$2698** | CAD **$4774** |

Caprina | Plan 8052

Old-World Meets New-World

Evocative of the adobe escapes of the Spanish Colonial vernacular, this exquisite villa invites a reconnection to nature. A few powerful renaissance details, such as spiral pilasters and patterned masonry, twist the traditional vocabulary to a more modern, eclectic motif. Rows of arched-top windows enhance the sidewalk presence of the home, and bring plenty of light to the interior.

Paneled doors lead to a grand foyer, which defies convention with a no-walls approach to the formal rooms. Coffered ceilings provide spatial separation and a visual link between the private and public realms. Dramatic views further define the interior and enable a rambling casual zone to meld into the scenery. A wraparound lanai connects rooms bordering the refreshing rear elevation, with an invitation to enjoy the outdoors. ❧

PHOTO ABOVE: The gourmet kitchen is open to both the dining nook and leisure room. Just outside, an outdoor kitchen offers the perfect place to barbecue.

PHOTO LEFT: Clever built-ins create a perfectly customized media center for leisure room enjoyment.

PHOTO LEFT: Slumped arches frame and delineate spaces throughout the home. Here, one frames the wet bar that provides fresh beverages to the nearby dining room.

PHOTO FAR LEFT: Retreating glass walls create a nearly seamless barrier to the outdoor living spaces beyond the leisure room.

PHOTO BELOW: An art niche provides the perfect display space near the kitchen, which resides under a detailed coffered ceiling.

PHOTO ABOVE: Bright and airy, the master bath features tall ceilings, dual sinks, a whirlpool bath, glass shower and plenty of sunshine.

PHOTO RIGHT: This master suite features a door to the pool and spa, which is also overlooked by the multiple windows of the sitting area.

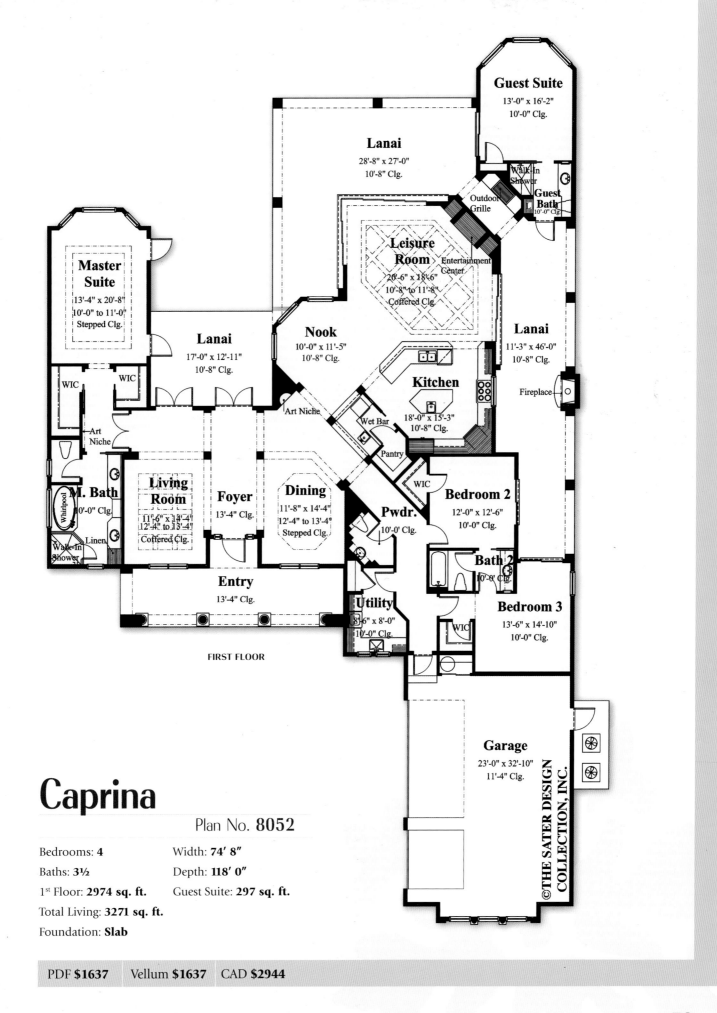

Guest Suite
13'-0" x 16'-2"
10'-0" Clg.

Lanai
28'-8" x 27'-0"
10'-8" Clg.

Walk-In Shower

Outdoor Grille

Guest Bath
10'-0" Clg.

Master Suite
13'-4" x 20'-8"
10'-0" to 11'-0"
Stepped Clg.

Lanai
17'-0" x 12'-11"
10'-8" Clg.

Nook
10'-0" x 11'-5"
10'-8" Clg.

Leisure Room
20'-6" x 18'-6"
10'-8" to 11'-8"
Coffered Clg.

Entertainment Center

Lanai
11'-3" x 46'-0"
10'-8" Clg.

Fireplace

WIC

WIC

Art Niche

Kitchen
18'-0" x 15'-3"
10'-8" Clg.

Art Niche

Wet Bar

Pantry

M. Bath
10'-0" Clg.

Living Room
11'-6" x 14'-4"
12'-4" to 13'-4"
Coffered Clg.

Foyer
13'-4" Clg.

Dining
11'-8" x 14'-4"
12'-4" to 13'-4"
Stepped Clg.

Pwdr.
10'-0" Clg.

WIC

Bedroom 2
12'-0" x 12'-6"
10'-0" Clg.

Whirlpool

Linen

Walk-In Shower

Entry
13'-4" Clg.

Bath 2
10'-0" Clg.

Utility
8'-6" x 8'-0"
10'-0" Clg.

WIC

Bedroom 3
13'-6" x 14'-10"
10'-0" Clg.

FIRST FLOOR

Garage
23'-0" x 32'-10"
11'-4" Clg.

©THE SATER DESIGN COLLECTION, INC.

Caprina

Plan No. **8052**

Bedrooms: **4**

Baths: **3½**

1st Floor: **2974 sq. ft.**

Total Living: **3271 sq. ft.**

Foundation: **Slab**

Width: **74' 8"**

Depth: **118' 0"**

Guest Suite: **297 sq. ft.**

PDF **$1637**   Vellum **$1637**   CAD **$2944**

Commanding Views

The elegant European façade will provide an old-world flair to any streetscape. Arches line the cloister flowing from the detached guest suite to the barrel-vault entry of this innovative design. Inside, the grand salon welcomes with commanding views past the loggia and a two-sided fireplace shared with the study. A walk-in wet bar adjoins the kitchen and provides a servery to the formal areas. Retreating glass walls open the leisure room to the outside amenities.

Multiple connections to the outdoors are present throughout the plan courtesy of French doors, walls of windows, and retreating walls of glass. To the left of the plan the master wing is an indulgent retreat for the owners, particularly with its luxurious his-and-hers amenities located throughout the spacious retreat. Two additional guest suites have ensuite baths and are located on the opposite side of the plan, enhancing privacy for all. ❖

PHOTO ABOVE: This beautiful outdoor living area also offers a separate pool bath and an outdoor kitchen area with an eating bar.

PHOTO LEFT: The formal dining room is open, and yet secluded by a distinguished ceiling, with a wet bar providing refreshments.

PHOTO LEFT: Two kitchen islands, one with an eating bar, dual sinks, and plentiful cabinetry come together to make this spacious kitchen spectacular.

PHOTO FAR LEFT: Formal dining occasions are sure to be memorable beneath the elegant stepped ceiling, with a built-in buffet server to ease entertaining.

PHOTO BELOW: Adjacent to the kitchen is the casual dining nook featuring a bayed, mitered glass window to the lanai, as well as a built-in niche to house a buffet server and showcase artwork.

PHOTO ABOVE: A luxurious master bath retreat boasts a center tub, walk-in shower, dual vanities and also overlooks a privacy garden complete with a tranquil fountain.

PHOTO RIGHT: A quiet haven, the sumptuous master suite enjoys access to a private sitting area and a door to the loggia.

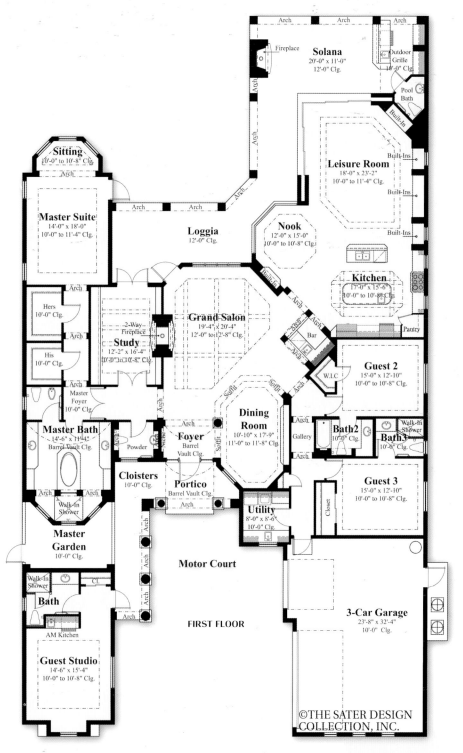

FIRST FLOOR

Sitting
10'-0" to 10'-8" Clg.

Arch

Master Suite
14'-0" x 18'-0"
10'-0" to 11'-4" Clg.

Loggia
12'-0" Clg.

Arch

Nook
12'-0" x 15'-0"
10'-0" to 10'-8" Clg.

Solana
20'-0" x 11'-0"
12'-0" Clg.

Fireplace

Arch

Outdoor Grille
14'-0" Clg.

Pool Bath

Built-In

Leisure Room
18'-0" x 23'-2"
10'-0" to 11'-4" Clg.

Built-Ins

Built-Ins

Built-Ins

Hers
10'-0" Clg.

2-Way Fireplace

Study
12'-2" x 16'-4"
10'-0" to 10'-8" Clg.

Grand Salon
19'-4" x 20'-4"
12'-0" to 12'-8" Clg.

Kitchen
17'-0" x 15'-6"
10'-0" to 10'-8" Clg.

His
10'-0" Clg.

Bar

W.I.C

Pantry

Guest 2
15'-0" x 12'-10"
10'-0" to 10'-8" Clg.

Master Foyer
10'-0" Clg.

Master Bath
14'-6" x 11'-4"
Barrel Vault Clg.

Powder

Foyer
Barrel Vault Clg.

Dining Room
10'-10" x 17'-9"
11'-0" to 11'-8" Clg.

Gallery

Bath 2
10'-0" Clg.

Bath 3
10'-6" Clg.

Walk-In Shower

Walk-In Shower

Cloisters
10'-0" Clg.

Portico
Barrel Vault Clg.

Arch

Guest 3
15'-0" x 12'-10"
10'-0" to 10'-8" Clg.

Closet

Master Garden
10'-0" Clg.

Utility
8'-0" x 8'-6"
10'-0" Clg.

Motor Court

Walk-In Shower

Cl.

Bath

AM Kitchen

3-Car Garage
23'-8" x 32'-4"
10'-0" Clg.

Guest Studio
14'-6" x 15'-4"
10'-0" to 10'-8" Clg.

©THE SATER DESIGN COLLECTION, INC.

PHOTO ABOVE: Walls of windows and retreating glass walls offer views of the serene loggia and pool from throughout the home.

Palazzo Ripoli

Plan No. 8074

Bedrooms: **4**

Baths: **4 full, 2 half**

1st Floor: **4266 sq. ft.**

Total Living: **4266 sq. ft.**

Foundation: **Slab**

Width: **69' 10"**

Depth: **120' 0"**

| PDF **$2773** | Vellum **$2773** | CAD **$4906** |

Not available for construction in Lee or Collier counties, Florida.

Handcrafted Details

This mid-sized European plan lives large with a wealth of well-appointed indoor and outdoor living space. A triple-arch entry, cupola and carved eave brackets set the atmosphere that is continued inside the home with multiple columns and rich, beamed ceilings.

An elegant foyer welcomes guests to the home, while the Grand Room's windows and French doors provide views of the amenity-rich courtyard. The solana hosts a spacious outdoor kitchen and fireplace beneath a distinctive tray ceiling.

The airy kitchen boasts a roomy island and is open to the casual dining nook and leisure room, but also offers easy access to the formal living and dining rooms. Built-ins throughout the home, such as the family valet near the rear-loading garage and the entertainment center in the leisure room, add utility, storage space and enduring value to the home.

An expansive master retreat offers the owners a luxe master bath with his-and-hers sinks as well as a central spa tub. An elegant art niche foyer features the perfect place to set the mood for relaxation.

Two secondary bedrooms upstairs share a divided bath, computer desk and dramatic balcony overlooking the living room. In the courtyard, the rear, detached suite can function as private guest quarters.

PHOTO ABOVE: The casual leisure room offers a family-friendly space for watching movies and playing games, with the nearby kitchen offering snacks.

PHOTO LEFT: A stunning living room offers expansive rear views, kitchen access and a balcony overlook. Columns and arches help define the space.

PHOTO LEFT AND BELOW: An inviting, open kitchen at the heart of the home is sure to delight. Wide countertops offer plenty of prep space and the island offers a second sink. A spacious corner pantry offers easy storage space. A pass-through to the great room eases entertaining and enhances the airiness of the space.

PHOTO FAR LEFT: A stately, two-story fireplace anchors the room while a modern take on clerestory windows keep the formal living room infused with daylight.

PHOTO ABOVE: An elegant art niche foyer sets the mood for relaxation immediately upon entering the owners' suite. A quiet haven, the private quarters boast a closet designed for two and direct access to the courtyard.

PHOTO RIGHT: Elegant and refined, the master bath features a central tub, dual vanities, a roomy shower and plenty of sunshine.

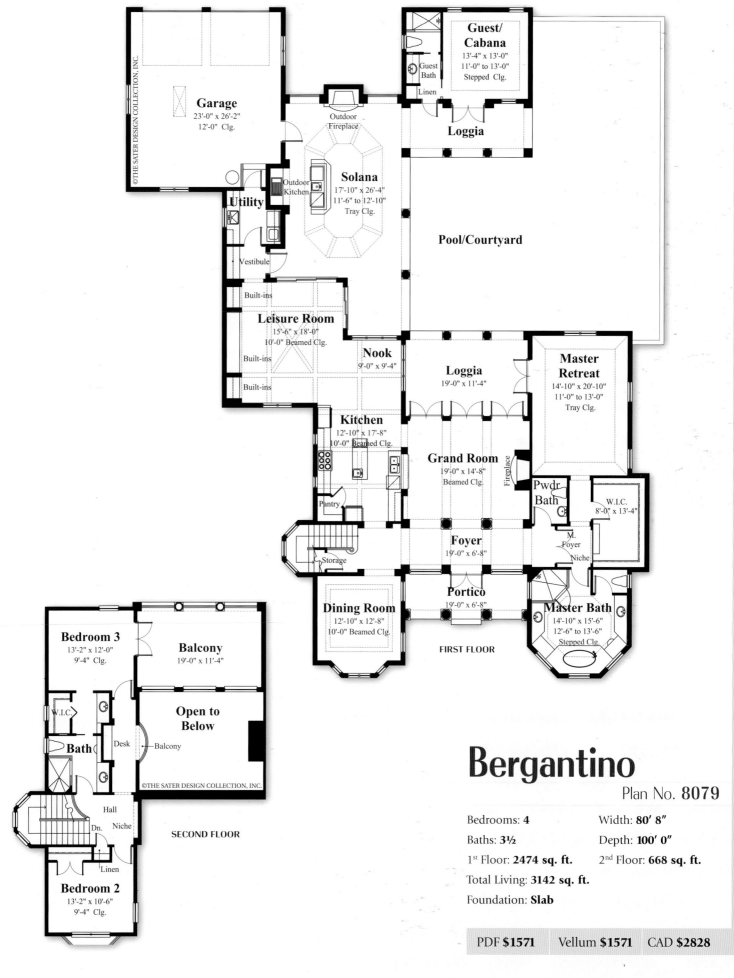

©THE SATER DESIGN COLLECTION, INC.

Garage
23'-0" x 26'-2"
12'-0" Clg.

Guest/Cabana
13'-4" x 13'-0"
11'-0" to 13'-0"
Stepped Clg.

Guest Bath

Linen

Loggia

Outdoor Fireplace

Solana
17'-10" x 26'-4"
11'-6" to 12'-10"
Tray Clg.

Outdoor Kitchen

Utility

Vestibule

Pool/Courtyard

Built-ins

Leisure Room
15'-6" x 18'-0"
10'-0" Beamed Clg.

Built-ins

Nook
9'-0" x 9'-4"

Loggia
19'-0" x 11'-4"

Master Retreat
14'-10" x 20'-10"
11'-0" to 13'-0"
Tray Clg.

Built-ins

Kitchen
12'-10" x 17'-8"
10'-0" Beamed Clg.

Grand Room
19'-0" x 14'-8"
Beamed Clg.

Fireplace

Pwdr Bath

W.I.C.
8'-0" x 13'-4"

Pantry

Storage

Foyer
19'-0" x 6'-8"

M. Foyer

Niche

Portico
19'-0" x 6'-8"

Dining Room
12'-10" x 12'-8"
10'-0" Beamed Clg.

Master Bath
14'-10" x 15'-6"
12'-6" to 13'-6"
Stepped Clg.

FIRST FLOOR

Bedroom 3
13'-2" x 12'-0"
9'-4" Clg.

Balcony
19'-0" x 11'-4"

W.I.C.

Bath

Desk

Balcony

Open to Below

©THE SATER DESIGN COLLECTION, INC.

Hall

Dn.

Niche

SECOND FLOOR

Linen

Bedroom 2
13'-2" x 10'-6"
9'-4" Clg.

Bergantino

Plan No. **8079**

Bedrooms: **4**	Width: **80' 8"**
Baths: **3½**	Depth: **100' 0"**
1ST Floor: **2474 sq. ft.**	2nd Floor: **668 sq. ft.**
Total Living: **3142 sq. ft.**	
Foundation: **Slab**	

| PDF **$1571** | Vellum **$1571** | CAD **$2828** |

Sherbrooke | Plan 6742

Unforgettable Vistas

Winner of four national design awards, *Sherbrooke* combines inviting outdoor living spaces with an impressive, open floor plan. Highly influenced by Italianate style, the layered elevation incorporates an array of details melded from renaissance themes. Pilasters line an arcade of windows that repeat the sculpted form of the entry. The open foyer grants extensive vistas through the living room, with wide outdoor panoramas that include the wrapping lanai. A graceful colonnade borders the formal dining room, which allows its own views to the front property.

Conveniently located near the dining room, state-of-the-art amenities prepare the gourmet kitchen for any occasion. With hardwood cabinetry, commercial-grade appliances and enough food-preparation space for two cooks, the kitchen easily serves the connected breakfast nook and leisure room. A stair hall connects the casual living space with secluded guest quarters and leads to a single glass door, which provides access to an outdoor kitchen. The entire wing opens through retreating doors to the side courtyard, which includes an outdoor fireplace.

On the opposite side of the plan, the owners' bedroom boasts a bay window with unimpeded views of the scenery and a step-up tray ceiling.

PHOTO ABOVE: A chef's dream, the kitchen has plenty of counter space, double ovens and a large walk-in pantry. The recessed window with window seat overlooks a courtyard with a stone fireplace.

PHOTO LEFT: The living room, with access to the lanai via two sets of French doors, is set apart from the dining and foyer area by Tuscan columns and made even more unique by an octagonal ceiling with inlaid wood.

PHOTO ABOVE LEFT: A private groin-vaulted foyer leads into the master retreat. Sitting under a step-up tray ceiling, the master retreat features sliding glass doors to the lanai, a cozy bay window sitting area, luxurious bath and spacious walk-in closets.

PHOTO ABOVE RIGHT: Topped with decorative corbels, a stately, ornately carved partition wall separates the Roman tub from a spacious walk-in shower designed for two.

PHOTO RIGHT: Unique ceiling details and decorative trimwork set this leisure room apart from the rest. Up the stairs is a flexible loft space which offers a second leisure area.

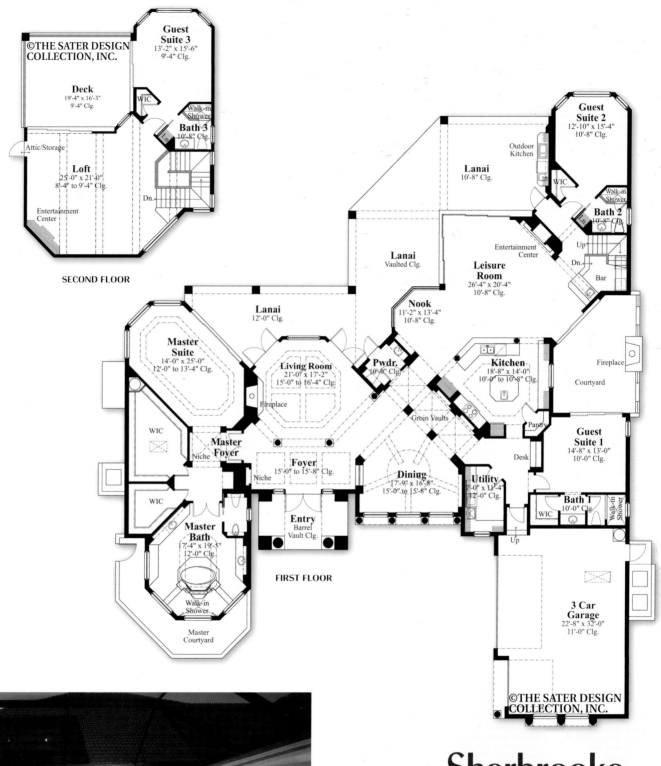

Guest Suite 3
13'-2" x 15'-6"
9'-4" Clg.

©THE SATER DESIGN COLLECTION, INC.

Deck
19'-4" x 16'-3"
9'-4" Clg.

WIC

Walk-in Shower

Bath 3
10'-8" Clg.

Attic/Storage

Loft
25'-0" x 21'-0"
8'-4" to 9'-4" Clg.

Entertainment Center

Dn.

SECOND FLOOR

Guest Suite 2
12'-10" x 15'-4"
10'-8" Clg.

Outdoor Kitchen

WIC

Walk-in Shower

Bath 2
10'-8" Clg.

Lanai
10'-8" Clg.

Entertainment Center

Up

Dn.

Bar

Leisure Room
26'-4" x 20'-4"
10'-8" Clg.

Lanai
Vaulted Clg.

Nook
11'-2" x 13'-4"
10'-8" Clg.

Fireplace

Courtyard

Lanai
12'-0" Clg.

Master Suite
14'-0" x 25'-0"
12'-0" to 13'-4" Clg.

Living Room
21'-0" x 17'-2"
15'-0" to 16'-4" Clg.

Pwdr.
10'-0" Clg.

Kitchen
18'-8" x 14'-0"
10'-0" to 10'-8" Clg.

Fireplace

WIC

Groin Vaults

Pantry

Desk

Guest Suite 1
14'-8" x 13'-0"
10'-0" Clg.

Master Foyer

Niche

WIC

Niche

Foyer
15'-0" to 15'-8" Clg.

Dining
17'-9" x 16'-8"
15'-0" to 15'-8" Clg.

Utility
x 11'-4"
12'-0" Clg.

Bath 1
10'-0" Clg.

WIC

Walk-in Shower

Master Bath
17'-4" x 19'-5"
12'-0" Clg.

Entry
Barrel Vault Clg.

Up

Walk-in Shower

Master Courtyard

FIRST FLOOR

3 Car Garage
22'-8" x 32'-0"
11'-0" Clg.

©THE SATER DESIGN COLLECTION, INC.

PHOTO ABOVE: The rear of the home offers a multitude of windows and doors to enjoy the rear lanai.

Sherbrooke

Plan No. **6742**

Bedrooms: **4**	Width: **91' 4"**
Baths: **4½**	Depth: **109' 0"**
1st Floor: **3943 sq. ft.**	2nd Floor: **859 sq. ft.**
Total Living: **4802 sq. ft.**	
Foundation: **Slab**	

Dramatic Spaces

Warm and intimate, *Kinsey* delights with perfectly thought out family living spaces, elegant and functional interior details, a Mediterranean façade and portico entry. Multiple connections with the outdoors provide great opportunities for lazy afternoons, cozy evening gatherings and festive large-scale entertaining.

The interior of this home is filled with unique architectural details intended to provide easy living amidst elegant appointments. In the kitchen, an angled counter, center island and sophisticated appliances please the most discerning cook, while Tuscan details—like the medallion and trim on the hood above the corner stove—add a subtle and sophisticated Mediterranean

spark to the room. Adjacent is a windowed eating nook and leisure room with open access to the lanai. A built-in entertainment center, dry bar and a server niche guarantee easy entertaining.

In contrast with the kitchen's informal nature, the dining and formal living room offer an opulent setting for entertaining. Stepped ceilings soar over both rooms, and disappearing glass doors open the living room to the lanai.

To ensure privacy, the master retreat is tucked away from the main living spaces and secondary bedrooms.

PHOTO ABOVE: This gourmet kitchen features a bounty of both preparation and storage space. Its location provides easy service to the nook, leisure room and dining room.

PHOTO LEFT: The leisure room flows seamlessly into the gourmet kitchen, providing a delightful environment for festive entertaining as well as cozy family movie nights.

PHOTO ABOVE: The intimate master suite gets an entire wing of the home and boasts a bay-windowed bedroom, walk-in wardrobe with adjacent dressing area, and a corner tub facing a private garden.

PHOTO ABOVE: Sleek granite crowns a dual vanity and makeup desk set under an arching mirror with sophisticated sconce lighting.

PHOTO ABOVE: A place for casual dining, the nook is enhanced by a built-in server niche, a bayed window overlooking the lanai, and an open layout.

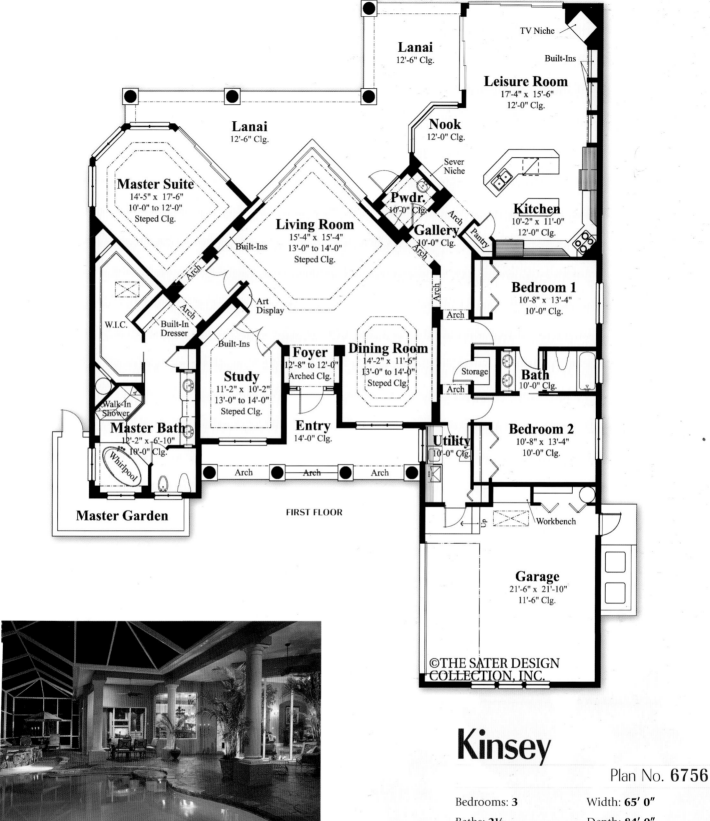

Lanai
12'-6" Clg.

Lanai
12'-6" Clg.

TV Niche

Built-Ins

Leisure Room
17'-4" x 15'-6"
12'-0" Clg.

Nook
12'-0" Clg.

Sever Niche

Master Suite
14'-5" x 17'-6"
10'-0" to 12'-0"
Steped Clg.

Pwdr.
10'-0" Clg.

Kitchen
10'-2" x 11'-0"
12'-0" Clg.

Living Room
15'-4" x 15'-4"
13'-0" to 14'-0"
Steped Clg.

Built-Ins

Gallery
10'-0" Clg.

Arch

Pantry

Arch

Bedroom 1
10'-8" x 13'-4"
10'-0" Clg.

Arch

Arch

Art Display

W.I.C.

Built-In Dresser

Storage

Bath
10'-0" Clg.

Built-Ins

Foyer
12'-8" to 12'-0"
Arched Clg.

Dining Room
14'-2" x 11'-6"
13'-0" to 14'-0"
Steped Clg.

Arch

Study
11'-2" x 10'-2"
13'-0" to 14'-0"
Steped Clg.

Walk-In Shower

Master Bath
12'-2" x 6'-10"
10'-0" Clg.

Whirlpool

Entry
14'-0" Clg.

Utility
10'-0" Clg.

Bedroom 2
10'-8" x 13'-4"
10'-0" Clg.

Master Garden

Arch   Arch   Arch

FIRST FLOOR

Up

Workbench

Garage
21'-6" x 21'-10"
11'-6" Clg.

©THE SATER DESIGN COLLECTION, INC.

PHOTO ABOVE: The winding, covered lanai embraces the home's rear rooms and free flowing pool, while offering cozy sitting and dining areas for every occasion.

Kinsey

Plan No. **6756**

Bedrooms: **3**	Width: **65' 0"**
Baths: **2½**	Depth: **84' 0"**
1st Floor: **2907 sq. ft.**	
Total Living: **2907 sq. ft.**	
Foundation: **Slab**	

PDF **$1455**   Vellum **$1455**   CAD **$2616**

Visit us on the web at www.saterdesign.com   **99**

Toscana | Plan 6758

Compact Luxury

This home celebrates the outdoors, with a floor plan that provides smart transitions between public and private realms while keeping the wide-open views in mind. Past the deeply recessed entry, the foyer opens to the great room with retreating glass doors, calling attention to the views beyond the pool. A coffered ceiling soars above the room and a tile-front fireplace with a coffered mantle fills up the spacious room with warmth on chilly evenings. Just steps away, guests can enjoy drinks from the wet bar as they make their way into the formal dining room.

Away from the public rooms, the common living space takes into account the lifestyle of the modern family. The leisure room boasts

built-ins for media components and retreating glass walls provide for easy transitions to the spacious loggia. A wraparound serving bar connects the leisure room to the state-of-the-art kitchen. Plenty of storage space and a center prep island make meal preparation easy.

Past the leisure room, the guest bedrooms share a full bath. On the opposite side of the home, an art-niche foyer leads to the private master retreat. Sliding glass doors open the generous suite to the loggia. The perfect place to begin and end your day, the spa-like master bath offers refuge in a bumped out whirlpool tub and a walk-in shower.

PHOTO ABOVE: Sleek in its simplicity, this contemporary gourmet kitchen boasts ample countertops, custom cabinets and state-of-the-art appliances.

PHOTO LEFT: The charming leisure room space is in the midst of the action, open to both the dining nook and kitchen.

PHOTO ABOVE LEFT: A striking tray ceiling creates a sheltering canopy in this generous master suite, while retreating glass doors offer convenient access to the breezy wraparound loggia.

PHOTO ABOVE RIGHT: His-and-hers vanities bookend the garden tub and walk-in shower in the octagonal-shaped master bath, a place of rest and respite at the end of a hectic day.

PHOTO RIGHT: A tile-front fireplace, with a coffered mantel that serves as an art niche, is the centerpiece of an airy great room made even more spacious by retreating glass doors to the rear loggia.

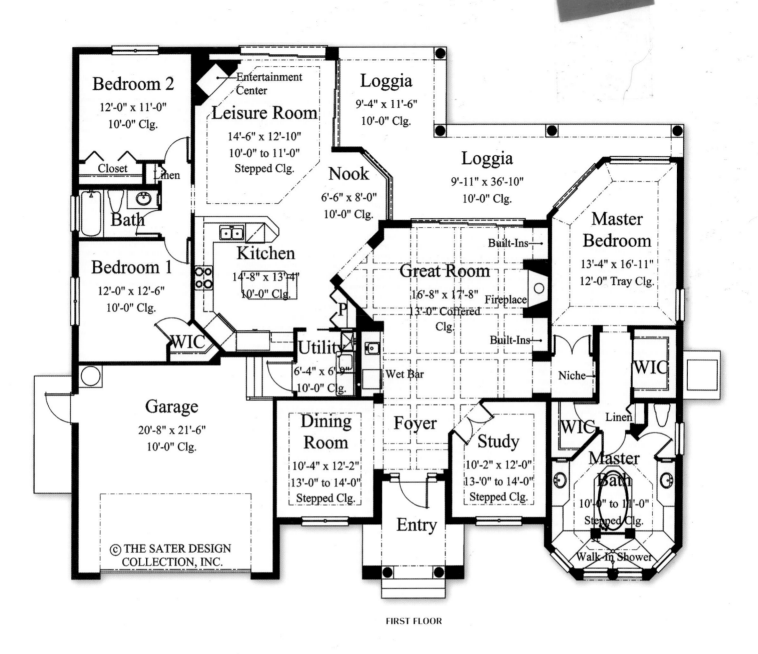

Bedroom 2
12'-0" x 11'-0"
10'-0" Clg.

Closet

Linen

Bath

Bedroom 1
12'-0" x 12'-6"
10'-0" Clg.

WIC

Kitchen
14'-8" x 13'-4"
10'-0" Clg.

Entertainment Center

Leisure Room
14'-6" x 12'-10"
10'-0" to 11'-0"
Stepped Clg.

Nook
6'-6" x 8'-0"
10'-0" Clg.

P

Utility
6'-4" x 6'-9"
10'-0" Clg.

Wet Bar

Loggia
9'-4" x 11'-6"
10'-0" Clg.

Loggia
9'-11" x 36'-10"
10'-0" Clg.

Built-Ins

Great Room
16'-8" x 17'-8"
13'-0" Coffered Clg.

Fireplace

Built-Ins

Niche

Master Bedroom
13'-4" x 16'-11"
12'-0" Tray Clg.

WIC

WIC

Linen

Garage
20'-8" x 21'-6"
10'-0" Clg.

© THE SATER DESIGN COLLECTION, INC.

Dining Room
10'-4" x 12'-2"
13'-0" to 14'-0"
Stepped Clg.

Foyer

Study
10'-2" x 12'-0"
13'-0" to 14'-0"
Stepped Clg.

Entry

Master Bath
10'-0" to 11'-0"
Stepped Clg.

Walk-In Shower

FIRST FLOOR

PHOTO ABOVE: Multiple retreating glass doors erase the boundaries between interior and exterior spaces.

Toscana

Plan No. 6758

Bedrooms: **3**	Width: **64' 10"**
Baths: **2**	Depth: **55' 2"**
1st Floor: **2331 sq. ft.**	
Total Living: **2331 sq. ft.**	
Foundation: **Slab**	

PDF **$1167**   Vellum **$1167**   CAD **$2098**

Deauville | Plan 6778

Family-Friendly

Repeating arches elevate the façade of this Italianate-style home, found in circle-head transoms topping the forward-looking windows, arched openings lining the portico and even framing the garage doors. Inside, stepped ceilings elevate the custom-home feel while visually dividing open spaces.

Just past the foyer, the living room features elegant built-ins, a fireplace or entertainment center and retreating glass walls to the loggia. A spacious butler's pantry connects the formal dining room to the gourmet-caliber kitchen. Nearby, a family-friendly leisure room opens to the loggia, making indoor/outdoor entertaining easy.

Away from the public realms, the master retreat enjoys the entire right wing of the home. This pampering suite offers a beautiful art niche foyer, two walk-in closets and a luxurious bathroom with a central spa tub.

Three uniquely-angled secondary bedrooms share two extra-functional bathrooms, configured so each bedroom has direct access: one doubles as a pool bath and the other is Jack-and-Jill style. For added convenience, the utility room is also located on this side of the home.

PHOTO ABOVE: State-of-the-art appliances make an understated appearance in the gourmet kitchen, inconspicuously supporting the chef in his or her culinary endeavors.

PHOTO LEFT: Gracefully arched built-ins, like beautiful bookends, complement a carved art niche over the mantel of this charming living room fireplace.

PHOTO ABOVE LEFT: If there ever was a reason to stay in bed, this is it: a positively mesmerizing twelve-foot stepped ceiling with recessed lighting is a sight to behold.

PHOTO ABOVE RIGHT: The master bath features a mammoth walk-in shower, step-up garden tub and generous his-and-hers walk-in closets.

PHOTO RIGHT: Double doors in the study open onto the portico, revealing shapely balusters and a picture-perfect view of the star-filled night sky.

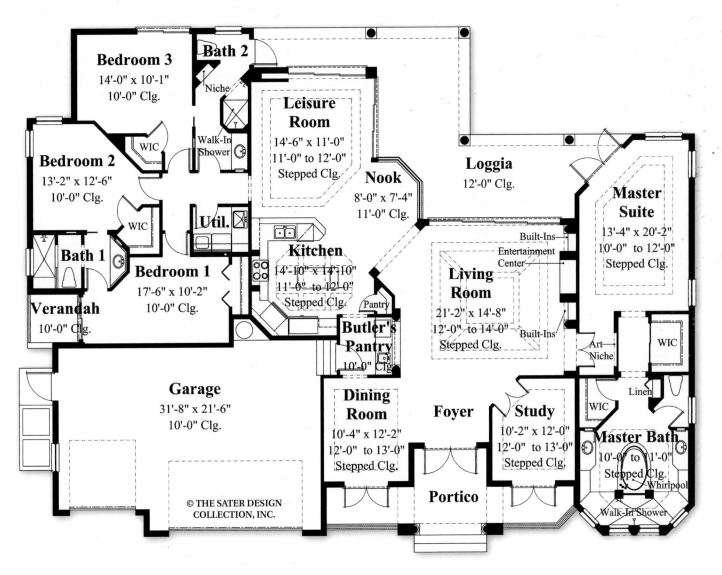

Bedroom 3
14'-0" x 10'-1"
10'-0" Clg.

Bath 2

Niche

Walk-In Shower

WIC

Bedroom 2
13'-2" x 12'-6"
10'-0" Clg.

WIC

Util.

Leisure Room
14'-6" x 11'-0"
11'-0" to 12'-0"
Stepped Clg.

Nook
8'-0" x 7'-4"
11'-0" Clg.

Loggia
12'-0" Clg.

Master Suite
13'-4" x 20'-2"
10'-0" to 12'-0"
Stepped Clg.

Kitchen
14'-10" x 14'-10"
11'-0" to 12'-0"
Stepped Clg.

Pantry

Built-Ins
Entertainment Center

Living Room
21'-2" x 14'-8"
12'-0" to 14'-0"
Stepped Clg.

Built-Ins

Bath 1

Bedroom 1
17'-6" x 10'-2"
10'-0" Clg.

Verandah
10'-0" Clg.

Butler's Pantry
10'-0" Clg.

Art Niche

WIC

WIC

Linen

Garage
31'-8" x 21'-6"
10'-0" Clg.

Dining Room
10'-4" x 12'-2"
12'-0" to 13'-0"
Stepped Clg.

Foyer

Study
10'-2" x 12'-0"
12'-0" to 13'-0"
Stepped Clg.

Master Bath
10'-0" to 11'-0"
Stepped Clg.
Whirlpool

Walk-In Shower

© THE SATER DESIGN COLLECTION, INC.

Portico

FIRST FLOOR

PHOTO ABOVE: Large expanses of glass create a breathtaking façade along the rambling loggia, which is supported by stately Tuscan columns.

Deauville

Plan No. 6778

Bedrooms: **4**   Width: **80' 10"**

Baths: **3**   Depth: **59' 10"**

1ST Floor: **2908 sq. ft.**

Total Living: **2908 sq. ft.**

Foundation: **Slab**

PDF **$1454**   Vellum **$1454**   CAD **$2617**

Serene & Spacious

A striking mix of arches, columns, carved balusters and arch-top windows foretell of the beauty waiting within this Mediterranean home. A view-oriented design, guests are immediately greeted with stunning vistas past the wall of curved glass to the wraparound verandah. A two-sided fireplace warms the formal areas comprised of the living and dining rooms, its boundary with the foyer defined by a line of decorative columns.

Arched entryways lead to the generous common living area. A beautiful and functional gourmet kitchen boasts a center prep island, walk-in pantry and a wraparound eating bar to the leisure room. The kitchen's open connection with the nook and leisure room creates a family-friendly environment that's perfect for large family get-togethers as well as intimate movie nights for two. Retreating glass walls further expand the area to the wraparound verandah. The outdoor kitchen is located just outside the leisure room, making indoor/outdoor entertaining a breeze.

Nearby, three guest suites offer friends and family a quiet place to relax at the end of the day. On the opposite side of the home, the master suite is a four-star retreat designed to pamper the homeowners after a busy day.

PHOTO ABOVE: Arched entryways lead to the state-of-the-art kitchen, which boasts black granite countertops, carved-wood cabinets, a stainless-steel double oven and built-in refrigerator.

PHOTO LEFT: Earth tones—as well as a two-sided fireplace—warm the living and dining area. A line of columns creates a boundary between the foyer and living areas.

PHOTO ABOVE: Arch-top windows and retreating glass doors invite the exterior landscape into the master bedroom, transforming the outdoors into an ever-changing work of art for this elegant retreat.

PHOTO BELOW: Both sides of the leisure room open to covered outdoor living space, allowing residents to enjoy the wide views from inside and out.

PHOTO ABOVE: With its scenic view of the master garden, the master bath becomes a private oasis.

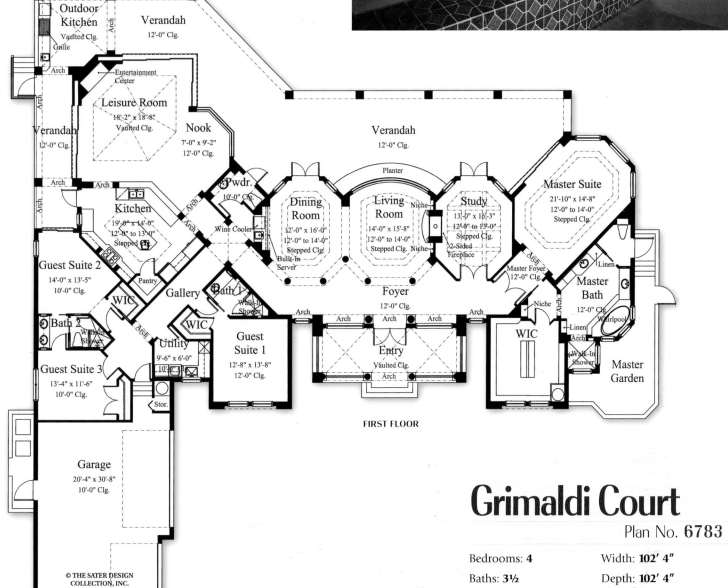

FIRST FLOOR

© THE SATER DESIGN COLLECTION, INC.

Grimaldi Court

Plan No. 6783

Bedrooms: **4**	Width: **102' 4"**
Baths: **3½**	Depth: **102' 4"**
1st Floor: **3817 sq. ft.**	
Total Living: **3817 sq. ft.**	
Foundation: **Slab**	

PDF **$2481**	Vellum **$2481**	CAD **$4390**

Quintessential Beauty

The repetition of graceful arches and elegant columns, stonework and a tile roof present an elegant façade for this stately Mediterranean-inspired home. The entry's dramatic barrel-vaulted ceiling begins a welcoming introduction; the foyer with its sweeping views of the scenery beyond the living room windows gives a warming embrace.

The casual areas of this home are to the left of the plan, including the leisure room, guest wing, and kitchen with its large island and pantry. An elegant gallery leads to two guest rooms, each with private full bathrooms and spacious walk-in closets.

The arches and columns from the façade add a flourish to interior spaces, defining boundaries between the open living room and dining room, creating a dramatic entry or a finishing touch to a niche. A covered veranda rambles freely along the rear of this home, providing secluded areas for intimate conversation or larger gathering spots for grand soirees. A scenic backdrop for six rooms, this outdoor area is showcased through floor-to-ceiling windows, including curved walls of glass in the nook and living room, as well as French doors from the dining room and private study, and a sliding glass door from the master suite.

PHOTO ABOVE: An air of serenity prevails throughout the neo-Mediterranean interior, expressed perfectly in the living room. Floor-to-ceiling glass permits nature to intrude, and grants spacious views of the veranda.

PHOTO LEFT: Superior outdoor entertaining abounds beneath a groin-vaulted ceiling in the outdoor kitchen with a roomy eating bar.

PHOTO ABOVE: The elongated master bedroom features a pocketing sliding glass door to the veranda as well as a sitting bay with multiple windows.

PHOTO RIGHT: Sand-hued cabinets and countertops subdue a seamless bay window that permits views of a lush private garden outside the master bath.

PHOTO RIGHT: A covered veranda rambles freely along the rear of this home, providing areas for intimate conversations or large gatherings.

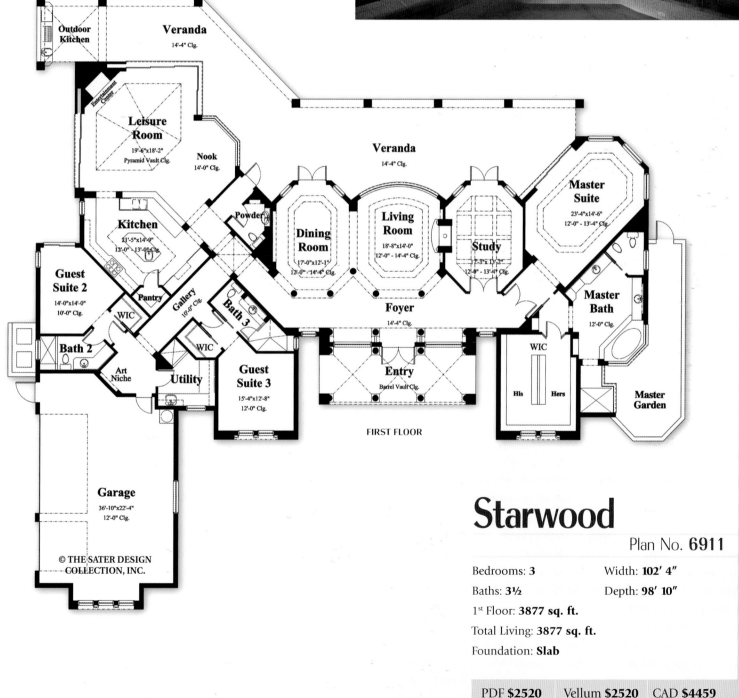

Outdoor Kitchen

Veranda
14'-4" Clg.

Leisure Room
19'-6"x18'-2"
Pyramid Vault Clg.

Nook
14'-0" Clg.

Veranda
14'-4" Clg.

Master Suite
23'-4"x14'-6"
12'-0" - 13'-4" Clg.

Kitchen
21'-5"x14'-9"
12'-0" - 13'-0" Clg.

Powder

Dining Room
17'-0"x12'-1"
12'-0" -14'-4" Clg.

Living Room
18'-8"x14'-0"
12'-0" - 14'-4" Clg.

Study
17'-3"x 13'-2"
12'-0" - 13'-4" Clg.

Guest Suite 2
14'-0"x14'-0"
10'-0" Clg.

Pantry

Gallery
10'-0" Clg.

Bath 3

WIC

Foyer
14'-4" Clg.

Master Bath
12'-0" Clg.

WIC

Bath 2

WIC

Art Niche

Utility

Guest Suite 3
15'-4"x12'-8"
12'-0" Clg.

Entry
Barrel Vault Clg.

WIC

His **Hers**

Master Garden

FIRST FLOOR

Garage
36'-10"x22'-4"
12'-0" Clg.

© THE SATER DESIGN COLLECTION, INC.

Starwood

Plan No. **6911**

Bedrooms: **3**	Width: **102' 4"**
Baths: **3½**	Depth: **98' 10"**
1st Floor: **3877 sq. ft.**	
Total Living: **3877 sq. ft.**	
Foundation: **Slab**	

PDF **$2520**	Vellum **$2520**	CAD **$4459**

Saraceno | Plan 6929

Luxurious Tradition

Arches and simple lines dominate the classic architecture of this home with corbels, banding, and hipped roofs providing visual excitement. Inside, a thoughtful plan arranges social areas and guest rooms to the left and the master suite and study to the right.

Private pockets of gathering areas are created by the gentle movement of the home's rear elevation, while a different perspective is experienced from the second floor deck. Designed to celebrate outdoor living and the views from inside, the rear elevation of this home is punctuated heavily by windows and sliding glass doors. These large openings provide wide open views of the home's surroundings and serve to bring the outside in.

Designed for entertaining, an open floor plan between the living and leisure rooms allows a wet bar to serve as the staging area for refreshments and hors d'oeuvres. Boundaries between these spaces are subtly defined by columns and changing ceilings. Natural light streams into the leisure room through zero-corner sliding glass doors and a second story band of vertical windows, opening up this room to the outdoors. This drama is heightened by a 22-foot coffered ceiling. A second floor loft overlooks the leisure room, and provides a private retreat for the fourth bedroom.

PHOTO ABOVE: A functional kitchen space features angled counters in varied heights, multiple sinks, a central island, plenty of seating and a walk-in pantry.

PHOTO LEFT: Just steps from the wet bar, dining room and kitchen, the living room is an entertainment hub. The space also beautifully opens to, and showcases, the rear view.

PHOTO ABOVE LEFT: Dignity characterizes the master suite, where two tray ceilings, dramatic windows and a sliding wall adjacent to the veranda define the room as a worthy retreat.

PHOTO ABOVE RIGHT: A unique shower floats effortlessly in a sea of glass, with soothing views to the privacy garden that are shared by the elegant, marble-encased bathtub.

PHOTO RIGHT: Natural light streams into the leisure room through zero-corner sliding glass doors and a second story band of vertical windows, opening up this room to the outdoors.

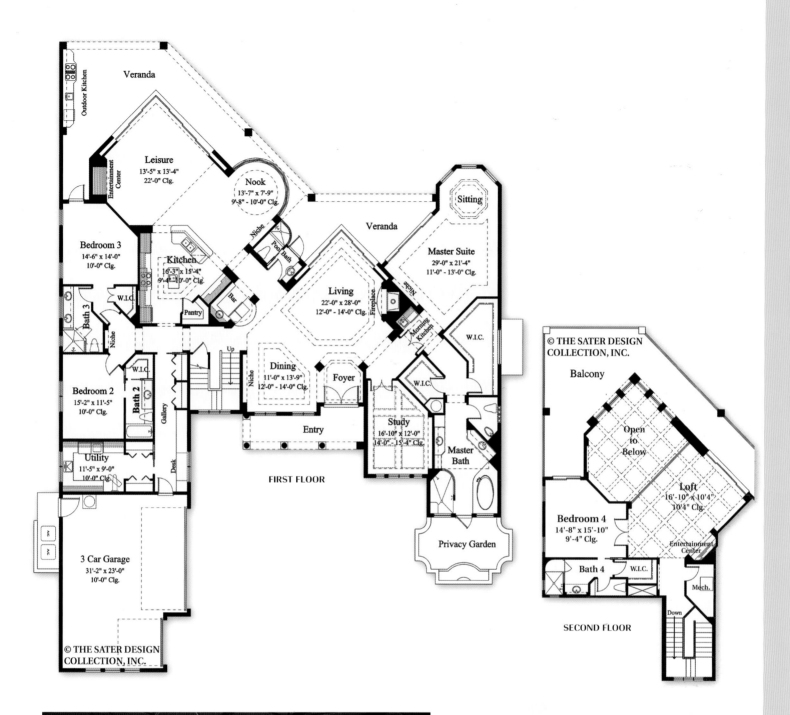

FIRST FLOOR

Veranda
Outdoor Kitchen
Leisure
13'-5" x 13'-4"
22'-0" Clg.
Nook
13'-7" x 7'-9"
9'-8" - 10'-0" Clg.
Entertainment Center
Bedroom 3
14'-6" x 14'-0"
10'-0" Clg.
Kitchen
16'-3" x 15'-4"
9'-4" - 10'-0" Clg.
Bar
Pantry
Niche
W.I.C.
Bath 3
Sitting
Veranda
Master Suite
29'-0" x 21'-4"
11'-0" - 13'-0" Clg.
Pool Bath
Living
22'-0" x 28'-0"
12'-0" - 14'-0" Clg.
Fireplace
Niche
Morning Kitchen
W.I.C.
Niche
Bedroom 2
15'-2" x 11'-5"
10'-0" Clg.
Bath 2
W.I.C.
Gallery
Up
Dining
11'-0" x 13'-9"
12'-0" - 14'-0" Clg.
Niche
Foyer
Study
16'-10" x 12'-0"
14'-0" - 15'-4" Clg.
W.I.C.
Desk
Utility
11'-5" x 9'-0"
10'-0" Clg.
Entry
Master Bath
3 Car Garage
31'-2" x 23'-0"
10'-0" Clg.
Privacy Garden

© THE SATER DESIGN COLLECTION, INC.

SECOND FLOOR

© THE SATER DESIGN COLLECTION, INC.
Balcony
Open to Below
Loft
16'-10" x 10'4"
10'4" Clg.
Bedroom 4
14'-8" x 15'-10"
9'-4" Clg.
Entertainment Center
Bath 4
W.I.C.
Mech.
Down

Saraceno

Plan No. **6929**

Bedrooms: **4**	Width: **81' 10"**
Baths: **5**	Depth: **113' 0"**
1st Floor: **4137 sq. ft.**	2nd Floor: **876 sq. ft.**
Total Living: **5013 sq. ft.**	
Foundation: **Slab**	

PHOTO ABOVE: An abundance of glass – in windows, nooks and disappearing walls to major living spaces – allows this home to celebrate the outdoors. The meandering veranda includes an outdoor kitchen.

PDF **$5013**	Vellum **$5013**	CAD **$8522**

Unexpected Architecture

A barrel-tile roof, graceful arches, rope columns and stone accents impart a distinctively Mediterranean flavor to the exterior of *Lindley*. Emphasizing openness, this design provides subtle definition between the formal and common living areas of the home as well as melding together indoor and outdoor areas, extending views and erasing boundaries.

Past the foyer, the formal living room enjoys expansive views through to the backyard. Rope columns lend a touch of formality to the more casual areas of the plan, adding architectural interest to spaces that define the perimeters between the leisure room, kitchen and nook.

A split-floor plan ensures privacy for the homeowners and guest alike. The entire right wing of the home is dedicated to the master retreat that features a private garden, spa-like bath, sitting room and access to the lanai. On the opposite wing of the home, French doors open onto a private courtyard, which is accessed by one of two guest bedrooms.

PHOTO ABOVE: The unique shape of the space, combined with the wide windows and warm color scheme, makes for an inviting, yet surprising, take on the modern gourmet kitchen.

PHOTO LEFT: A pyramid ceiling, sculpted recesses, built-in niches and cabinetry add texture to the leisure room area.

PHOTO ABOVE: A spacious master suite seamlessly blends a room-sized sitting space with a bounty of views and access to a private lanai.

PHOTO BELOW: Sitting under a pyramid ceiling, the lanai offers guests cool beverages from the outdoor kitchen and warmth by the fireplace.

PHOTO ABOVE: An art niche and sculpture add an air of repose to this open master bath. A chaise lounge helps amplify the sense of luxury created by a step-down shower and spa-style tub.

PHOTO ABOVE: Unexpected architecture creates seamless boundaries between a koi pond bordered with lush planters and outdoor living spaces, which include an alfresco dining area.

FIRST FLOOR

©THE SATER DESIGN COLLECTION, INC.

Deck

Bedroom 4
16'-8" x 13'-8"
9'-0" Ceiling

Bonus Room
11'-0" x 22'-5"
15'-6" Ceiling

Bath 4

Open to Below

©THE SATER DESIGN COLLECTION, INC.

SECOND FLOOR

Lindley

Plan No. 6930

Bedrooms: **4**

Baths: **4½**

1st Floor: **5265 sq. ft.**

Total Living: **6011 sq. ft.**

Foundation: **Slab**

Width: **99' 4"**

Depth: **140' 0"**

2nd Floor: **746 sq. ft.**

| PDF **$6011** | Vellum **$6011** | CAD **$10219** |

Relaxation Beckons

A romantic courtyard welcomes all into this unforgettable, view-oriented design. Stone steps, scrolling wrought iron, cast-stone ornamentals, dentil molding and a magnificent cupola add captivating details to the front façade.

Inside, past the barrel-vaulted foyer, the formal living room boasts a two-story coffered ceiling, fireplace, and a wall of windows and doors connecting to the veranda. A butler's pantry, wet bar and formal dining room are situated close by. The central rotunda connects the public, formal realm with an upper-level game and guest wing, which opens to a wide deck overlooking the pool, veranda and koi pond.

Two more guest suites are found on the left side of the floor plan (where a side family entry increases the pattern of circulation through the guest wing), as is the kitchen, leisure room and nook. These open spaces are expanded by zero-corner sliding glass doors that pocket into the walls and open the common living area onto the veranda.

For added privacy, the master suite is located on the opposite wing. A three-sided fireplace warms the sitting area adjacent to the suite. Dual walk-in closets, a dressing area and a spa-like bath ensure the homeowners will always feel pampered.

PHOTO ABOVE: A grand rotunda links the main level with the game room, designed as a desirable getaway for family members and guests.

PHOTO LEFT: A warming fireplace anchors the two-story formal living room with built-in art niches to highlight favorite pieces.

PHOTO ABOVE: Intended for relaxation—and rejuvenation—the master bath is a luxurious getaway. Dramatic stained glass separates the bathtub from a hidden steam room, while a private garden, two vanities and a separate make-up area complete the retreat.

PHOTO RIGHT: Sculpted arches add depth and dimension to the master bedroom, and a peninsular fireplace borders a sitting area framed by views of the side and rear properties. Sliding glass doors open the master bedroom to the veranda and views of the coastal preserve.

PHOTO ABOVE: Open to the leisure room and deck, the veranda features a sheltered outdoor eating area and a fireplace with a plush sitting area.

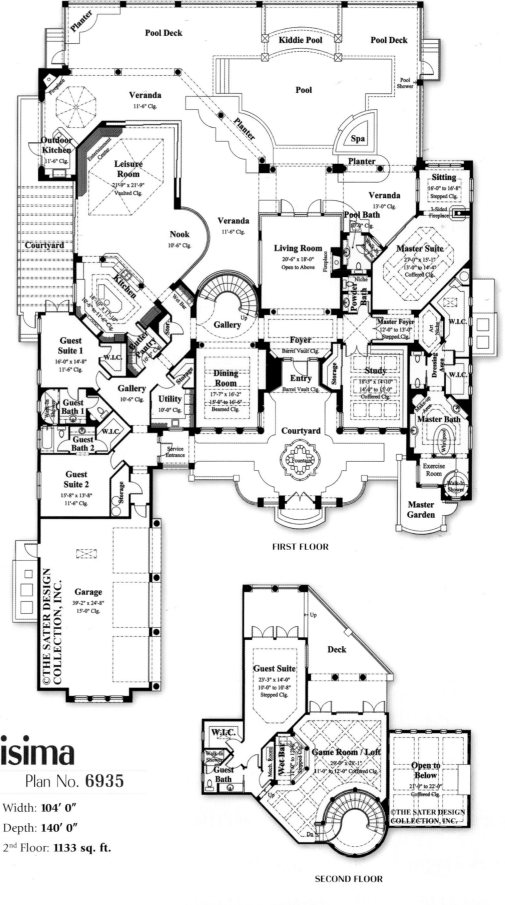

FIRST FLOOR

SECOND FLOOR

©THE SATER DESIGN COLLECTION, INC.

Casa Bellisima

Plan No. 6935

Bedrooms: **4**

Baths: **5½**

1st Floor: **5391 sq. ft.**

Total Living: **6524 sq. ft.**

Foundation: **Slab**

Width: **104' 0"**

Depth: **140' 0"**

2nd Floor: **1133 sq. ft.**

PDF **$6524**   Vellum **$6524**   CAD **$11091**

Simply Spellbinding

With many luxe design features—carved ceilings, large rooms and 21st-century electronics—the strength of this design is its unique capacity to merge indoor living areas with outer spaces through a fluid perimeter of retreating glass walls and windows. Immediately upon entry, the grand foyer leads to the formal living and dining rooms and witnesses views that extend to the veranda, pool and beyond.

To the left of the formal rooms, a wet bar and butler's pantry ease the spatial transition to the casual living space. A family-friendly zone, the kitchen flows into the generous leisure room, nook and out to the verandah. Nearby, two guest suites feature full baths and walk-in closets.

Tucked away on the other side of the home, the master wing is a truly luxurious retreat. Special features—a morning kitchen, a spa-like bath with a private garden and quiet sitting area create a sanctuary that is hard to leave. Upstairs, a spacious loft with a wet bar is a versatile space that connects two guest suites and opens to an outer deck.

PHOTO ABOVE: A customized wall of niches provides space for artwork, a media center, an angled fireplace and a cozy window seat in the leisure room. Sliding glass walls extend the space.

PHOTO LEFT: Flowing smoothly into the expansive leisure room and a glass-walled breakfast nook, the kitchen offers numerous amenities in a functional configuration.

PHOTO ABOVE LEFT: An embracing arch leads the way into a cozy sitting area that offers stirring views through a series of vertical windows.

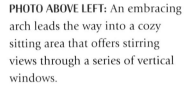

PHOTO ABOVE RIGHT: A spa-style tub encased in wood and marble floats before a glass door leading to a private garden. A walk-in shower is encased in intensely hued natural materials and a curved glass wall.

PHOTO RIGHT: Dual outdoor living areas boast a wealth of amenities: outdoor kitchen and dining on the lower level and a roomy upper deck off of the flexible loft space.

PHOTO ABOVE: A corbelled roofline and upper deck framed in wrought iron extend the home out and upward, while the multi-angled veranda edges a free-form pool.

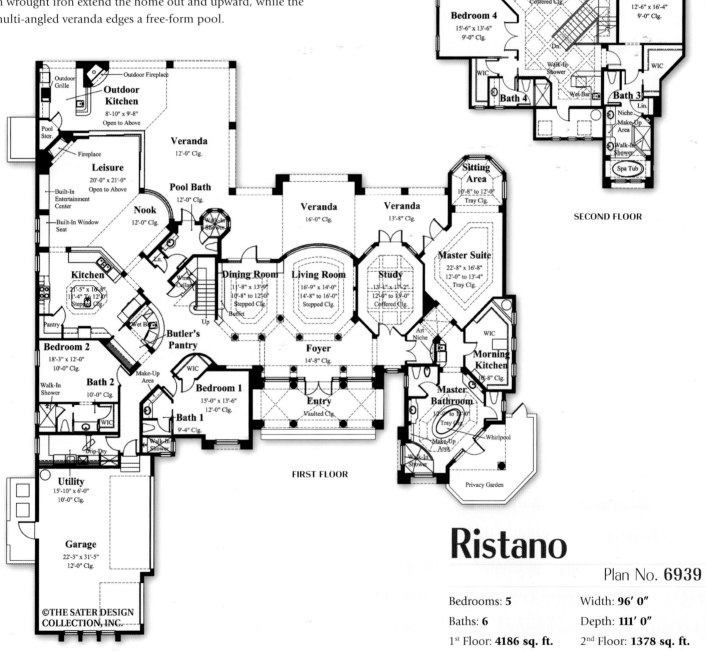

Deck
26'-10" x 30'-2"
9'-0" Clg.

Open to Below

©THE SATER DESIGN COLLECTION, INC.

22'-4" to 23'-4"
Coffered Clg.
Open to Below

Loft
9'-0" to 10'-0"
Coffered Clg.

Bedroom 3
12'-6" x 16'-4"
9'-0" Clg.

Bedroom 4
15'-6" x 13'-6"
9'-0" Clg.

Dn

Walk-In Shower

WIC

WIC

Bath 4

Wet Bar

Bath 3

Niche

Make-Up Area

Walk-In Shower

Lin.

Spa Tub

SECOND FLOOR

Outdoor Grille

Outdoor Fireplace

Outdoor Kitchen
8'-10" x 9'-8"
Open to Above

Pool Stor.

Fireplace

Veranda
12'-0" Clg.

Leisure
20'-0" x 21'-0"
Open to Above

Built-In Entertainment Center

Built-In Window Seat

Nook
12'-0" Clg.

Pool Bath
12'-0" Clg.

Walk-In Shower

Sitting Area
10'-8" to 12'-0"
Tray Clg.

Veranda
16'-0" Clg.

Veranda
13'-8" Clg.

Kitchen
21'-5" x 16'-8"
11'-4" To 12'-0"
Stepped Clg.

Wine Cellar

Dining Room
11'-8" x 13'-9"
10'-8" to 12'-0"
Stepped Clg.

Living Room
16'-9" x 14'-0"
14'-8" to 16'-0"
Stepped Clg.

Study
13'-1" x 17'-2"
12'-0" to 13'-0"
Coffered Clg.

Master Suite
22'-8" x 16'-8"
12'-0" to 13'-4"
Tray Clg.

Pantry

Wet Bar

Butler's Pantry

Up

Buffet

Foyer
14'-8" Clg.

Art Niche

WIC

Morning Kitchen
18'-8" Clg.

Bedroom 2
18'-3" x 12'-0"
10'-0" Clg.

Walk-In Shower

Make-Up Area

WIC

Bedroom 1
15'-0" x 13'-6"
12'-0" Clg.

Master Bathroom
12'-0" to 14'-0"
Tray Clg.

Bath 2
10'-0" Clg.

WIC

Bath 1
9'-4" Clg.

Walk-In Shower

Entry
Vaulted Clg.

Make-Up Area

Whirlpool

Drip-Dry

Walk-In Shower

Walk-In Shower

Utility
15'-10" x 6'-0"
10'-0" Clg.

FIRST FLOOR

Privacy Garden

Garage
22'-3" x 31'-5"
12'-0" Clg.

©THE SATER DESIGN COLLECTION, INC.

Ristano

Plan No. **6939**

Bedrooms: **5**　　　　Width: **96' 0"**

Baths: **6**　　　　Depth: **111' 0"**

1st Floor: **4186 sq. ft.**　　2nd Floor: **1378 sq. ft.**

Total Living: **5564 sq. ft.**

Foundation: **Slab**

PDF **$5564**　　Vellum **$5564**　　CAD **$9459**

Stately & Refined

Mediterranean and Moorish influences come together to grant *Pontedera* its unique character and expansive graciousness, while 21st century features such as the two-story leisure room and high-tech gourmet kitchen lend balance and cutting-edge style.

The dining room offers numerous entertaining options with its generous size and a beautiful niche designed to house a custom, built-in buffet and dramatic mirror. Tall arched windows with forward views provide soothing natural light and a lovely frame for tropical sunsets. Entertainment options are plentiful outdoors, where the solana hosts a full kitchen, complete with built-in grille and serving counter. Accessed through zero-corner pocket sliding doors in the leisure room, the solana offers a protected outdoor living space for cooking, dining and great conversations by the fire.

This riverfront manor captures the essence of refined living with its majestic façade, rich in Mediterranean details and stunning interior features that speak of exceptional living in each and every room. Designed to celebrate one-of-a-kind architecture and embrace the outdoors, *Pontedera* is a home that indulges, inspires and nurtures. ◈

PHOTO ABOVE: The diamond-shaped leisure room has two retreating glass walls on either side of the built-in entertainment center. A second leisure area is found in the loft upstairs.

PHOTO LEFT: Polished stone columns are the only boundary separating the spacious gourmet kitchen from the view-oriented nook and leisure room.

PHOTO ABOVE LEFT: An expansive window wall and built-in server niche highlight the simple elegance of the sizeable dining room.

PHOTO ABOVE RIGHT: Serenity is the theme of the opulent master bath, where a freestanding spa tub views a lush, private garden.

PHOTO RIGHT: A complete outdoor kitchen, sheltered beneath the loggia's roof, makes any day the perfect day for a barbecue. The solana's fireplace is the perfect place to retire with dessert.

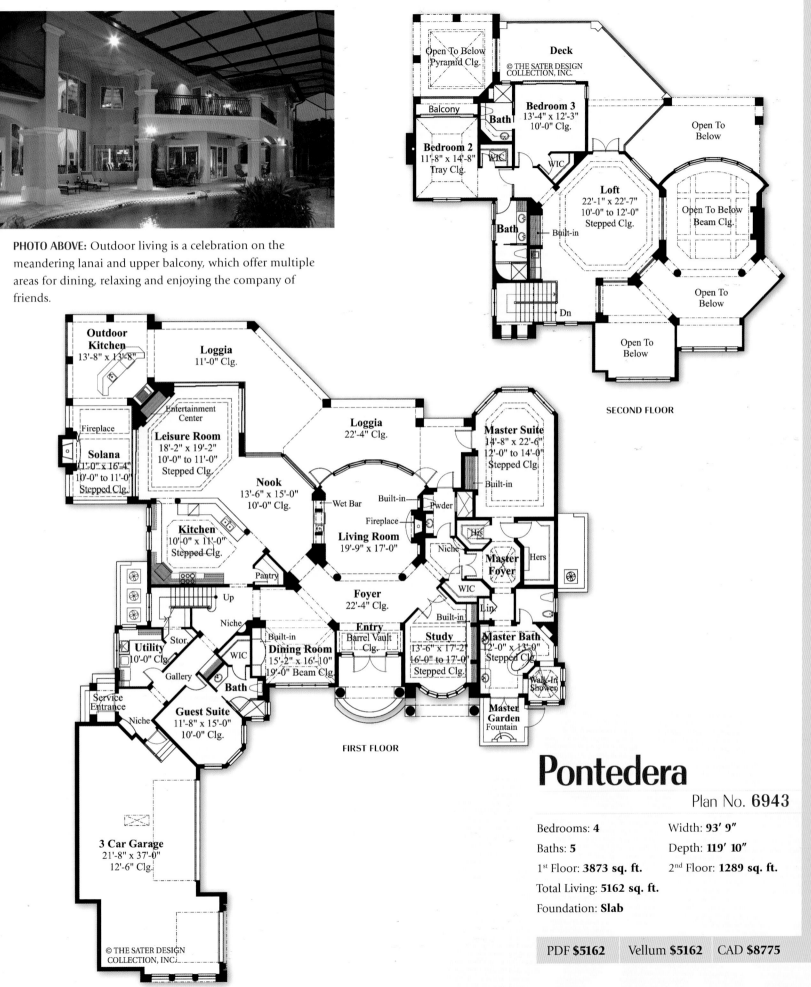

SECOND FLOOR

PHOTO ABOVE: Outdoor living is a celebration on the meandering lanai and upper balcony, which offer multiple areas for dining, relaxing and enjoying the company of friends.

FIRST FLOOR

Pontedera

Plan No. 6943

Bedrooms: **4**	Width: **93' 9"**
Baths: **5**	Depth: **119' 10"**
1st Floor: **3873 sq. ft.**	2nd Floor: **1289 sq. ft.**
Total Living: **5162 sq. ft.**	
Foundation: **Slab**	

PDF $5162	Vellum $5162	CAD $8775

Cataldi | Plan 6946

Resplendent Respite

Cataldi classically demonstrates the New Mediterranean style. It artfully blends modern amenities – such as whirlpool baths and spacious family zones – with classical Mediterranean design elements such as turrets, gracefully arched openings, colorful low-pitched gabled roofs, abundant stonework, vaulted ceilings, rustic wall surfaces of stucco and stone, deep Roman-arched windows and breezy arcades.

Welcoming visitors to this stately manor home is a grand entry turret, its impressive entablature supported by stone columns and flanked by breezy arcades. Sunny chiffon stucco contrasts beautifully with a colorful, red barrel-tile roof. The Mediterranean strength and dignity

of the exterior is carried throughout the interior as well.

The floor plan includes a spacious great room that features a stone-arched coffer and exposed wood beam ceiling and easy access to the dining area. The well-appointed gourmet kitchen offers more-than-ample food preparation, storage and gathering space, while two bedrooms with walk-in closets and individual baths provide guests with their own private living space.

PHOTO ABOVE: A festive tile backsplash, sleek granite countertop and scenic views through the breakfast nook's bay window make this gourmet kitchen the perfect place for preparing a formal meal or enjoying a casual gathering.

PHOTO LEFT: The generous great room is adjacent to the kitchen and flows into the gallery, which in turn flows into the formal dining area. Volume ceilings add to the spaciousness, giving each area its own unique character.

PHOTO ABOVE LEFT: Tucked away from the guest bedrooms, the master bedroom pampers with floor-to-ceiling bay windows, forming the boundaries for a cozy sitting nook.

PHOTO ABOVE RIGHT: Beauty is in the details. Intricately carved organic stone materials give the master bath both boldness and intimacy, crafting an environment perfect for relaxation and rejuvenation.

PHOTO RIGHT: Adjacent to the master sits this private study, elegantly appointed with custom built-ins and a dramatic stepped ceiling, which can be either the perfect place to relax with a good book or the ideal home office.

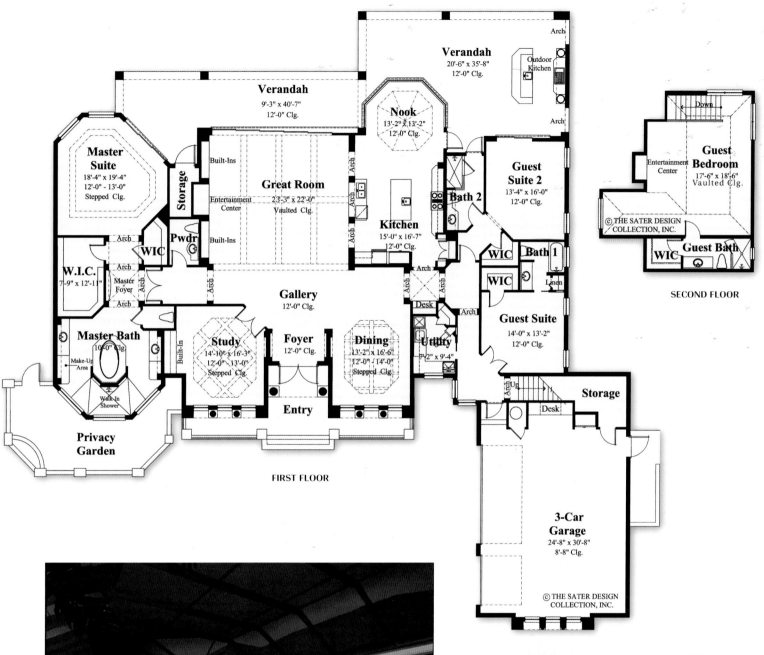

FIRST FLOOR

Verandah
9'-3" x 40'-7"
12'-0" Clg.

Verandah
20'-6" x 35'-8"
12'-0" Clg.

Outdoor Kitchen

Arch

Arch

Nook
13'-2" x 13'-2"
12'-0" Clg.

Master Suite
18'-4" x 19'-4"
12'-0" - 13'-0"
Stepped Clg.

Storage

Built-Ins

Great Room
23'-3" x 22'-0"
Vaulted Clg.

Entertainment Center

Built-Ins

Arch

Arch

Kitchen
15'-0" x 16'-7"
12'-0" Clg.

Bath 2

Guest Suite 2
13'-4" x 16'-0"
12'-0" Clg.

Pwdr

Arch

WIC

Arch

WIC

Arch

W.I.C.
7'-9" x 12'-11"

Master Foyer

Arch

Arch

Gallery
12'-0" Clg.

Arch

Arch

WIC

Bath 1

Linen

Desk

Arch

Guest Suite
14'-0" x 13'-2"
12'-0" Clg.

Master Bath
10'-0"

Make-Up Area

Built-In

Study
14'-10" x 16'-3"
12'-0" - 13'-0"
Stepped Clg.

Foyer
12'-0" Clg.

Dining
13'-2" x 16'-6"
12'-0" - 14'-0"
Stepped Clg.

Utility
7'-2" x 9'-4"

Walk-In Shower

Entry

Arch Up

Desk

Storage

Privacy Garden

© THE SATER DESIGN COLLECTION, INC.

3-Car Garage
24'-8" x 30'-8"
8'-8" Clg.

SECOND FLOOR

Down

Entertainment Center

Guest Bedroom
17'-6" x 18'-6"
Vaulted Clg.

© THE SATER DESIGN COLLECTION, INC.

WIC

Guest Bath

PHOTO ABOVE: The wraparound verandah forms the boundary between the gracious indoors and an inviting backyard pool with spa.

Cataldi

Plan No. **6946**

Bedrooms: **4**   Width: **105' 9"**

Baths: **4½**   Depth: **100' 9"**

1st Floor: **3947 sq. ft.**   2nd Floor: **546 sq. ft.**

Total Living: **4493 sq. ft.**

Foundation: **Slab**

PDF **$2859**   Vellum **$2859**   CAD **$5058**

Not available for construction in Lee or Collier counties, Florida.

Sancho | Plan 6947

Enchanting Escape

The influence of Spanish Colonial style is clearly evident in this rambling home that truly welcomes the outside in. Lush planters greet visitors as they enter an engaging entry made even grander by a decorative, second-story, wrought iron balcony. Further accenting the great outdoors is an expansive covered loggia that wraps the rear elevation.

Inside, this home is all about luxurious and relaxed living, with rooms that exceed expectation in both design and function. While maintaining convenient access to the formal dining room, the gourmet-caliber kitchen resides under an octagonal ceiling and is adjacent to the leisure room, wet bar and breakfast nook. This combination space is the hub of the home, perfect for intimate family gatherings and large-scale entertaining. Parties flow easily outside, through two walls of pocketing glass framing the leisure room and connecting to a spacious loggia that boasts both a solana and outdoor kitchen. Alternately, private moments may be shared in the butterfly garden adjacent to the leisure room and kitchen.

PHOTO ABOVE: A charming chiminea-style fireplace warms the outdoor kitchen and adjacent sitting area. Just steps from the leisure room and guest study, this outdoor room is perfect for occasions both lively and relaxing.

PHOTO LEFT: With spacious swirled granite countertops, ample storage space and a convenient butcher-block center island, this octagonal gourmet kitchen is friendly to chefs, family and friends alike.

PHOTO ABOVE LEFT: An elegant
bedroom with a bay windowed
sitting area is at the core of a
sprawling master suite. The retreat
also boasts dual walk-in closets
(one with a stacked washer and
dryer), a study and spa-like bath.

PHOTO ABOVE RIGHT: Located
directly off of the foyer, soft lighting
makes the faux-painted walls of the
formal dining room glow under the
beamed octagonal-shaped ceiling.

PHOTO RIGHT: Optional his-and-
hers studies feature custom-wood
built-ins, wrought-iron accents and
access to the loggia through double
doors.

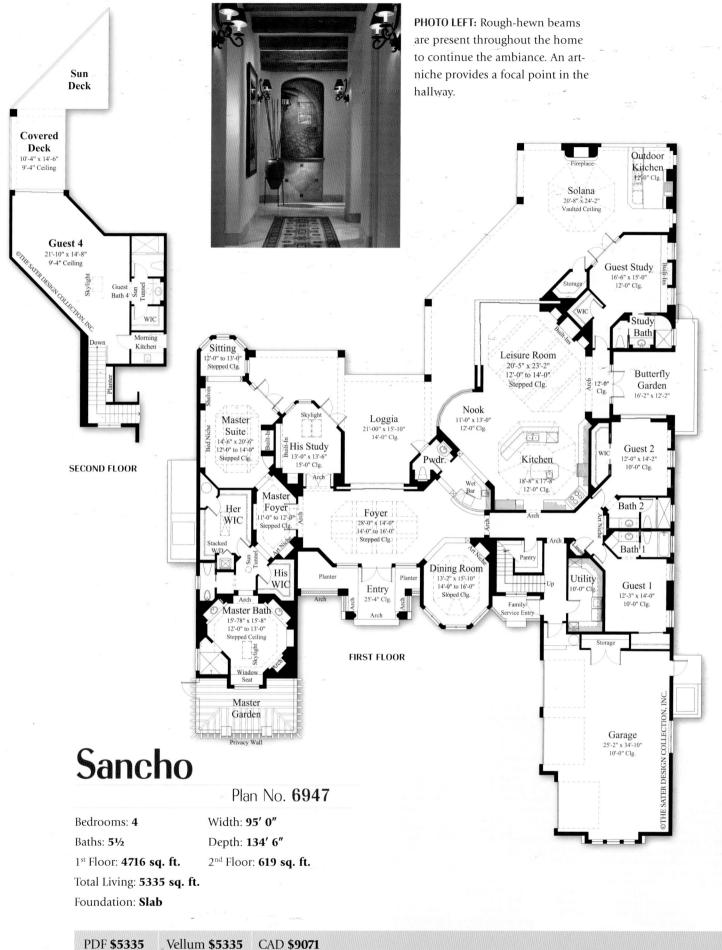

PHOTO LEFT: Rough-hewn beams are present throughout the home to continue the ambiance. An art-niche provides a focal point in the hallway.

Sun Deck

Covered Deck
10'-4" x 14'-6"
9'-4" Ceiling

Guest 4
21'-10" x 14'-8"
9'-4" Ceiling

© THE SATER DESIGN COLLECTION, INC.

Skylight

Guest Bath 4

Sun Tunnel

WIC

Morning Kitchen

Down

Planter

SECOND FLOOR

Outdoor Kitchen
12'-0" Clg.

Fireplace

Solana
20'-8" x 24'-2"
Vaulted Ceiling

Storage

Guest Study
16'-6" x 15'-0"
12'-0" Clg.

Built-Ins

WIC

Study Bath

Built-Ins

Leisure Room
20'-5" x 23'-2"
12'-0" to 14'-0"
Stepped Clg.

Butterfly Garden
16'-2" x 12'-2"

Arch

12'-0" Clg.

Sitting
12'-0" to 13'-0"
Stepped Clg.

Shelves

Bed Niche

Master Suite
14'-6" x 20'-6"
12'-0" to 14'-0"
Stepped Clg.

Built-In

His Study
13'-0" x 13'-6"
15'-0" Clg.

Skylight

Loggia
21'-00" x 15'-10"
14'-0" Clg.

Nook
11'-0" x 13'-0"
12'-0" Clg.

Kitchen
18'-8" x 17'-8"
12'-0" Clg.

WIC

Guest 2
12'-0" x 14'-2"
10'-0" Clg.

Pwdr.

Wet Bar

Arch

Her WIC

Master Foyer
11'-0" to 12'-0"
Stepped Clg.

Arch

Art Niche

Foyer
28'-0" x 14'-0"
14'-0" to 16'-0"
Stepped Clg.

Arch

Bath 2

Art Niche

Bath 1

Stacked W/D

Sun Tunnel

His WIC

Planter

Entry
25'-4" Clg.

Planter

Dining Room
13'-2" x 15'-10"
14'-0" to 16'-0"
Sloped Clg.

Art Niche

Pantry

Arch

Up

Utility
10'-0" Clg.

Guest 1
12'-3" x 14'-0"
10'-0" Clg.

Arch

Arch

Arch

Arch

Family Service Entry

Arch

Master Bath
15'-78" x 15'-8"
12'-0" to 13'-0"
Stepped Ceiling

Skylight

Window Seat

Storage

FIRST FLOOR

Master Garden

Privacy Wall

Garage
25'-2" x 34'-10"
10'-0" Clg.

© THE SATER DESIGN COLLECTION, INC.

Sancho

Plan No. **6947**

Bedrooms: **4**   Width: **95' 0"**

Baths: **5½**   Depth: **134' 6"**

1st Floor: **4716 sq. ft.**   2nd Floor: **619 sq. ft.**

Total Living: **5335 sq. ft.**

Foundation: **Slab**

PDF **$5335**   Vellum **$5335**   CAD **$9071**

Substantial Grandeur

This stately home is sure to make an impression in any neighborhood, with fanlight windows that provide a light counterpoint to the portico's weighty stonework.

An open configuration of bayed formal rooms at the front of the plan offers forward and rear views through wide windows under unique ceiling details for elegant entertaining anytime. A gourmet-caliber kitchen offers a food-preparation island, as well as a walk-in pantry to ease service.

Plentiful outdoor living space is found in the rambling rear veranda with an outdoor kitchen, as well as a side courtyard accessed through the leisure room. Retreating walls of glass

fully open rooms to the outdoors. For indoor casual activities, a cozy leisure room and flexible loft space with wet bar are sure to fit the bill.

A spacious owner's suite offers a view-oriented bedroom, light-filled and feature-rich bath and two roomy walk-in closets tucked behind the enclave's regal double-door entry.

Three guest suites with ensuite baths are sequestered to the boundaries of the common areas, affording everyone the ultimate in privacy.

PHOTO ABOVE: Gleaming granite countertops and a Tuscan-flavored tile backsplash are luxurious appointments to a kitchen that's also ultra-functional with its extended serving counter and center prep-island.

PHOTO LEFT: Lavish get-togethers, as well as cozy family nights, are memory-makers in this leisure room with its coffered ceiling, rich stone floor, striking entertainment niche and disappearing glass walls to the courtyard.

PHOTO ABOVE: It's hard to tell where the bedroom ends and the great outdoors begin in this large light-flooded master retreat. The sitting area is perfect for a good book – and even an afternoon nap.

PHOTO BELOW: An absolutely extraordinary fireplace, dramatic pergolas of carved Tuscan columns and wood canopies, and a warm brick floor all merge to create a courtyard worthy of royalty.

PHOTO ABOVE: A center garden tub and walk-in shower behind a marble wall make an impressive statement in this ultra luxurious master bath, which also features his-and-hers vanities and arch-top transom windows.

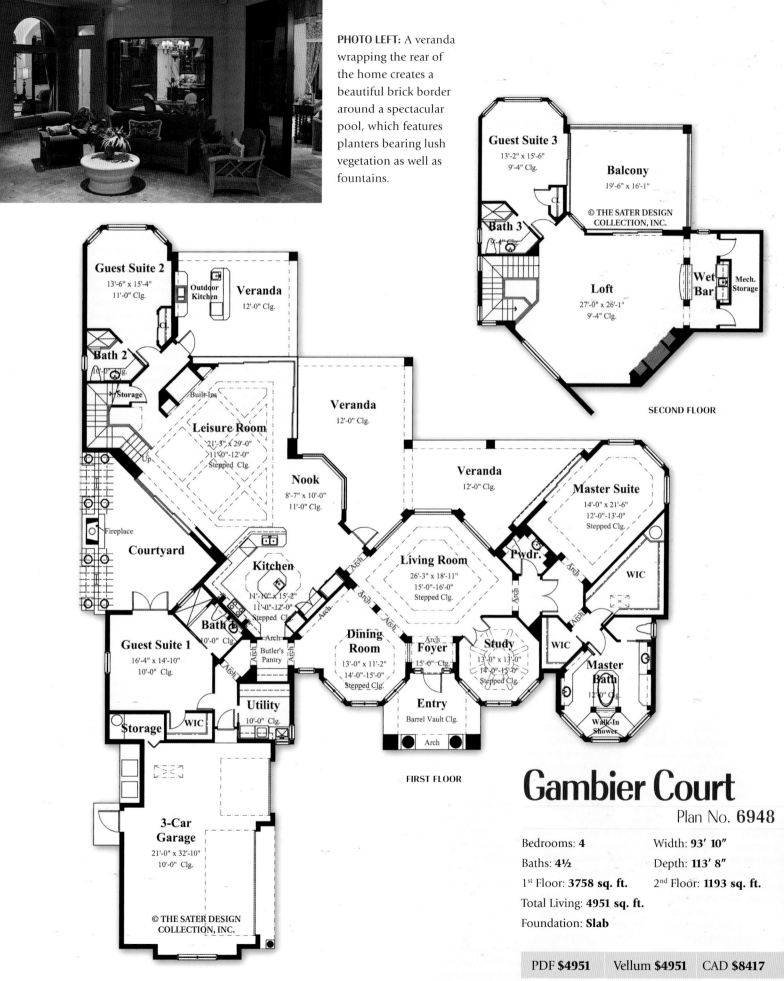

PHOTO LEFT: A veranda wrapping the rear of the home creates a beautiful brick border around a spectacular pool, which features planters bearing lush vegetation as well as fountains.

Guest Suite 3
13'-2" x 15'-6"
9'-4" Clg.

Balcony
19'-6" x 16'-1"

© THE SATER DESIGN
COLLECTION, INC.

Bath 3
9'-4" Clg.

Loft
27'-0" x 26'-1"
9'-4" Clg.

Wet Bar

Mech. Storage

SECOND FLOOR

Guest Suite 2
13'-6" x 15'-4"
11'-0" Clg.

Outdoor Kitchen

Veranda
12'-0" Clg.

Bath 2
10'-0" Clg.

Storage

Built-Ins

Leisure Room
21'-3" x 29'-0"
11'-0"-12'-0"
Stepped Clg.

Veranda
12'-0" Clg.

Nook
8'-7" x 10'-0"
11'-0" Clg.

Veranda
12'-0" Clg.

Master Suite
14'-0" x 21'-6"
12'-0"-13'-0"
Stepped Clg.

Up

Fireplace

Courtyard

Kitchen
11'-10" x 15'-2"
11'-0"-12'-0"
Stepped Clg.

Living Room
26'-3" x 18'-11"
15'-0"-16'-0"
Stepped Clg.

Pwdr.

Arch

WIC

Bath

Guest Suite 1
16'-4" x 14'-10"
10'-0" Clg.

Butler's Pantry

Arch

Dining Room
13'-0" x 11'-2"
14'-0"-15'-0"
Stepped Clg.

Arch

Foyer
15'-0" Clg.

Study
13'-0" x 13'-0"
14'-0"-15'-0"
Stepped Clg.

WIC

Master Bath
12'-0" Clg.

Utility
10'-0" Clg.

Storage

WIC

Entry
Barrel Vault Clg.

Arch

Walk-In Shower

FIRST FLOOR

3-Car Garage
21'-0" x 32'-10"
10'-0" Clg.

© THE SATER DESIGN
COLLECTION, INC.

Gambier Court

Plan No. 6948

Bedrooms: **4**	Width: **93' 10"**
Baths: **4½**	Depth: **113' 8"**
1st Floor: **3758 sq. ft.**	2nd Floor: **1193 sq. ft.**
Total Living: **4951 sq. ft.**	
Foundation: **Slab**	

PDF **$4951**   Vellum **$4951**   CAD **$8417**

Not available for construction in Lee or Collier counties, Florida.

Unique Arrangement

A stately entry distinguishes this Mediterranean estate from the rest. Varied rooflines and wrought iron accents provide visual interest in the façade. Guests are welcomed into the formal living room, where a soaring ceiling and walls of glass are sure to make a lasting impression.

The kitchen is open to a casual dining nook and leisure room, an open arrangement that provides a family-friendly atmosphere. Stairs lead from the leisure room to the roomy upstairs loft with wet bar.

The master retreat offers a host of features in a rambling arrangement that encompasses one entire side of the home. Three self-contained guest suites are not only secluded from the master, they're also secluded from each other, offering the ultimate in privacy for overnight guests.

Outdoor living is at its finest in *Cantadora*, with retreating glass walls eliminating boundaries between inside and out, as well as walls of windows highlighting the beautiful outdoors. Amenities include an outdoor kitchen under the veranda and an outdoor fireplace in the courtyard.

PHOTO ABOVE: Casual and comfortable, yet equipped to meet any culinary challenge, the kitchen flows into both the leisure room and the breakfast nook. The gleaming, carved-wood hood provides a beautiful focal point.

PHOTO LEFT: The leisure room has it all, from custom built-ins for media equipment to an outdoor kitchen located just beyond retreating glass walls.

PHOTO ABOVE: A uniquely-shaped master retreat offers an elegant getaway for the owners. The amenity-rich suite offers private veranda access.

PHOTO BELOW: This view of the living room from the formal dining area speaks volumes abut the design's blending of interior and exterior spaces. A sixteen-foot stepped ceiling and expansive glass create a seamless boundary between indoors and out.

PHOTO ABOVE: A regal master bath features an elevated marble garden tub and elegant walk-in shower framed by handsome columns.

PHOTO LEFT:
Architectural lighting gives the rear elevation a warm glow in the early evening hours.

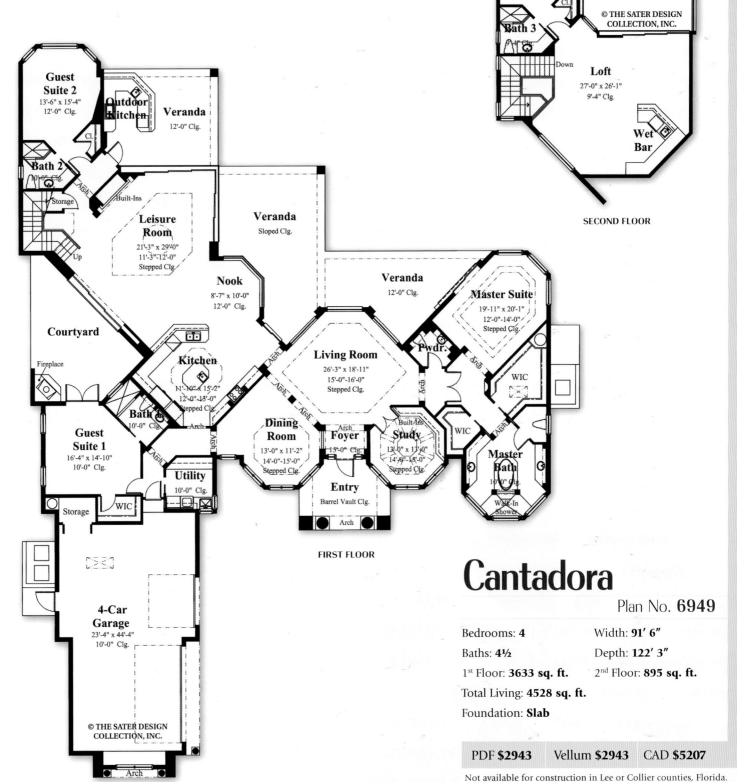

Guest Suite 3
13'-2" x 15'-6"
9'-4" Clg.

Balcony
19'-6" x 16'-1"

© THE SATER DESIGN COLLECTION, INC.

Bath 3

Down

Loft
27'-0" x 26'-1"
9'-4" Clg.

Wet Bar

SECOND FLOOR

Guest Suite 2
13'-6" x 15'-4"
12'-0" Clg.

Outdoor Kitchen

Veranda
12'-0" Clg.

Bath 2
10'-0" Clg.

Storage

Built-Ins

Leisure Room
21'-3" x 29'-0"
11'-3"-12'-0"
Stepped Clg.

Veranda
Sloped Clg.

Up

Nook
8'-7" x 10'-0"
12'-0" Clg.

Veranda
12'-0" Clg.

Master Suite
19'-11" x 20'-1"
12'-0"-14'-0"
Stepped Clg.

Courtyard

Fireplace

Kitchen
11'-10" x 15'-2"
12'-0"-13'-0"
Stepped Clg.

Living Room
26'-3" x 18'-11"
15'-0"-16'-0"
Stepped Clg.

Pwdr.

WIC

Bath
10'-0" Clg.

Guest Suite 1
16'-4" x 14'-10"
10'-0" Clg.

Dining Room
13'-0" x 11'-2"
14'-0"-15'-0"
Stepped Clg.

Foyer
15'-0" Clg.

Study
13'-0" x 13'-0"
14'-0"-15'-0"
Stepped Clg.

WIC

Master Bath
10'-0" Clg.

Built-Ins

Utility
10'-0" Clg.

Storage

WIC

Entry
Barrel Vault Clg.

Arch

Walk-In Shower

FIRST FLOOR

4-Car Garage
23'-4" x 44'-4"
10'-0" Clg.

© THE SATER DESIGN COLLECTION, INC.

Arch

Cantadora

Plan No. 6949

Bedrooms: **4**   Width: **91' 6"**

Baths: **4½**   Depth: **122' 3"**

1st Floor: **3633 sq. ft.**   2nd Floor: **895 sq. ft.**

Total Living: **4528 sq. ft.**

Foundation: **Slab**

| PDF **$2943** | Vellum **$2943** | CAD **$5207** |

Not available for construction in Lee or Collier counties, Florida.

A Stunning Portico

An entry distinguished by a barrel-vault ceiling sets the stage for the timeless detailing found throughout *Ravello*. Arches, soffits and extraordinary ceiling treatments elevate the atmosphere throughout the home. An art niche is the focal point at one end of the central gallery hall, lined with arches and columns, while the luxurious master retreat's double-door entry is located at the opposite end.

Formal rooms are located front and center, with a stunning, uniquely-shaped living room greeting guests. A two-sided fireplace is shared with the private study that offers a built-in desk and custom shelving. The formal dining room features

French doors to the verandah and proximity to a wet bar with custom wine cellar. The view-oriented design offers plentiful connections to the rear outdoor living space beneath the spacious verandah, with French doors, retreating glass walls and walls of bowed glass throughout the plan.

Casual living space is also abundant, with a wide-open leisure room, kitchen and dining nook on the first floor, and a game room connecting two upper-level bedrooms. Outdoor living space includes a fireplace and a full outdoor kitchen.

PHOTO ABOVE: When the glass walls are retreated, the indoor leisure room spills out into the outdoor living space, resulting in one tremendous, wide-open room with no differentiation between the inside and outside.

PHOTO LEFT: One of the most important characteristics of *Ravello* is how the outdoors is visible from every room. In lieu of cabinetry over the kitchen's eating bar which could have potentially obstructed the extended views, a large, custom-designed furniture piece was built into an adjacent wall for additional storage.

PHOTO ABOVE: A spacious master bedroom finds privacy in a secluded first-floor location and convenience in abundant indulgences, including a built-in bed niche, view-oriented sitting room and verandah access.

PHOTO RIGHT: The luxurious master bath boasts the modern amenities owners will expect in a daily retreat: dual vanities and built-in storage overlooking a private, pergola-covered garden.

PHOTO ABOVE: Wide arched openings and linear columns enhance the verandah, which wraps around the back of the house from the master suite and library to the living and dining rooms and family wing.

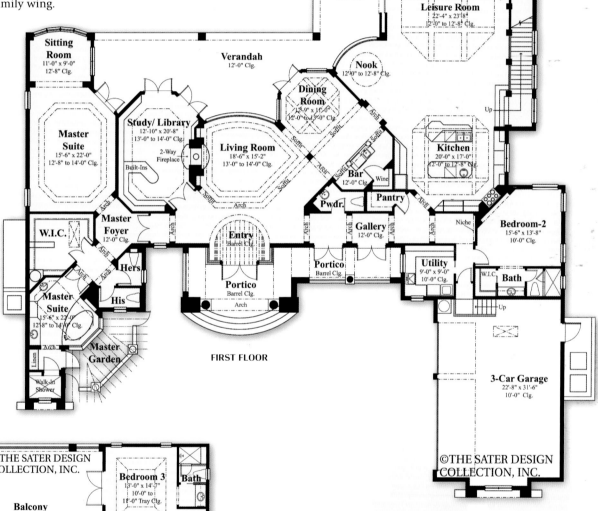

Solana
39'-8" x 15'-0"
12'-0" to 12'-8" Clg.

Fireplace Outdoor Kitchen Grille

Pool Bath

Storage

Verandah
12'-0" Clg.

Leisure Room
22'-4" x 23'-8"
12'-0" to 12'-8" Clg.

Sitting Room
11'-0" x 9'-0"
12'-8" Clg.

Verandah
12'-0" Clg.

Nook
12'-10" to 12'-8" Clg.

Up

Dining Room
12'-9" x 11'-0"
12'-0" to 13'-0" Clg.

Master Suite
15'-6" x 22'-0"
12'-8" to 14'-0" Clg.

Study/ Library
12'-10" x 20'-8"
13'-0" to 14'-0" Clg.

2-Way Fireplace

Built-Ins

Living Room
18'-6" x 15'-2"
13'-0" to 14'-0" Clg.

Kitchen
20'-0" x 17'-0"
12'-0" to 12'-8" Clg.

Bar
12'-0" Clg.

Wine

Master Foyer
12'-0" Clg.

Pwdr.

Pantry

Niche

Bedroom-2
15'-6" x 13'-8"
10'-0" Clg.

W.I.C.

Hers

Entry
Barrel Clg.

Gallery
12'-0" Clg.

Portico
Barrel Clg.

Utility
9'-0" x 9'-0"
10'-0" Clg.

W.I.C. Bath

His

Master Suite
15'-6" x 22'-0"
12'-8" to 14'-0" Clg.

Portico
Barrel Clg.

Arch

Up

Master Garden

Linen

Walk-in Shower

FIRST FLOOR

3-Car Garage
22'-8" x 31'-6"
10'-0" Clg.

©THE SATER DESIGN COLLECTION, INC.

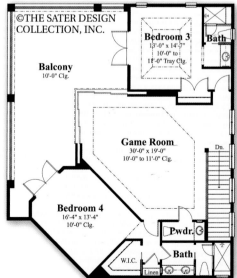

©THE SATER DESIGN COLLECTION, INC.

Balcony
10'-0" Clg.

Bedroom 3
13'-0" x 14'-7"
10'-0" to 11'-0" Tray Clg.

Bath

Game Room
30'-0" x 19'-0"
10'-0" to 11'-0" Clg.

Dn.

Bedroom 4
16'-4" x 13'-4"
10'-0" Clg.

Pwdr.

Bath

W.I.C. Linen

SECOND FLOOR

Ravello

Plan No. **6952**

Bedrooms: **4**	Width: **100' 0"**
Baths: **4 full, 3 half**	Depth: **113' 0"**
1st Floor: **4196 sq. ft.**	2nd Floor: **1270 sq. ft.**
Total Living: **5466 sq. ft.**	
Foundation: **Slab**	

PDF **$5466**	Vellum **$5466**	CAD **$9292**

Dimora | Plan 6954

Genuinely View-Oriented

Corbelled cornices, decorative quoin elements and keystone enhanced arches, coupled with a capriciously hipped roofline reinforce the home's Italian-inspired design. The true essence of the home is the amalgamation of interior and exterior spaces, thus maximizing the spatiality and functionality of the home. While myriad windows and glass doors strengthen the constant connection between the inside and outdoors, the study, dining and living rooms transition freely into one another.

To the left of the foyer, the wet bar differentiates the informal and formal venues. In the kitchen and family room, retreating glass walls open onto the covered lanai and pool deck, creating a "room without walls." To the right of the foyer, the master suite, with its large sitting alcove, oversized walk-in closet, luxuriously appointed bath and private courtyard, is a serene milieu that is unsurpassed.

PHOTO ABOVE: Retreating glass walls seemingly pull the outdoors inside toward the family room, kitchen and nook, creating a large, wide-open living space. Enhanced by custom millwork elements, the family room's exaggerated sloped tray ceiling creates a cozy ambiance.

PHOTO LEFT: The kitchen, with its octagonal-shaped, beamed coffered ceiling and center prep island, opens up into the family room and nook. The angled breakfast bar and arched side entries define the exclusivity of the separate spaces while at the same time joining them as one.

PHOTO ABOVE: Through a row of windows in the bay-shaped sitting alcove, as well as through a pair of adjacent French doors, a profusion of sunlight explodes in the luxuriously detailed master suite.

PHOTO RIGHT: In the center of the room, the tile surround and deck of the oval-shaped tub incorporates the same intricate detailing as in the stunning walk-in shower.

PHOTO RIGHT: The loggia, with its corresponding columns and broadly arched openings, spans from one side of the home to the other, strengthening the transition and connectivity of the indoors to the outdoors through copious window walls and entryways.

Verandah
12'-0" Clg.

Outdoor Kitchen

Built-In

Leisure Room
18'-8" x 15'-5"
12'-0" to 13'-4" Clg.

2-Sided Fireplace

Nook
9'-0" x 7'-6"
12'-0" Clg.

Verandah
50'-6" x 12'-4"
12'-0" Clg.

Sitting
10'-2" x 9'-0"
10'-0" to 12'-0"
Sloped Clg.

Kitchen
16'-2" x 14'-8"
12'-0" to 13'-0"
Stepped Clg.

Pool Bath

Dining Room
11'-0" x 18'-4"
12'-0" to 14'-0"
Stepped Clg.

Living Room
14'-6" x 18'-4"
12'-0" to 14'-0"
Stepped Clg.

Study
12'-6" x 16'-10"
12'-0" to 13'-0"
Stepped Clg.

Master Suite
15'-10" x 22'-10"
12'-0" to 14'-0"
Stepped Clg.

Pantry

Wet Bar

Butler's Pantry

W.I.C.

Niche

Foyer
12'-0" Clg.

Master Foyer

Morning Kitchen

W.I.C.

Bedroom 3
12'-0" x 14'-0"
10'-0" Clg.

Bedroom 1
13'-6" x 16'-8"
12'-0" Clg.

Entry
Barrel Vault Clg.

Master Bath
13'-6" x 14'-6"
12'-0" to 13'-4"
Stepped Clg.

Bath 3

W.I.C.

Bath 1

Walk-In Shower

Private Garden

Bedroom 2
12'-0" x 13'-4"
10'-0" Clg.

Utility

Walk-In Shower

Bath 2

FIRST FLOOR

3-Car Garage
22'-4" x 32'-0"
10'-0" Clg.

©THE SATER DESIGN COLLECTION, INC.

Dimora

Plan No. **6954**

Bedrooms: **4**	Width: **94' 2"**
Baths: **5**	Depth: **131' 6"**
1st Floor: **4664 sq. ft.**	
Total Living: **4664 sq. ft.**	
Foundation: **Slab**	

La Serena | Plan 8076

Authentically Italian

Hipped rooflines, carved eave brackets and a turret evoke a sense of the past in this Italianate-style design. Inside, an engaging blend of old and new prevails where beamed and coffered ceilings play counterpoint to modern amenities—cutting-edge appliances in the kitchen, a state-of-the-art utility room and retreating glass walls in the leisure room.

Past the dramatic entryway, columns line the formal rooms and foyer. The hand-carved fireplace is nestled between built-in cabinetry and lies underneath the cove-lit coffered-ceiling. Nearby, the leisure room is an open and comfortable retreat for family and guests.

Centrally located between the main living areas, snacks are just a few feet away in the kitchen, retreating glass walls open up to the lanai—making indoor/outdoor entertaining a breeze and a fun-filled game room lays just beyond the art-niche foyer.

A split-bedroom floor plan ensures privacy to the master wing of the home. A generous walk-in closet provides ample storage while the master bath features luxe amenities. On the opposite wing, three guest bedrooms offer plenty of space for overnight guests.

PHOTO ABOVE: : Sitting under an octagonal coffered ceiling, the leisure room is an open and comfortable retreat for family and guests.

PHOTO LEFT: The kitchen features a step-up tray ceiling, spacious pantry, state-of-the-art appliances, a convenient island workstation and an eating counter.

PHOTO ABOVE: A split-bedroom floor plan provides privacy to the master wing of the home. Muted lighting creates a relaxing environment while the sitting nook provides a quiet spot for reading.

PHOTO RIGHT: To create a warm and organic feel, earth-toned slate tiles flow throughout the entire master bath. A cove-lit tray ceiling, walk-in shower, spa-style tub and his-and-hers vanities complete the luxurious retreat.

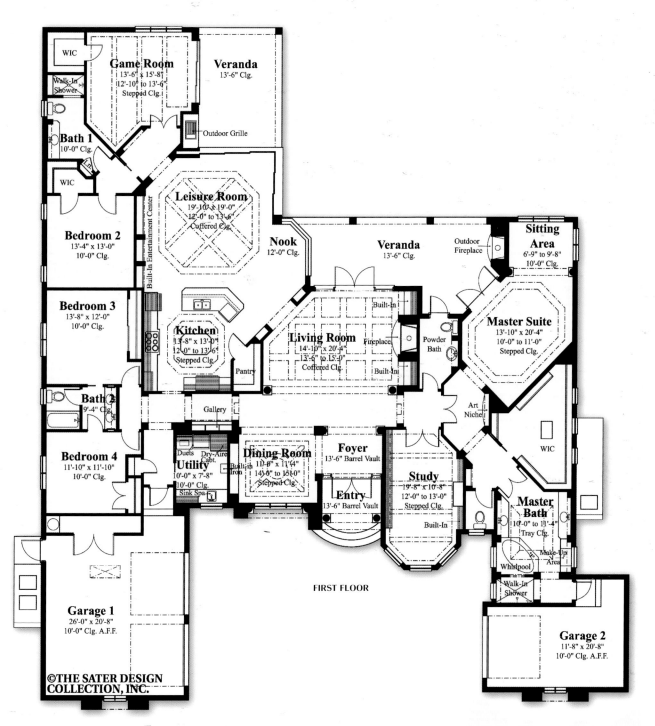

WIC

Game Room
13'-6" x 15'-8"
12'-10" to 13'-6"
Stepped Clg.

Veranda
13'-6" Clg.

Walk-In Shower

Bath 1
10'-0" Clg.

WIC

Outdoor Grille

Leisure Room
19'-10" x 19'-0"
12'-0" to 13'-6"
Coffered Clg.

Nook
12'-0" Clg.

Veranda
13'-6" Clg.

Outdoor Fireplace

Sitting Area
6'-9" to 9'-8"
10'-0" Clg.

Bedroom 2
13'-4" x 13'-0"
10'-0" Clg.

Built-In Entertainment Center

Bedroom 3
13'-8" x 12'-0"
10'-0" Clg.

Kitchen
13'-8" x 13'-0"
12'-0" to 13'-6"
Stepped Clg.

Pantry

Living Room
14'-10" x 20'-4"
13'-6" to 15'-0"
Coffered Clg.

Built-In

Fireplace

Built-In

Powder Bath

Master Suite
13'-10" x 20'-4"
10'-0" to 11'-0"
Stepped Clg.

Bath 2
9'-4" Clg.

Gallery

Art Niche

WIC

Bedroom 4
11'-10" x 11'-10"
10'-0" Clg.

Duets
Dry-Aire Cabt.

Utility
10'-0" x 7'-8"
10'-0" Clg.
Sink Spa.

Built-In Iron

Dining Room
11'-0" x 11'-4"
14'-0" to 16'-0"
Stepped Clg.

Foyer
13'-6" Barrel Vault

Study
19'-8" x 10'-8"
12'-0" to 13'-0"
Stepped Clg.

Built-In

Master Bath
10'-0" to 11'-4"
Tray Clg.

Make-Up Area

Entry
13'-6" Barrel Vault

Whirlpool

Walk-In Shower

FIRST FLOOR

Garage 1
26'-0" x 20'-8"
10'-0" Clg. A.F.F.

Garage 2
11'-8" x 20'-8"
10'-0" Clg. A.F.F.

©THE SATER DESIGN
COLLECTION, INC.

PHOTO LEFT: Accessible from the master bedroom, formal living, leisure and game rooms—the spacious lanai features amenities designed especially for entertaining and relaxing.

La Serena

Plan No. **8076**

Bedrooms: **4** Width: **88' 0"**

Baths: **3½** Depth: **98' 8"**

1st Floor: **4049 sq. ft.**

Total Living: **4049 sq. ft.**

Foundation: **Slab**

PDF **$2632**   Vellum **$2632**   CAD **$4656**

illustrated designs

Beautifully rendered plans articulate Mediterranean design loud and clear. Spanish, Tuscan, Moorish, and Andalusian influences are present throughout.

© The Sater Design Collection, Inc.

After a house has been designed, CAD operators take over and create computer generated mechanical drawings of every aspect of the house. This includes different views of the exterior called elevations. The front elevation is then given to an artist.

The artist then takes the one dimensional image of the front elevation and creates a three dimensional view of the house. The artist will add detail to the elevation such as roof tile, surface texture and landscaping.

Finally, the artist will add color to the image. At this stage the image is no longer called an elevation, it is now referred to as a color rendering. The finished color rendering adds life to the image, making it easier for us to envision the finished home.

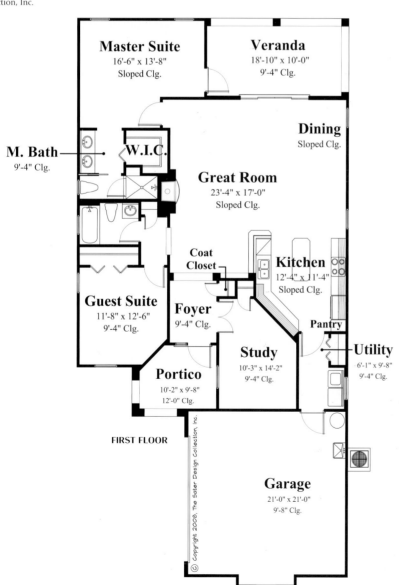

Master Suite
16'-6" x 13'-8"
Sloped Clg.

Veranda
18'-10" x 10'-0"
9'-4" Clg.

M. Bath
9'-4" Clg.

W.I.C.

Dining
Sloped Clg.

Great Room
23'-4" x 17'-0"
Sloped Clg.

Coat Closet

Kitchen
12'-4" x 11'-4"
Sloped Clg.

Guest Suite
11'-8" x 12'-6"
9'-4" Clg.

Foyer
9'-4" Clg.

Pantry

Utility
6'-1" x 9'-8"
9'-4" Clg.

Study
10'-3" x 14'-2"
9'-4" Clg.

Portico
10'-2" x 9'-8"
12'-0" Clg.

FIRST FLOOR

Garage
21'-0" x 21'-0"
9'-8" Clg.

Arezzo

Plan No. **6547**

This Mediterranean home features the details that count: arched passageways lead from room to room, a spacious kitchen offers a central island, the great room's fireplace warms the dining area as well and a covered rear veranda offers sheltered outdoor space. The master suite offers private veranda access, and a bathroom designed for two.

Bedrooms: **2**	Width: **36' 0"**
Baths: **2**	Depth: **73' 4"**

1st Floor: **1497 sq. ft.**

Total Living: **1497 sq. ft.**

Foundation: **Slab**

PDF **$875**	Vellum **$875**	CAD **$1347**

ALTERNATE ELEVATION - PLAN #6548

Riviera dei Fiori

Plan No. 6809

Inspired by Mediterranean architecture, sun-splashed columns and balustrades call to mind an earlier era. The main level contains an open arrangement of the gourmet kitchen, dining room and great room with a built-in fireplace as well as a study and one guest room. On the second floor, the master retreat offers up sublime relaxation to the owners while another guest suite provides additional accommodations.

Bedrooms: **3**	Width: **46' 0"**
Baths: **3**	Depth: **51' 0"**
1st Floor: **1542 sq. ft.**	2nd Floor: **971 sq. ft.**
Total Living: **2513 sq. ft.**	
Foundation: **Island Basement**	

PDF **$1257**	Vellum **$1257**	CAD **$2262**

REAR ELEVATION

© Sater Design Collection, Inc.

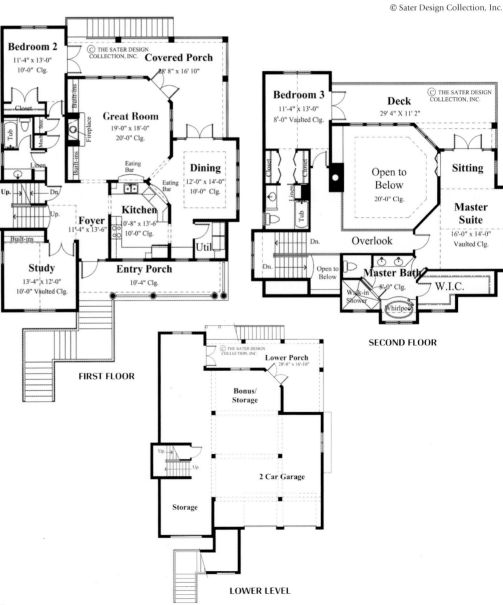

Bedroom 2
11'-4" x 13'-0"
10'-0" Clg.

Covered Porch
28' 8" x 16' 10"

Great Room
19'-0" x 18'-0"
20'-0" Clg.

Dining
12'-0" x 14'-0"
10'-0" Clg.

Kitchen
0'-8" x 13'-6"
10'-0" Clg.

Foyer
11'-4" x 13'-6"
10'-0" Clg.

Study
13'-4" x 12'-0"
10'-0" Vaulted Clg.

Entry Porch
10'-4" Clg.

Util.

FIRST FLOOR

Bedroom 3
11'-4" x 13'-0"
8'-0" Vaulted Clg.

Deck
29' 4" X 11' 2"

Open to Below
20'-0" Clg.

Sitting

Master Suite
16'-0" x 14'-0"
Vaulted Clg.

Overlook

Open to Below

Master Bath
8'-0" Clg.

Walk-in Shower

Whirlpool

W.I.C.

SECOND FLOOR

Lower Porch
28'-8" x 16'-10"

Bonus/ Storage

2 Car Garage

Storage

LOWER LEVEL

Veranda
18'-10" x 11'-0"
9'-4" Clg.

Master Suite
16'-6" x 14'-4"
Sloped Clg.

W.I.C.

M. Bath
9'-4" Clg.

Great Room
23'-4" x 17'-2"
Sloped Clg.

Dining
Sloped Clg.

Bath
9'-4" Clg.

Kitchen
12'-0" x 11'-4"
Sloped Clg.

Coat Closet

Pantry

Utility
5'-6" x 12'-2"
9'-4" Clg.

Study
10'-10" x 14'-8"
9'-4" Clg.

Foyer
9'-4" Clg.

Guest Suite
11'-8" x 13'-0"
9'-4" Clg.

Portico
18'-6" x 9'-8"
11'-0" Clg.

FIRST FLOOR

Garage
21'-4" x 21'-0"
9'-8" Clg.

Como

Plan No. **6549**

This compact plan lives larger than its footprint thanks to an open fusion of living space within. A uniquely shaped kitchen offers an island and eating bar. The great room opens to a covered veranda perfect for outdoor entertaining through two sets of sliders. The master suite offers a unique ceiling, dual vanities and a walk-in closet.

Bedrooms: **2**	Width: **36' 0"**
Baths: **2**	Depth: **80' 8"**
1st Floor: **1753 sq. ft.**	
Total Living: **1753 sq. ft.**	
Foundation: **Slab**	

PDF **$877**	Vellum **$877**	CAD **$1578**

ALTERNATE ELEVATION - PLAN #6550

© Sater Design Collection, Inc.

Wulfert Point

Plan No. 6688

A Charleston Row courtyard complete with a sundeck, spa and lap pool make this villa a relaxing retreat. Inside, arches and columns provide definition to the kitchen, dining and great rooms. French doors extend the living areas to the covered porch. The second level includes two guest bedrooms and the master suite. A bonus room over the garage offers many options.

Bedrooms: **4**

Baths: **3½**

1st Floor: **1293 sq. ft.**

Guest Suite: **426 sq. ft.**

Total Living: **2873 sq. ft.**

Foundation: **Slab**

Width: **50' 0"**

Depth: **90' 0"**

2nd Floor: **1154 sq. ft.**

| PDF **$1437** | Vellum **$1437** | CAD **$2586** |

REAR ELEVATION

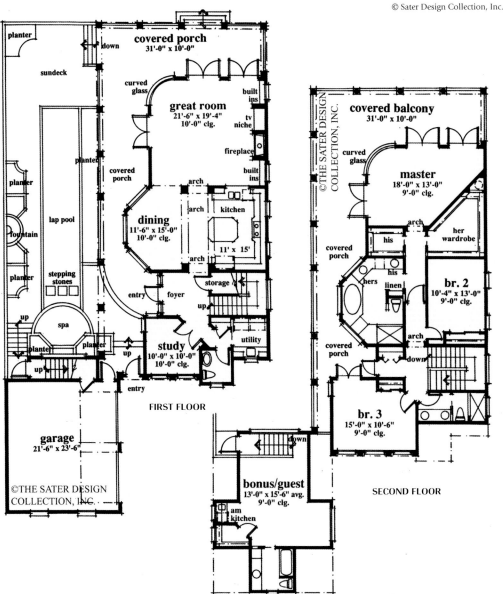

FIRST FLOOR

SECOND FLOOR

©THE SATER DESIGN COLLECTION, INC.

© Sater Design Collection, Inc.

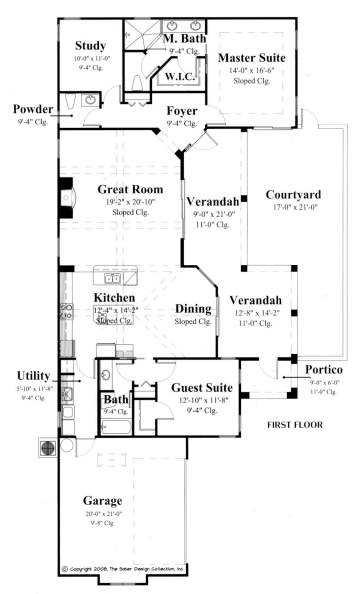

Study
10'-0" x 11'-0"
9'-4" Clg.

M. Bath
9'-4" Clg.

W.I.C.

Master Suite
14'-0" x 16'-6"
Sloped Clg.

Powder
9'-4" Clg.

Foyer
9'-4" Clg.

Great Room
19'-2" x 20'-10"
Sloped Clg.

Verandah
9'-0" x 21'-0"
11'-0" Clg.

Courtyard
17'-0" x 21'-0"

Kitchen
12'-4" x 14'-2"
Sloped Clg.

Dining
Sloped Clg.

Verandah
12'-8" x 14'-2"
11'-0" Clg.

Utility
5'-10" x 11'-8"
9'-4" Clg.

Bath
9'-4" Clg.

Guest Suite
12'-10" x 11'-8"
9'-4" Clg.

Portico
9'-0" x 6'-0"
11'-0" Clg.

FIRST FLOOR

Garage
20'-0" x 21'-0"
9'-8" Clg.

© Copyright 2008, The Sater Design Collection, Inc.

Empoli

Plan No. 6551

This courtyard plan offers a unique home centered around a beautiful outdoor living space. An open arrangement of the kitchen, dining area and great room is accented by ceiling treatments throughout the space. The master suite is secluded to the rear of the plan, while the guest suite is on the opposite side of the home to maximize privacy.

Bedrooms: **2**   Width: **38' 0"**

Baths: **2½**   Depth: **87' 4"**

1st Floor: **1790 sq. ft.**

Total Living: **1790 sq. ft.**

Foundation: **Slab**

| PDF **$895** | Vellum **$895** | CAD **$1611** |

REAR ELEVATION

© Sater Design Collection, Inc.

Florenze

Plan No. 6552

This courtyard plan offers a unique home centered around a beautiful outdoor living space. An open arrangement of the kitchen, dining area and great room is accented by ceiling treatments throughout the space. The master suite is secluded to the rear of the plan, while the guest suite is on the opposite side of the home to maximize privacy.

Bedrooms: **2**

Baths: **2½**

1st Floor: **1790 sq. ft.**

Total Living: **1790 sq. ft.**

Foundation: **Slab**

Width: **38' 0"**

Depth: **87' 4"**

| PDF **$895** | Vellum **$895** | CAD **$1611** |

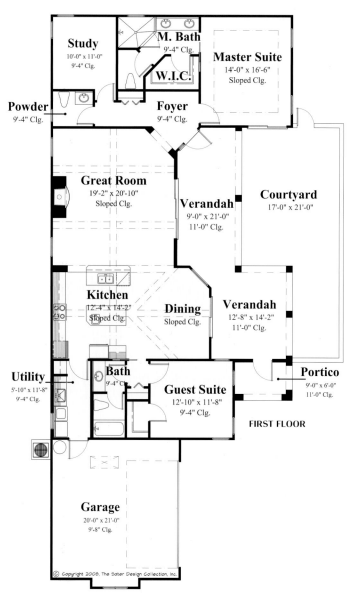

REAR ELEVATION

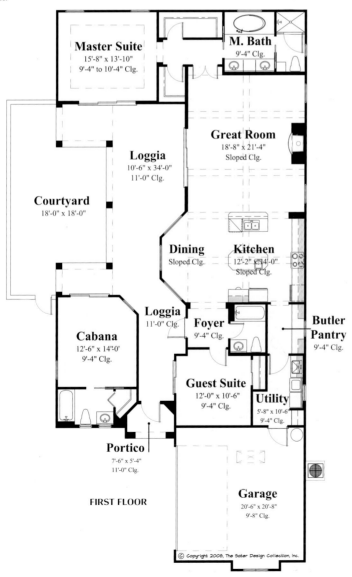

Master Suite
15'-8" x 13'-10"
9'-4" to 10'-4" Clg.

M. Bath
9'-4" Clg.

Great Room
18'-8" x 21'-4"
Sloped Clg.

Loggia
10'-6" x 34'-0"
11'-0" Clg.

Courtyard
18'-0" x 18'-0"

Dining
Sloped Clg.

Kitchen
12'-2" x 14'-0"
Sloped Clg.

Loggia
11'-0" Clg.

Foyer
9'-4" Clg.

Butler Pantry
9'-4" Clg.

Cabana
12'-6" x 14'-0'
9'-4" Clg.

Guest Suite
12'-0" x 10'-6"
9'-4" Clg.

Utility
5'-8" x 10'-6"
9'-4" Clg.

Portico
7'-6" x 5'-4"
11'-0" Clg.

FIRST FLOOR

Garage
20'-6" x 20'-8"
9'-8" Clg.

Gavello

Plan No. **6553**

This Mediterranean design features views of the private courtyard throughout the living areas. Sliding glass doors open rooms to the secluded outdoor living space. Despite its smaller size, amenities like a great room fireplace, butler's pantry and his-and-hers master closets offer luxurious living.

Bedrooms: **2**

Baths: **3**

1st Floor: **1629 sq. ft.**

Total Living: **1892 sq. ft.**

Foundation: **Slab**

Width: **40' 0"**

Depth: **87' 4"**

Cabana: **263 sq. ft.**

| PDF **$946** | Vellum **$946** | CAD **$1703** |

REAR ELEVATION

Lizzano

Plan No. **6554**

This Mediterranean design features views of the private courtyard throughout the living areas. Sliding glass doors open rooms to the secluded outdoor living space. Despite its smaller size, amenities like a great room fireplace, butler's pantry and his-and-hers master closets offer luxurious living within the home. A cabana is sure to impress as a guest suite or detached home office.

Bedrooms: **2**	Width: **40' 0"**
Baths: **3**	Depth: **87' 4"**
1st Floor: **1629 sq. ft.**	Cabana: **263 sq. ft.**
Total Living: **1892 sq. ft.**	
Foundation: **Slab**	

PDF **$946**	Vellum **$946**	CAD **$1703**

REAR ELEVATION

© Sater Design Collection, Inc.

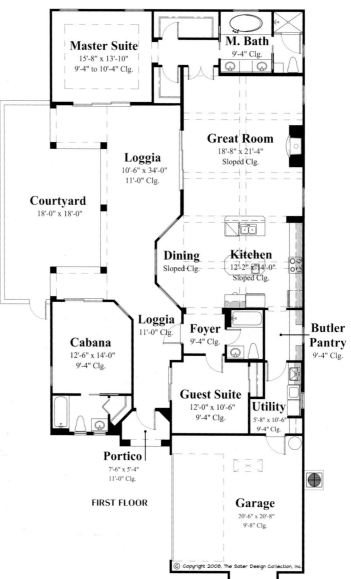

Master Suite
15'-8" x 13'-10"
9'-4" to 10'-4" Clg.

M. Bath
9'-4" Clg.

Great Room
18'-8" x 21'-4"
Sloped Clg.

Loggia
10'-6" x 34'-0"
11'-0" Clg.

Courtyard
18'-0" x 18'-0"

Dining
Sloped Clg.

Kitchen
12'-2" x 14'-0"
Sloped Clg.

Loggia
11'-0" Clg.

Foyer
9'-4" Clg.

Butler Pantry
9'-4" Clg.

Cabana
12'-6" x 14'-0"
9'-4" Clg.

Guest Suite
12'-0" x 10'-6"
9'-4" Clg.

Utility
5'-8" x 10'-6"
9'-4" Clg.

Portico
7'-6" x 5'-4"
11'-0" Clg.

FIRST FLOOR

Garage
20'-6" x 20'-8"
9'-8" Clg.

© Copyright 2008, The Sater Design Collection, Inc.

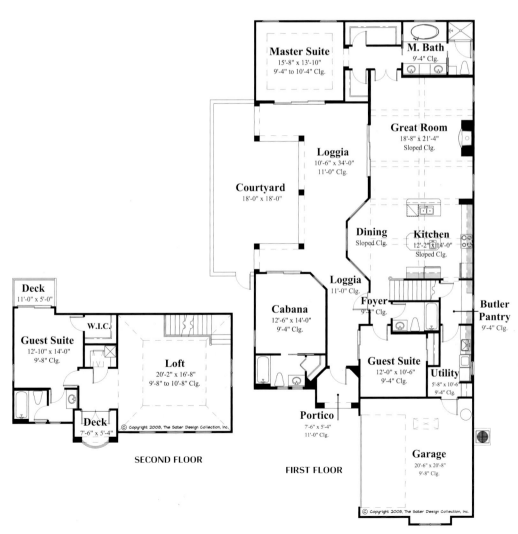

Master Suite
15'-8" x 13'-10"
9'-4" to 10'-4" Clg.

M. Bath
9'-4" Clg.

Great Room
18'-8" x 21'-4"
Sloped Clg.

Loggia
10'-6" x 34'-0"
11'-0" Clg.

Courtyard
18'-0" x 18'-0"

Dining
Sloped Clg.

Kitchen
12'-2" x 14'-0"
Sloped Clg.

Deck
11'-0" x 5'-0"

W.I.C.

Guest Suite
12'-10" x 14'-0"
9'-8" Clg.

Loft
20'-2" x 16'-8"
9'-8" to 10'-8" Clg.

Loggia
11'-0" Clg.

Cabana
12'-6" x 14'-0"
9'-4" Clg.

Foyer
9'-4" Clg.

Butler Pantry
9'-4" Clg.

Deck
7'-6" x 5'-4"

Guest Suite
12'-0" x 10'-6"
9'-4" Clg.

Utility
5'-8" x 10'-6"
9'-4" Clg.

Portico
7'-6" x 5'-4"
11'-0" Clg.

Garage
20'-6" x 20'-8"
9'-8" Clg.

© Copyright 2008, The Sater Design Collection, Inc.

SECOND FLOOR

FIRST FLOOR

Melito

Plan No. 6555

This narrow courtyard home creates a private sanctuary to enjoy the outdoors. An open arrangement of living space creates an airy atmosphere. A flexible loft is on the second floor, while a separate cabana on the first floor makes luxe guest quarters. The rambling master suite takes up the entire rear of the plan, but offers a private entrance to the courtyard.

Bedrooms: **3**

Baths: **4**

1st Floor: **1664 sq. ft.**

Cabana: **263 sq. ft.**

Total Living: **2676 sq. ft.**

Foundation: **Slab**

Width: **40' 0"**

Depth: **89' 0"**

2nd Floor: **749 sq. ft.**

PDF **$1338**   Vellum **$1338**   CAD **$2408**

REAR ELEVATION

© Sater Design Collection, Inc.

Pelago

Plan No. 6556

This narrow courtyard home creates a private sanctuary to enjoy the outdoors. An open arrangement of living space creates an airy atmosphere. A flexible loft is on the second floor, while a separate cabana on the first floor makes luxe guest quarters. The rambling master suite takes up the entire rear of the plan, but offers a private entrance to the courtyard.

Bedrooms: **3**

Baths: **4**

1st Floor: **1664 sq. ft.**

Cabana: **263 sq. ft.**

Total Living: **2676 sq. ft.**

Foundation: **Slab**

Width: **40' 0"**

Depth: **89' 0"**

2nd Floor: **749 sq. ft.**

| PDF **$1338** | Vellum **$1338** | CAD **$2408** |

REAR ELEVATION

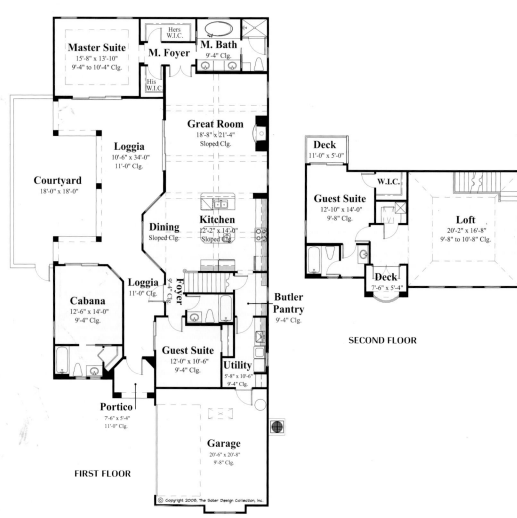

FIRST FLOOR

SECOND FLOOR

© Sater Design Collection, Inc.

Ventana

Plan No. 6925

Rope molding gives Romanesque flair to the pointed-arch entry in this detail-rich Mediterranean manor. The foyer is grand under a barrel-vault ceiling and leads to a living room walled by in glass. The guest suites and family spaces are to the right, with the leisure room opening to a veranda and an outdoor kitchen. The master suite is commanding with stepped ceilings, two walk-in closets and a luxurious bath where a centered tub "floats" under a tray ceiling.

Bedrooms: **4**	Width: **101′ 4″**
Baths: **4½**	Depth: **120′ 8″**
1st Floor: **4369 sq. ft.**	2nd Floor: **640 sq. ft.**
Total Living: **5009 sq. ft.**	
Foundation: **Slab**	

PDF **$5009**	Vellum **$5009**	CAD **$8515**

REAR ELEVATION

FIRST FLOOR

Veranda
35'-8" x 11'-8"
12'-0" Clg.

Outdoor Kitchen

Stor.

Fireplace

Leisure Room
22'-0" x 24'-0"
22'-4"-23'-4"
Stepped Clg.

Entertainment Center

Nook
9'-8" x 11'-2"
12'-0" Clg.

Desk

Kitchen
16'-4" x 21'-2"
11'-3"-12'-0"
Stepped Clg.

Veranda
62'-5" x 20'-6"
12'-0" Clg.

Master Suite
20'-0" x 14'-4"
14'-0"-16'-0"
Stepped Clg.

Study
16'-4" x 13'-0"
14'-0"-15'-0"
Stepped Clg.

Living Room
17'-6" x 16'-2"
Stepped Clg.

Dining Room
16'-10" x 14'-0"
14'-0"-16'-0"
Stepped Clg.

Pwdr.

Wet Bar

Pantry

WIC
10'-4" x 9'-2"

Art Niche

WIC

Built-Ins

Foyer
12'-8" to 17'-10"
Barrel Vault Clg.

Entry

Glass Wall

Wine Cellar

Guest Suite 1
13'-2" x 14'-2"
12'-0" Clg.

Bath 2

WIC

Bath 1

WIC

Master Bath
18'-11" x 18'-8"
10'-0"-17'-0" Tray Clg.

Linen

Walk-In Shower

Guest Suite 2
12'-8" x 16'-6"
10'-0" Clg.

Utility
14'-2" x 7'-2"

Privacy Garden

Storage

Garage
39'-6" x 22'-8"
10'-0" Clg.

© THE SATER DESIGN COLLECTION, INC.

SECOND FLOOR

Deck
28'-2" x 13'-7"

© THE SATER DESIGN COLLECTION, INC.

Lanai
13'-6" x 23'-4"
9'-0" Clg.

Open To Below

Loft
22'-5" x 19'-6"
9'-0"-10'-0"
Stepped Clg.

Bath 3

Guest Suite 3
16'-0" x 11'-10"
9'-0" Clg.

WIC

Salcito

Plan No. 6787

This charming courtyard home features private, family and guest spaces filled with Mediterranean design details and open connections to a central loggia with fountain pool. The leisure room has a two-story boxed-beamed ceiling, a wall of built-ins, and retreating glass doors that make it one with the loggia. Nearby, the formal dining and living rooms open to a private lanai. The second level includes a study, guest bedrooms and a loft.

Bedrooms: **4**

Baths: **4½**

1st Floor: **2087 sq. ft.**

Guest Suite: **272 sq. ft.**

Total Living: **3458 sq. ft.**

Foundation: **Slab**

Width: **45' 0"**

Depth: **94' 0"**

2nd Floor: **1099 sq. ft.**

PDF **$1729**	Vellum **$1729**	CAD **$3112**

REAR ELEVATION

FIRST FLOOR

©THE SATER DESIGN COLLECTION, INC.

SECOND FLOOR

©THE SATER DESIGN COLLECTION, INC.

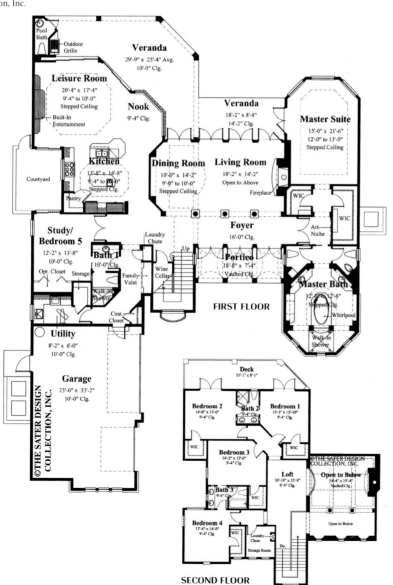

Pool Bath

Outdoor Grille

Veranda
29'-9" x 25'-4" Avg.
10'-0" Clg.

Leisure Room
20'-4" x 17'-4"
9'-4" to 10'-0"
Stepped Ceiling

Built-In Entertainment

Nook
9'-4" Clg.

Veranda
18'-2" x 8'-8"
14'-2" Clg.

Master Suite
15'-0" x 21'-6"
12'-0" to 13'-0"
Stepped Ceiling

Kitchen
13'-8" x 14'-8"
9'-4" to 10'-0"
Stepped Clg.

Courtyard

Pantry

Dining Room
10'-0" x 14'-2"
9'-0" to 10'-0"
Stepped Ceiling

Living Room
18'-2" x 14'-2"
Open to Above

Fireplace

WIC

WIC

Study/ Bedroom 5
12'-2" x 13'-8"
10'-0" Clg.

Opt. Closet   Storage

Bath 1
10'-0" Clg.

Laundry Chute

Foyer
16'-0" Clg.

Art Niche

Up

Family Valet

Walk-In Shower

Wine Cellar

Portico
18'-8" x 7'-4"
Vaulted Clg.

Master Bath
12'-0" x 22'-8"
Stepped Clg.

Whirlpool

FIRST FLOOR

Coat Closet

Walk-In Shower

Utility
8'-2" x 6'-0"
10'-0" Clg.

Garage
23'-0" x 33'-2"
10'-0" Clg.

Deck
35'-1" x 8'-1"

Bedroom 2
14'-0" x 13'-0"
9'-4" Clg.

Bath 2
9'-4" Clg.

Bedroom 1
13'-5" x 13'-10"
9'-4" Clg.

WIC   WIC

Bedroom 3
16'-2" x 12'-0"
9'-4" Clg.

Bath 3
9'-4" Clg.

WIC

Loft
10'-10" x 13'-8"
9'-4" Clg.

Open to Below
18'-4" x 19'-4"
Vaulted Clg.

Bedroom 4
12'-4" x 14'-0"
9'-4" Clg.

WIC

Laundry Chute

Dn.

Storage Room

Open to Below

SECOND FLOOR

Massimo

Plan No. 8057

Colonial lines evoke the ancient forms of the houses of Tuscany, yet this grand manor steps boldly into the present. A side courtyard complements a veranda that wraps around the rear of the plan, bordered by walls of glass. French doors open the central living and dining space to the world outside. Upstairs, guest bedrooms open to a shared deck with rear-property views, while a spacious loft overlooks the living room below.

Bedrooms: **6**   Width: **69' 4"**

Baths: **4½**   Depth: **95' 4"**

1st Floor: **2920 sq. ft.**   2nd Floor: **1478 sq. ft.**

Total Living: **4398 sq. ft.**

Foundation: **Slab**

PDF $2859	Vellum $2859	CAD $5058

REAR ELEVATION

© Sater Design Collection, Inc.

Napier

Plan No. **6926**

A unique two-story master suite makes this home fabulous. The bedroom and spectacular bath with private garden are downstairs; a den, exercise room, half-bath and deck are above. Across the home, another second-level space includes a full bedroom suite with deck, plus a media room or fourth bedroom also with a private bath and balcony. The main floor has every amenity imaginable surrounded by vast outdoor spaces.

Bedrooms: **4**	Width: **140' 7"**
Baths: **5½**	Depth: **116' 10"**
1st Floor: **5155 sq. ft.**	2nd Floor: **1937 sq. ft.**
Total Living: **7092 sq. ft.**	
Foundation: **Slab**	

PDF **$8865**	Vellum **$8865**	CAD **$14184**

REAR ELEVATION

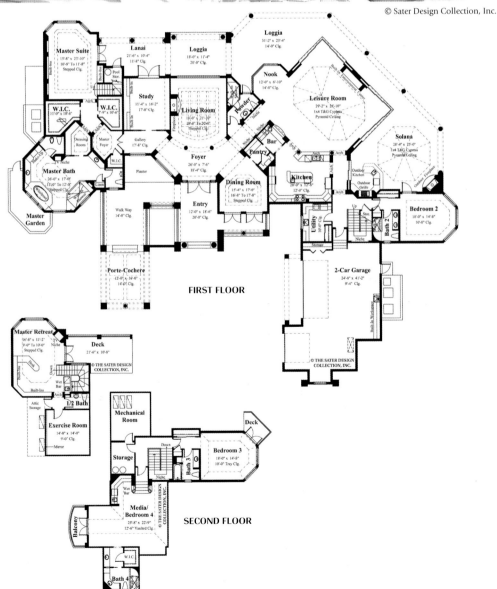

FIRST FLOOR

SECOND FLOOR

© THE SATER DESIGN COLLECTION, INC.

© Sater Design Collection, Inc.

Rosario

Plan No. 6784

Arches, columns and a corner courtyard combine to create a striking street presence. Inside, a smart floor plan loaded with glass walls and windows enhances indoor-outdoor living. Past the foyer, the formal living and dining rooms are divided by a floating bar and bordered by pocketing glass walls to the lanai. A butler's pantry connects the formal rooms to the kitchen, ensuring easy entertaining.

Bedrooms: **3**	Width: **65' 0"**
Baths: **3½**	Depth: **90' 6"**
1st Floor: **3184 sq. ft.**	
Total Living: **3184 sq. ft.**	
Foundation: **Slab**	

PDF $1592	Vellum $1592	CAD $2866

REAR ELEVATION

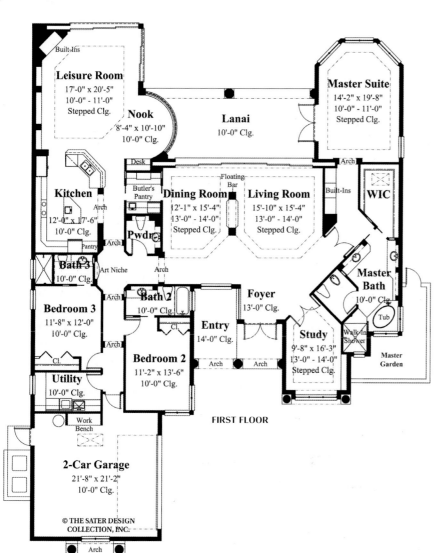

Leisure Room
17'-0" x 20'-5"
10'-0" - 11'-0"
Stepped Clg.

Built-Ins

Nook
8'-4" x 10'-10"
10'-0" Clg.

Lanai
10'-0" Clg.

Master Suite
14'-2" x 19'-8"
10'-0" - 11'-0"
Stepped Clg.

Desk

Floating Bar

Arch

Kitchen
12'-0" x 17'-6"
10'-0" Clg.

Butler's Pantry

Dining Room
12'-1" x 15'-4"
13'-0" - 14'-0"
Stepped Clg.

Living Room
15'-10" x 15'-4"
13'-0" - 14'-0"
Stepped Clg.

Built-Ins

WIC

Arch

Pwdr

Pantry

Arch

Bath 3
10'-0" Clg.

Art Niche

Arch

Bath 2
10'-0" Clg.

Foyer
13'-0" Clg.

Master Bath
10'-0" Clg.

Tub

Bedroom 3
11'-8" x 12'-0"
10'-0" Clg.

Cl.

Entry
14'-0" Clg.

Study
9'-8" x 16'-3"
13'-0" - 14'-0"
Stepped Clg.

Walk-In Shower

Cl.

Arch

Bedroom 2
11'-2" x 13'-6"
10'-0" Clg.

Arch

Arch

Master Garden

Cl.

Utility
10'-0" Clg.

Work Bench

FIRST FLOOR

2-Car Garage
21'-8" x 21'-2"
10'-0" Clg.

© THE SATER DESIGN COLLECTION, INC.

Arch

© Sater Design Collection, Inc.

La Posada

Plan No. 6785

Decorative pendants add one-of-a-kind detail to the entryway cornice. Inside, the living room, kitchen and leisure room flow together and offer uninterrupted access and views to the lanai through disappearing glass walls and mitered windows. An island and large walk-in pantry make the kitchen sparkle. Owners will enjoy privacy in a master suite tucked to one side of the home.

Bedrooms: **4**	Width: **60′ 4″**
Baths: **3**	Depth: **78′ 9″**

1ˢᵗ Floor: **2544 sq. ft.**

Total Living: **2544 sq. ft.**

Foundation: **Slab**

| PDF **$1272** | Vellum **$1272** | CAD **$2290** |

REAR ELEVATION

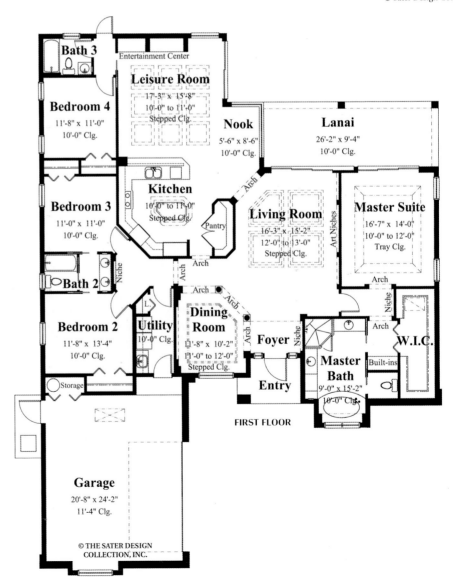

Bath 3

Leisure Room
17′-3″ x 15′-8″
10′-0″ to 11′-0″
Stepped Clg.

Entertainment Center

Bedroom 4
11′-8″ x 11′-0″
10′-0″ Clg.

Nook
5′-6″ x 8′-6″
10′-0″ Clg.

Lanai
26′-2″ x 9′-4″
10′-0″ Clg.

Kitchen
10′-0″ to 11′-0″
Stepped Clg.

Pantry

Living Room
16′-3″ x 15′-2″
12′-0″ to 13′-0″
Stepped Clg.

Master Suite
16′-7″ x 14′-0″
10′-0″ to 12′-0″
Tray Clg.

Arch

Art Niches

Bedroom 3
11′-0″ x 11′-0″
10′-0″ Clg.

Niche

Arch

Bath 2

Arch

Niche

W.I.C.

Bedroom 2
11′-8″ x 13′-4″
10′-0″ Clg.

Utility
10′-0″ Clg.

Dining Room
11′-8″ x 10′-2″
11′-0″ to 12′-0″
Stepped Clg.

Arch

Foyer

Niche

Built-ins

Master Bath
9′-0″ x 15′-2″
10′-0″ Clg.

Storage

Entry

FIRST FLOOR

Garage
20′-8″ x 24′-2″
11′-4″ Clg.

© THE SATER DESIGN
COLLECTION, INC.

© Sater Design Collection, Inc.

Guest Bath
10'-0" Clg.

Guest Suite
12'-2" x 12'-6"
10'-0" Clg.

WIC   WIC

Bedroom 2
12'-2" x 12'-1"
10'-0" Clg.

Kitchen
14'-0" x 15'-0"
10'-0" to 10'-8"
Stepped Clg.

Leisure Room
15'-0" x 20'-6"
10'-0" to 11'-0"
Stepped Clg.

Nook
10'-0" Clg.

Lanai
37'-10" x 12'-2"
10'-0" Clg.

Grille

Master Suite
15'-10" x 15'-2"
10'-0" to 11'-0"
Stepped Clg.

Built-in

Living Room
17'-6" x 15'-2"
12'-0" to 13'-4"
Stepped Clg.

Fireplace

Pantry

Built-in

Art Niche

Bath 1

WIC

Linen

Bedroom 1
14'-2" x 11'-11"
10'-0" Clg.

Dining Room
11'-4" x 13'-2"
12'-0" to 12'-8"
Stepped Clg.

Foyer
12'-8" Clg.

Pwdr.

Linen

Master Bath
9'-4" x 10'-0"
Stepped Clg.

Whirlpool

Privacy Garden

Walk-In Shower

Dressing Area

Utility
12'-8" x 5'-8"
10'-0" Clg.

Family Valet

Stor.

Entry
Barrel Clg.

Study
11'-2" x 17'-6"
Beamed Clg.

FIRST FLOOR

Garage
22'-0" x 31'-4"
10'-0" Clg.

©THE SATER DESIGN COLLECTION, INC.

Simone

Plan No. **8059**

Stacked stone gables dramatically define the neighborhood presence of this Italian villa. Beyond the entry, the plan offers well-defined rooms and wide-open spaces, with views of nature everywhere. Columns define the boundaries of the formal dining room, permitting interior vistas as well as easy service from the kitchen. Retreating glass doors provide views and expand the living and leisure rooms onto the spacious lanai, where guests can enjoy meals al fresco by the built-in grille.

Bedrooms: **4**   Width: **67' 0"**

Baths: **3½**   Depth: **91' 8"**

1st Floor: **3231 sq. ft.**

Total Living: **3231 sq. ft.**

Foundation: **Slab**

| PDF **$1617** | Vellum **$1617** | CAD **$2908** |

REAR ELEVATION

© Sater Design Collection, Inc.

Bartolini

Plan No. 8022

Trefoil windows and a deeply sculpted portico set off a lyrical Italian aesthetic inspired by 15th-century forms and an oceanfront attitude. Inside, three sets of French doors open the great room to the courtyard and terrace. A private wing that includes the kitchen and morning nook also opens to the outdoors. The master suite enjoys ample amounts of space, while the upper level harbors two guest suites, a loft and a bonus room.

Bedrooms: **3**

Baths: **2½**

1st Floor: **2084 sq. ft.**

Total Living: **2736 sq. ft.**

Bonus: **375 sq. ft.**

Foundation: **Slab or Optional Basement**

Width: **60' 6"**

Depth: **94' 0"**

2nd Floor: **652 sq. ft.**

| PDF **$1368** | Vellum **$1368** | CAD **$2462** |

REAR ELEVATION

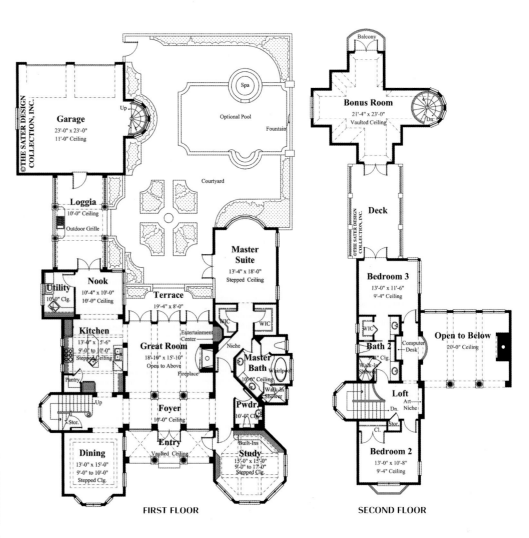

FIRST FLOOR

SECOND FLOOR

Corsini

Plan No. 8049

Corbels, columns and carved balusters rooted in a timeless Spanish vocabulary establish a striking street presence. Inside, the foyer opens to the great room, an outside-in space that brings in breezes and links with nature. A lateral arrangement of the kitchen, loggia, nook and formal dining room eases entertaining. To the right of the plan, the owners' wing opens to the terrace. The upper-level loft overlooks the great room and connects four guest bedrooms.

Bedrooms: **5**	Width: **71' 0"**
Baths: **3½**	Depth: **72' 0"**
1st Floor: **2163 sq. ft.**	2nd Floor: **1415 sq. ft.**

Total Living: **3578 sq. ft.**

Foundation: **Slab or Optional Basement**

PDF **$1789**	Vellum **$1789**	CAD **$3220**

REAR ELEVATION

FIRST FLOOR

Garage
23'-8" x 23'-0"
10'-0" Ceiling

© THE SATER DESIGN COLLECTION, INC.

Loggia
8'-4" x 23'-6"
10'-8" Ceiling
Outdoor Grille

Utility
8'-8" x 9'-6"
10'-0" Ceiling

Nook
11'-4" x 9'-0"
10'-8" Ceiling

Terrace
21'-4" x 12'-9"
Open to Above

Master Suite
13'-4" x 18'-0"
12'-0" to 14'-0"
Tray Ceiling

Kitchen
13'-0" x 15'-6"
10'-2" to 10'-8"
Beamed Ceiling

Pantry

Great Room
20'-10" x 16'-6"
Open to Above

Entertainment Center

WIC WIC

Dressing Mirror

M. Bath
10'-8" Ceiling

Fireplace

Art Niche

Walk-In Shower

Up

Stor.

Foyer
10'-8" Ceiling

Art Niche

Pwdr.
10'-0" Ceiling

Dining
13'-0" x 13'-0"
10'-0" to 14'-0"
Beamed Ceiling

Portico
21'-10" x 7'-0"
Groin Vault

Built-Ins

Study
13'-0" x 13'-6"
9'-8" to 10'-8"
Coffered Ceiling

SECOND FLOOR

Sun Deck

Bedroom 3
13'-0" x 11'-6"
9'-4" Ceiling

WIC

Bath 2
9'-4" Clg.

Walk-In Shower

© THE SATER DESIGN COLLECTION, INC.

Open to Below
23'-0" to 24'-0"
Beamed Ceiling

Computer Desk

Bedroom 5
13'-0" x 14'-0"
9'-4" Ceiling

Window Seat

Loft
9'-4" Clg.

Dn

Stor.

Balcony
8'-6" Clg.

Walk-In Shower

Bath 3
9'-4" Clg.

WIC

Bedroom 2
13'-0" x 11'-1"
9'-4" Ceiling

Bedroom 4
13'-0" x 11'-1"
9'-4" Ceiling

Laparelli

Plan No. 8035

Romantic elements reside throughout this Italian villa, melding style and views with a profound level of comfort. Arch-topped windows bring light into the forward formal spaces, while retreating glass walls on the lanai side extend both public and private realms outside. The kitchen serves the formal dining room via a gallery, while a wet bar announces the casual living space. The owners' retreat is an amenity-rich escape.

Bedrooms: **3**

Baths: **4**

1st Floor: **3942 sq. ft.**

Total Living: **3942 sq. ft.**

Foundation: **Slab**

Width: **83' 10"**

Depth: **106' 0"**

| PDF **$2562** | Vellum **$2562** | CAD **$4533** |

REAR ELEVATION

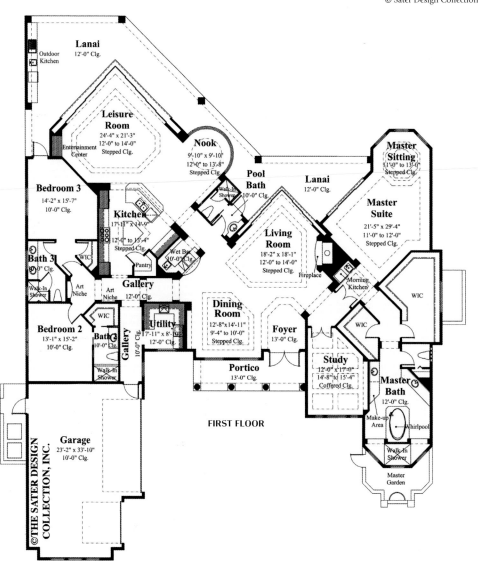

FIRST FLOOR

© THE SATER DESIGN COLLECTION, INC.

© Sater Design Collection, Inc.

Verrado

Plan No. **6918**

Stone balustrades create an entryway patio, making this home ultra-impressive. The interior impresses, too, with zero-corner pocket doors in the living room, a private master suite with a privacy garden, and a fabulous solana with an outdoor grill and fireplace. The second floor offers two guest rooms with a shared bath, a bonus room with its own lanai and deck, and even a second wet bar.

Bedrooms: **4** Width: **65' 0"**

Baths: **3½** Depth: **115' 0"**

1st Floor: **3008 sq. ft.** 2nd Floor: **987 sq. ft.**

Total Living: **3995 sq. ft.**

Foundation: **Slab or Optional Basement**

| PDF **$2597** | Vellum **$2597** | CAD **$4594** |

REAR ELEVATION

SECOND FLOOR

Deck
10'-0" x 14'-0"

© THE SATER DESIGN COLLECTION, INC.

Lanai
10'-0" x 12'-6"
10'-0" Clg.

Guest Suite 3
18'-4" x 12'-0"
10'-0" Clg.

WIC

Linen

Bonus Room
15'-6" x 22'-8"
10'-0" Clg.

Bath

Closet

Guest Suite 2
12'-4" x 12'-0"
10'-0" Clg.

Arch

Wet Bar
Popcorn Maker

Attic Storage

Down

FIRST FLOOR

Solana
28'-8" x 13'-10"
12'-0" Clg.

Outdoor Fireplace

Outdoor Grill

Leisure Room
18'-0" x 20'-0"
11'-0"-12'-0"
Stepped Clg.

Loggia
24'-5" x 15'-6"
14'-6" Clg.

Nook
8'-10" x 9'-10"
12'-0" Clg.

Kitchen
14'-9" x 15'-6"
12'-0" Clg.

Master Suite
19'-6" x 19'-4"
10'-0" - 12'-0"
Stepped Clg.

Living Room
18'-6" x 15'-6"
12'-8" - 14'-0"
Stepped Clg.

Pwdr

Wet Bar

Pantry

WIC
9'-10" x 14'-9"
10'-0" Clg.

Dining
12'-0" x 13'-0"
12'-8" - 14'-8"
Stepped Clg.

Up

Storage

Study
11'-0" x 16'-6"
12'-8" - 14'-8"
Stepped Clg.

Foyer
14'-0" Clg.

Niche

WIC

Bath

Master Bath
13'-8" x 17'-10"
10'-0" Clg.

Entry
16'-0" Clg.

Tub

Guest Suite
14'-4" x 11'-8"
10'-0" Clg.

Privacy Garden

Walk-In Shower

Utility

Arch

Arch

Arch

3 Car Garage
21'-0" x 37'-10"
11'-4" Clg.

© THE SATER DESIGN COLLECTION, INC.

© Sater Design Collection, Inc.

Bellini

Plan No. 8042

Classic architectural lines surround an entry portico inspired by original Italian villas. Ancient and modern elements come together throughout the interior, juxtaposing rusticated beamed ceilings with up-to-the-minute electronics. The combined living/dining room is anchored by a massive fireplace. A state-of-the-art kitchen overlooks the nook and spacious leisure room. Retreating glass walls open to a wraparound veranda.

Bedrooms: **3**	Width: **84' 0"**
Baths: **2 full, 2 half**	Depth: **92' 2"**
1st Floor: **3351 sq. ft.**	
Total Living: **3351 sq. ft.**	
Foundation: **Slab**	

PDF **$1677**	Vellum **$1677**	CAD **$3016**

REAR ELEVATION

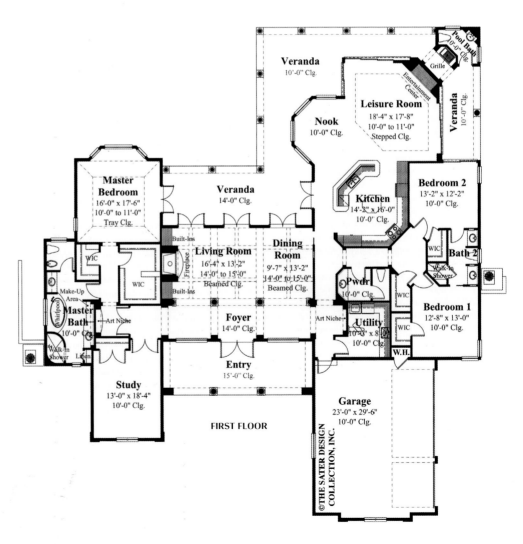

© Sater Design Collection, Inc.

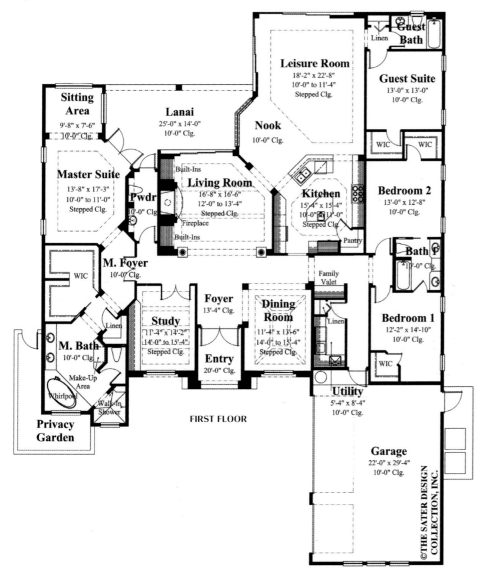

Leisure Room
18'-2" x 22'-8"
10'-0" to 11'-4"
Stepped Clg.

Guest Bath

Linen

Guest Suite
13'-0" x 13'-0"
10'-0" Clg.

Sitting Area
9'-8" x 7'-6"
10'-0" Clg.

Lanai
25'-0" x 14'-0"
10'-0" Clg.

Nook
10'-0" Clg.

WIC WIC

Master Suite
13'-8" x 17'-3"
10'-0" to 11'-0"
Stepped Clg.

Built-Ins

Pwdr
10'-0" Clg.

Living Room
16'-8" x 16'-6"
12'-0" to 13'-4"
Stepped Clg.

Fireplace

Built-Ins

Kitchen
15'-4" x 15'-4"
10'-0" to 11'-4"
Stepped Clg.

Bedroom 2
13'-0" x 12'-8"
10'-0" Clg.

Pantry

M. Foyer
10'-0" Clg.

WIC

Bath
10'-0" Clg.

Family Valet

Foyer
13'-4" Clg.

Study
11'-4" x 14'-2"
14'-0" to 15'-4"
Stepped Clg.

Dining Room
11'-4" x 13'-6"
14'-0" to 15'-4"
Stepped Clg.

Linen

Bedroom 1
12'-2" x 14'-10"
10'-0" Clg.

M. Bath
10'-0" Clg.

Make-Up Area

Whirlpool

Entry
20'-0" Clg.

WIC

Privacy Garden

Walk-In Shower

FIRST FLOOR

Utility
5'-4" x 8'-4"
10'-0" Clg.

© THE SATER DESIGN COLLECTION, INC.

Garage
22'-0" x 29'-4"
10'-0" Clg.

Martelli

Plan No. 8061

A sculpted, recessed entry defines the finely detailed Spanish eclectic façade, and a quatrefoil window confirms a Moorish influence. Inside, an open arrangement of the foyer and the formal rooms permits natural light to flow freely through the space. Walls of glass to the rear of the plan open the public and private realms to spectacular views, while nearby, the gourmet kitchen easily serves planned events both inside and out.

Bedrooms: **4**   Width: **68' 8"**

Baths: **3½**   Depth: **91' 8"**

1st Floor: **3497 sq. ft.**

Total Living: **3497 sq. ft.**

Foundation: **Slab**

PDF **$1749**	Vellum **$1749**	CAD **$3147**

REAR ELEVATION

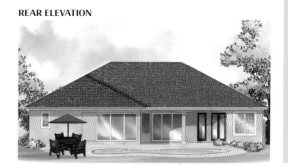

© Sater Design Collection, Inc.

Salina

Plan No. 8043

Hipped rooflines, carved eave brackets and varied gables evoke a sense of the past, while a blend of old and new prevails inside. Beamed and coffered ceilings juxtapose state-of-the-art amenities—a pass-thru wet bar, cutting-edge appliances in the kitchen, and a standalone media center between the leisure and game rooms. Rounded arches define the transitions between well-appointed rooms and open spaces.

Bedrooms: **4**	Width: **80' 0"**
Baths: **3½**	Depth: **104' 8"**

1st Floor: **3743 sq. ft.**

Total Living: **3743 sq. ft.**

Foundation: **Slab or Optional Basement**

PDF **$1873**	Vellum **$1873**	CAD **$3369**

REAR ELEVATION

OPTIONAL BEDROOM

Leisure Room
19'-8" x 15'-9"
Stepped Clg.

Optional Bedroom
12'-4" x 13'-11"
Flat Clg.

Entertainment Center

©THE SATER DESIGN COLLECTION, INC.

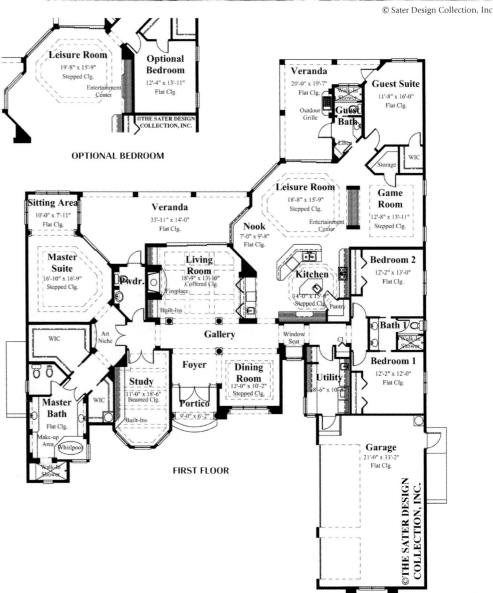

FIRST FLOOR

©THE SATER DESIGN COLLECTION, INC.

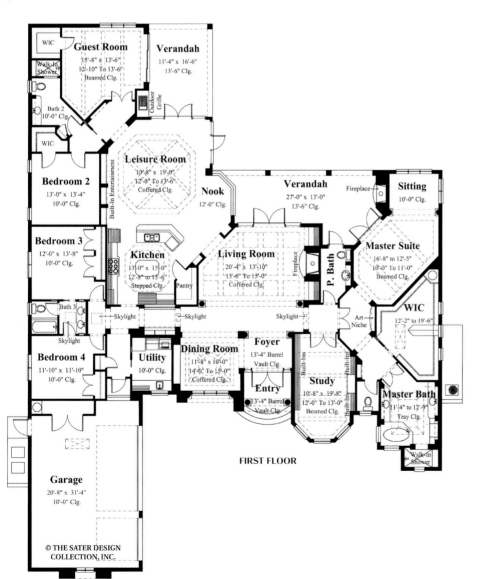

WIC

Guest Room
15'-8" x 13'-6"
12'-10" To 13'-6"
Beamed Clg.

Verandah
11'-4" x 16'-6"
13'-6" Clg.

Walk-In Shower

Outdoor Grille

Bath 2
10'-0" Clg.

WIC

Bedroom 2
13'-0" x 13'-4"
10'-0" Clg.

Leisure Room
19'-8" x 19'-0"
12'-0" To 13'-6"
Coffered Clg.

Nook
12'-0" Clg.

Verandah
27'-0" x 13'-0"
13'-6" Clg.

Fireplace

Sitting
10'-0" Clg.

Bedroom 3
12'-0" x 13'-8"
10'-0" Clg.

Built-In Entertainment

Kitchen
13'-0" x 15'-0"
12'-8" to 15'-6"
Stepped Clg.

Pantry

Living Room
20'-4" x 13'-10"
13'-6" To 15'-0"
Coffered Clg.

Fireplace

P. Bath

Master Suite
16'-8" to 12'-5"
10'-0" To 11'-0"
Beamed Clg.

Bath 3

Skylight

Skylight

Skylight

Art Niche

WIC
12'-2" to 19'-6"

Bedroom 4
11'-10" x 11'-10"
10'-0" Clg.

Utility
10'-0" Clg.

Dining Room
11'-8" x 10'-0"
14'-0" to 15'-0"
Coffered Clg.

Foyer
13'-4" Barrel
Vault Clg.

Built-Ins

Built-Ins

Entry
13'-4" Barrel
Vault Clg.

Study
10'-8" x 19'-8"
12'-0" To 13'-0"
Beamed Clg.

Master Bath
11'-4" x 12'-9"
Tray Clg.

Walk-In Shower

FIRST FLOOR

Garage
20'-8" x 31'-4"
10'-0" Clg.

Teodora

Plan No. 8066

A grand cupola, bay turret and a recessed arch entry adorn this Spanish-inspired home. Inside, rooms are embellished with fine details—built-in cabinetry, fireplaces, art niches and specialty ceilings. The kitchen features an eating bar that connects to the nook and spacious leisure room. Separate verandahs offer intimacy around an outdoor fireplace and a party center around a built-in grille. Three bedrooms plus a guest suite provide quiet spaces for family and friends.

Bedrooms: **5**   Width: **80' 0"**

Baths: **3½**   Depth: **104' 0"**

1st Floor: **3993 sq. ft.**

Total Living: **3993 sq. ft.**

Foundation: **Slab**

PDF $2595	Vellum $2595	CAD $4592

REAR ELEVATION

© Sater Design Collection, Inc.

Porta Rossa

Plan No. 8058

Decorative tile vents, spiral pilasters and wrought-iron window treatments achieve a seamless fusion with the powerful, new-century look of this modern revival elevation. Interior vistas mix it up with sunlight and fresh breezes through the plan, with walls of glass that extend living spaces to the outdoors. A family valet, conveniently located, provides the perfect place to drop your keys and packages.

Bedrooms: **4** Width: **67' 0"**

Baths: **3½** Depth: **91' 8"**

1st Floor: **3166 sq. ft.**

Total Living: **3166 sq. ft.**

Foundation: **Slab**

PDF **$1583**	Vellum **$1583**	CAD **$2849**

REAR ELEVATION

FIRST FLOOR

© Sater Design Collection, Inc.

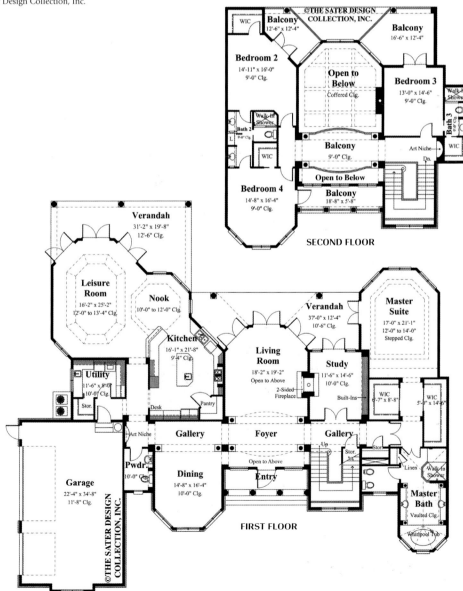

©THE SATER DESIGN COLLECTION, INC.

WIC

Balcony
12'-6" x 12'-4"

Balcony
16'-6" x 12'-4"

Bedroom 2
14'-11" x 16'-0"
9'-0" Clg.

Open to Below
Coffered Clg.

Bedroom 3
13'-0" x 14'-6"
9'-0" Clg.

Walk-In Shower

Walk-In Shower

Bath 2
9'-0" Clg.

WIC

Balcony
9'-0" Clg.

Bath 3
9'-0" Clg.

Art Niche

WIC

Bedroom 4
14'-8" x 16'-4"
9'-0" Clg.

Open to Below

Dn.

Balcony
18'-8" x 5'-8"

SECOND FLOOR

Verandah
31'-2" x 19'-8"
12'-6" Clg.

Leisure Room
16'-2" x 25'-2"
12'-0" to 13'-4" Clg.

Nook
10'-0" to 12'-0" Clg.

Kitchen
16'-1" x 21'-8"
9'-4" Clg.

Verandah
37'-0" x 12'-4"
10'-6" Clg.

Master Suite
17'-0" x 21'-1"
12'-0" to 14'-0"
Stepped Clg.

Desk

Living Room
18'-2" x 19'-2"
Open to Above

Study
11'-6" x 14'-6"
10'-0" Clg.

Utility
11'-6" x 8'-0"
10'-0" Clg.

Stor.

Pantry

2-Sided Fireplace

Built-Ins

WIC
9'-7" x 8'-8"

WIC
5'-0" x 14'-6"

Art Niche

Gallery

Foyer

Gallery

Up

Stor.

Stor.

Linen

Walk-In Shower

Pwdr.
10'-0" Clg.

Dining
14'-8" x 16'-4"
10'-0" Clg.

Open to Above

Entry

Master Bath
Vaulted Clg.

Garage
22'-4" x 34'-8"
11'-8" Clg.

Whirlpool Tub

©THE SATER DESIGN COLLECTION, INC.

FIRST FLOOR

Trevi

Plan No. 8065

Turrets frame the entry arcade of this magnificent manor. Inside, a mix of breezy, open spaces creates an at-home feeling that encourages all kinds of gatherings. A two-sided fireplace anchors the living room that extends out to the verandah through French doors. Varied ceiling treatments define rooms that defy their boundaries with walls of glass and unrestrained spaces. Columns whisper the edges of a gallery colonnade that runs nearly the width of the plan.

Bedrooms: **4**   Width: **95' 0"**

Baths: **3½**   Depth: **84' 0"**

1st Floor: **3581 sq. ft.**   2nd Floor: **1256 sq. ft.**

Total Living: **4837 sq. ft.**

Foundation: **Basement**

PDF **$4837**	Vellum **$4837**	CAD **$8223**

REAR ELEVATION

Raphaello

Plan No. 8037

Turrets integrate the layered elevation, which draws its inspiration from 16th-century forms, with symmetry, brackets and pilasters. New-world allocations of space defy tradition throughout the interior, creating a natural flow and easing everyday functions. Living spaces oriented to the rear of the plan take in expansive views through retreating glass walls and access the lanai. On the upper level, guest bedrooms open to a shared deck.

Bedrooms: **3**	Width: **72' 0"**
Baths: **3½**	Depth: **68' 3"**
1st Floor: **2250 sq. ft.**	2nd Floor: **663 sq. ft.**
Total Living: **2913 sq. ft.**	
Bonus: **351 sq. ft.**	
Foundation: **Slab**	

PDF **$1457**	Vellum **$1457**	CAD **$2622**

REAR ELEVATION

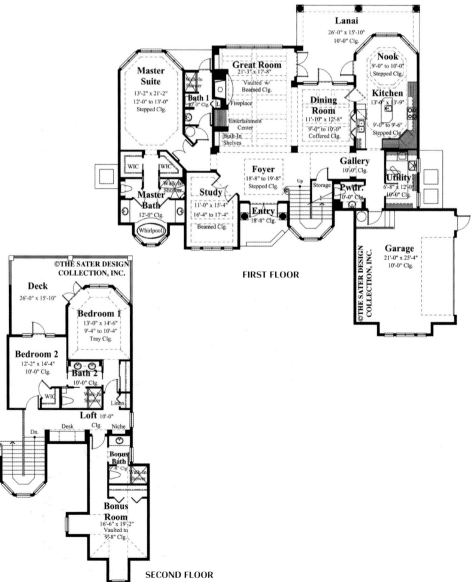

FIRST FLOOR

SECOND FLOOR

© Sater Design Collection, Inc.

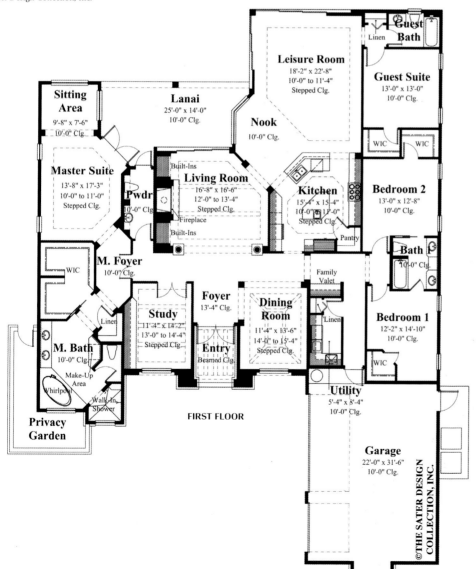

FIRST FLOOR

Sitting Area
9'-8" x 7'-6"
10'-0" Clg.

Master Suite
13'-8" x 17'-3"
10'-0" to 11'-0"
Stepped Clg.

Pwdr
10'-0" Clg.

M. Foyer
10'-0" Clg.

WIC

M. Bath
10'-0" Clg.

Make-Up Area

Whirlpool

Walk-In Shower

Linen

Privacy Garden

Lanai
25'-0" x 14'-0"
10'-0" Clg.

Nook
10'-0" Clg.

Built-Ins

Living Room
16'-8" x 16'-6"
12'-0" to 13'-4"
Stepped Clg.

Fireplace

Built-Ins

Study
11'-4" x 14'-2"
13'-0" to 14'-4"
Stepped Clg.

Foyer
13'-4" Clg.

Entry
Beamed Clg.

Dining Room
11'-4" x 13'-6"
14'-0" to 15'-4"
Stepped Clg.

Leisure Room
18'-2" x 22'-8"
10'-0" to 11'-4"
Stepped Clg.

Kitchen
15'-4" x 15'-4"
10'-0" to 12'-0"
Stepped Clg.

Pantry

Family Valet

Linen

Utility
5'-4" x 8'-4"
10'-0" Clg.

Guest Bath

Linen

Guest Suite
13'-0" x 13'-0"
10'-0" Clg.

WIC   WIC

Bedroom 2
13'-0" x 12'-8"
10'-0" Clg.

Bath
10'-0" Clg.

Bedroom 1
12'-2" x 14'-10"
10'-0" Clg.

WIC

Garage
22'-0" x 31'-6"
10'-0" Clg.

©THE SATER DESIGN COLLECTION, INC.

Santa Trinita

Plan No. 8063

Tuscan charm invites a feeling of home outside and in, with floor-to-ceiling windows letting in the sun. The front of the home features formal spaces intended for entertaining with richly textured amenities such as a stone-mantel fireplace, cabinetry and stepped ceilings. To the rear of the plan, the leisure room flows through retreating glass walls onto the lanai. A gallery hall runs the width of the plan, linking three guest bedrooms with the master suite.

Bedrooms: **4**   Width: **68' 8"**

Baths: **3½**   Depth: **91' 8"**

1st Floor: **3497 sq. ft.**

Total Living: **3497 sq. ft.**

Foundation: **Slab**

PDF **$1749**   Vellum **$1749**   CAD **$3147**

REAR ELEVATION

© Sater Design Collection, Inc.

Alessandra

Plan No. **8003**

Massive square columns frame a spectacular portico and pedimented window above the entry of this romantic villa. Well-defined formal rooms offer both intimacy and grandeur, while the casual zone provides a lose-the-shoes atmosphere. Defined by a series of sculpted arches, the central corridor extends the plan's sight lines to the leisure and the master wings. On the upper level, three guest quarters boast private decks.

Bedrooms: **4**　　　　Width: **85′ 0″**

Baths: **3½**　　　　Depth: **76′ 2″**

1st Floor: **2829 sq. ft.**　　2nd Floor: **1127 sq. ft.**

Total Living: **3956 sq. ft.**

Foundation: **Slab or Optional Basement**

| PDF **$2571** | Vellum **$2571** | CAD **$4549** |

REAR ELEVATION

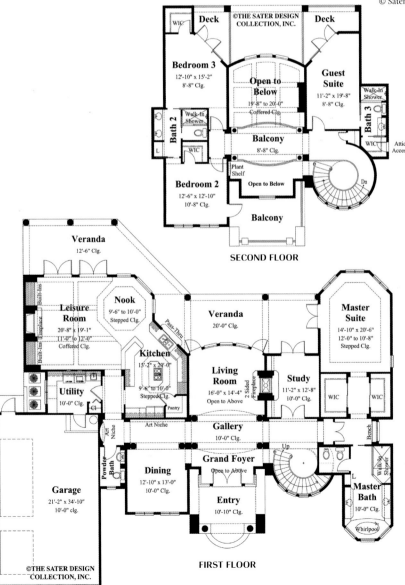

SECOND FLOOR

FIRST FLOOR

© Sater Design Collection, Inc.

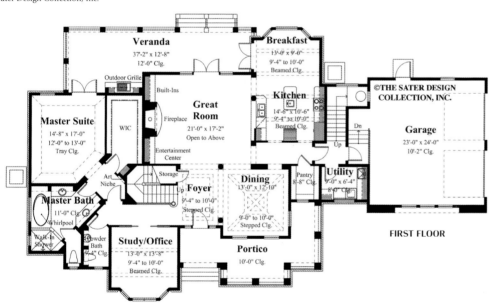

Veranda
37'-2" x 12'-8"
12'-0" Clg.

Outdoor Grille

Built-Ins

Great Room
21'-0" x 17'-2"
Open to Above

WIC

Fireplace

Master Suite
14'-8" x 17'-0"
12'-0" to 13'-0"
Tray Clg.

Art Niche

Entertainment Center

Storage

Master Bath
11'-0" Clg.
Whirlpool

Walk-In Shower

Powder Bath
9'-4" Clg.

Study/Office
13'-0" x 13'-8"
9'-4" to 10'-0"
Beamed Clg.

Up

Foyer
9'-4" to 10'-0"
Stepped Clg.

Dining
13'-0" x 12'-10"
9'-0" to 10'-0"
Stepped Clg.

Portico
10'-0" Clg.

Breakfast
13'-0" x 9'-0"
9'-4" to 10'-0"
Beamed Clg.

Kitchen
14'-6" x 10'-6"
9'-4" to 10'-0"
Beamed Clg.

Pantry
8'-8" Clg.

Utility
9'-0" x 6'-4"
8'-0" Clg.

Dn

Up

©THE SATER DESIGN COLLECTION, INC.

Garage
23'-0" x 24'-0"
10'-2" Clg.

FIRST FLOOR

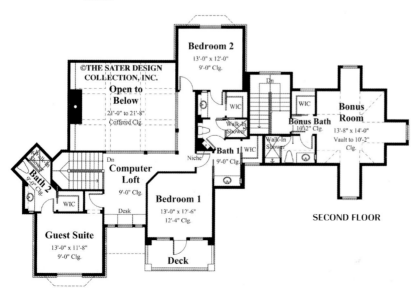

©THE SATER DESIGN COLLECTION, INC.

Bedroom 2
13'-0" x 12'-0"
9'-0" Clg.

Open to Below
21'-0" to 21'-8"
Coffered Clg.

Dn

WIC

WIC

Walk-In Shower

Bonus Bath
10'-2" Clg.

Bonus Room
13'-8" x 14'-0"
Vault to 10'-2" Clg.

Niche

Bath 1
9'-0" Clg.

WIC

Walk-In Shower

Bath 2
9'-0" Clg.

Dn

Computer Loft
9'-0" Clg.

Desk

WIC

Bedroom 1
13'-0" x 12'-6"
12'-4" Clg.

Guest Suite
13'-0" x 11'-8"
9'-0" Clg.

Desk

Deck

SECOND FLOOR

Chadbryne

Plan No. **8004**

Stacked stone and stucco capture the character of a rural Italian manor, influenced by the pastoral forms of Tuscany. Inside, an open foyer is defined by columns and arches, allowing views that extend past the veranda. Architectural details—a coffered ceiling above the two-story great room, an art niche and built-in cabinetry—contribute to the rusticated décor. State-of-the-art appliances in the kitchen play counterpoint to rough-hewn ceiling beams and stone accents in the nook and study.

Bedrooms: **4**   Width: **91' 0"**

Baths: **3½**   Depth: **52' 8"**

1st Floor: **2219 sq. ft.**   2nd Floor: **1085 sq. ft.**

Total Living: **3304 sq. ft.**

Bonus: **404 sq. ft.**

Foundation: **Slab or Optional Basement**

PDF **$1652**   Vellum **$1652**   CAD **$2974**

REAR ELEVATION

© Sater Design Collection, Inc.

Capucina

Plan No. **8010**

Stone accents complement the sculpted entry of this romantic, Italian Country manor. An open arrangement of the central living space, gallery and formal dining room permits views of the rear through a two-story bow window. French doors open the leisure room to the outdoors, while the nook grants access to a lanai shared with the master suite's sitting bay. Upstairs, a balcony hall connects the family bedrooms and guest quarters.

Bedrooms: **4**

Baths: **4½**

1st Floor: **2855 sq. ft.**

Total Living: **4011 sq. ft.**

Bonus Room: **371 sq. ft.**

Foundation: **Slab or Optional Basement**

Width: **71' 6"**

Depth: **83' 0"**

2nd Floor: **1156 sq. ft.**

PDF **$2607**   Vellum **$2607**   CAD **$4613**

REAR ELEVATION

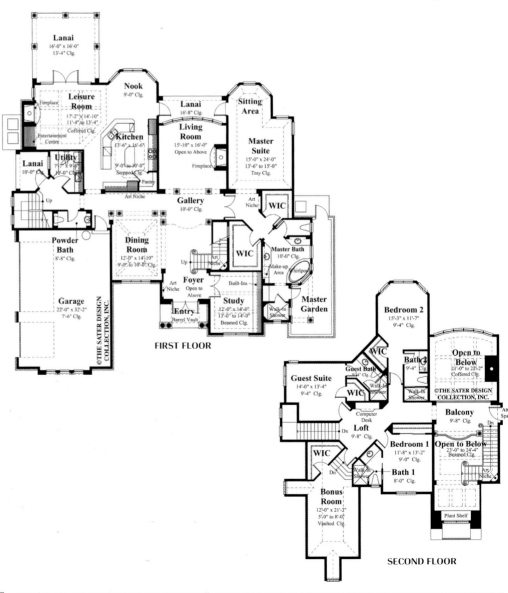

FIRST FLOOR

SECOND FLOOR

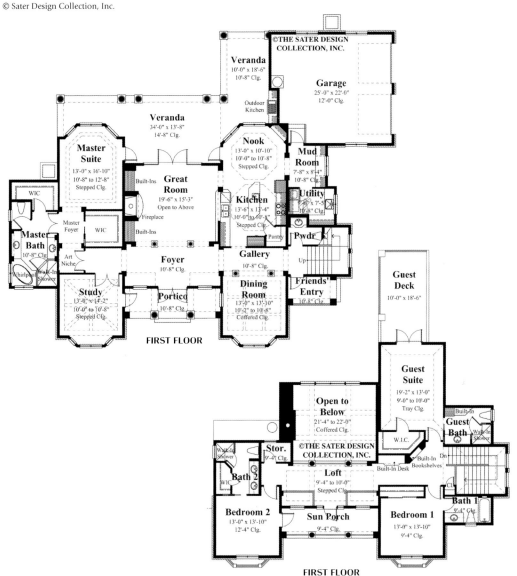

FIRST FLOOR

Veranda
10'-0" x 18'-6"
10'-8" Clg.

©THE SATER DESIGN COLLECTION, INC.

Garage
25'-0" x 22'-0"
12'-0" Clg.

Outdoor Kitchen

Veranda
34'-0" x 13'-8"
14'-8" Clg.

Nook
13'-0" x 10'-10"
10'-0" to 10'-8"
Stepped Clg.

Mud Room
7'-8" x 8'-4"
10'-8" Clg.

Master Suite
13'-0" x 16'-10"
10'-8" to 12'-8"
Stepped Clg.

WIC

Great Room
19'-6" x 15'-3"
Open to Above

Fireplace

Built-Ins

Kitchen
13'-6" x 13'-4"
10'-0" to 10'-8"
Stepped Clg.

Utility
9'-6" x 7'-5"
10'-8" Clg.

Master Foyer

WIC

Pantry

Master Bath
10'-8" Clg.

Art Niche

Whirlpool

Walk-In Shower

Foyer
10'-8" Clg.

Gallery
10'-8" Clg.

Pwdr

Up

Study
13'-0" x 14'-2"
10'-0" to 10'-8"
Stepped Clg.

Portico
10'-8" Clg.

Dining Room
13'-0" x 13'-10"
10'-2" to 10'-8"
Coffered Clg.

Friends' Entry
10'-8" Clg.

Guest Deck
10'-0" x 18'-6"

Open to Below
21'-4" to 22'-0"
Coffered Clg.

Guest Suite
19'-2" x 13'-0"
9'-0" to 10'-0"
Tray Clg.

Built-In

Guest Bath

Walk-In Shower

W.I.C.

©THE SATER DESIGN COLLECTION, INC.

Stor.
9'-4"

Walk-In Shower

Built-In Desk

Built-In Bookshelves

Dn

Bath 2

WIC

Loft
9'-4" to 10'-0"
Stepped Clg.

Cl.

Bedroom 2
13'-0" x 13'-10"
12'-4" Clg.

Sun Porch
9'-4" Clg.

Bedroom 1
13'-0" x 13'-10"
9'-4" Clg.

Bath 1
9'-4" Clg.

FIRST FLOOR

Vienna

Plan No. 8020

A dialogue between tradition and innovation, the Old World elements of this striking façade belie a form-and-function interior packed with new-century amenities. Parallel wings harbor private and public realms, connected by an airy great room and gallery-style foyer. An extended-hearth fireplace shares its beauty with the common living zone—the gourmet kitchen and morning nook. A sun porch on the upper level extends light to the loft, which links two bedroom suites and guest quarters.

Bedrooms: **4**	Width: **80' 0"**
Baths: **4½**	Depth: **63' 9"**
1st Floor: **2232 sq. ft.**	2nd Floor: **1269 sq. ft.**

Total Living: **3501 sq. ft.**

Foundation: **Slab or Optional Basement**

| PDF **$1751** | Vellum **$1751** | CAD **$3151** |

REAR ELEVATION

© Sater Design Collection, Inc.

Royal Palm

Plan No. **6727**

Triple arches in the entryway and windows to the right of the plan create a commanding presence for this spectacular home and its dominantly triangular rooflines. Elegant columns, traditional stucco and stone detailing reflect Mediterranean influences. Past the foyer, stepped ceilings define the formal rooms with retreating glass walls extending the space out to the lanai. The master retreat enjoys quiet seclusion in the far wing of the home.

Bedrooms: **3**   Width: **65′ 0″**

Baths: **2½**   Depth: **85′ 4″**

1st Floor: **2823 sq. ft.**

Total Living: **2823 sq. ft.**

Foundation: **Slab**

| PDF **$1413** | Vellum **$1413** | CAD **$2541** |

REAR ELEVATION

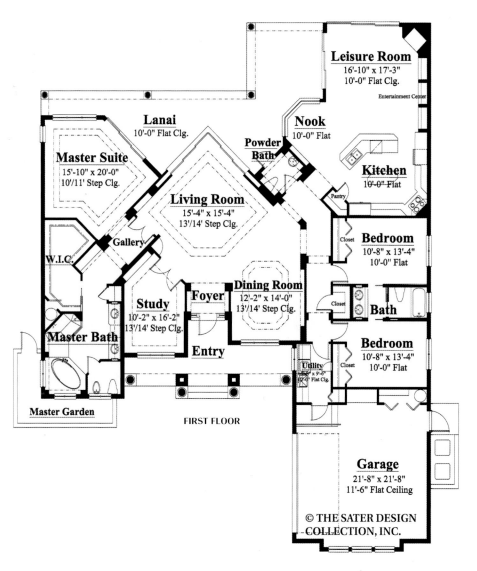

Leisure Room
16'-10" x 17'-3"
10'-0" Flat Clg.

Entertainment Center

Lanai
10'-0" Flat Clg.

Nook
10'-0" Flat

Powder Bath

Kitchen
10'-0" Flat

Master Suite
15'-10" x 20'-0"
10'/11' Step Clg.

Pantry

Living Room
15'-4" x 15'-4"
13'/14' Step Clg.

Gallery

W.I.C.

Closet

Bedroom
10'-8" x 13'-4"
10'-0" Flat

Closet

Bath

Study
10'-2" x 16'-2"
13'/14' Step Clg.

Foyer

Dining Room
12'-2" x 14'-0"
13'/14' Step Clg.

Master Bath

Entry

Bedroom
10'-8" x 13'-4"
10'-0" Flat

Closet

Utility

Master Garden

FIRST FLOOR

Garage
21'-8" x 21'-8"
11'-6" Flat Ceiling

© THE SATER DESIGN COLLECTION, INC.

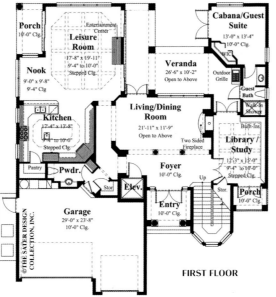

Porch
10'-0" Clg.

Entertainment Center

Leisure Room
17'-8" x 19'-11"
9'-4" to 10'-0"
Stepped Clg.

Nook
9'-0" x 9'-8"
9'-4" Clg.

Kitchen
17'-4" x 13'-8"
to 10'-0"
Stepped Clg.

Pantry

Pwdr.

Garage
29'-0" x 23'-8"
10'-0" Clg.

©THE SATER DESIGN COLLECTION, INC.

Cabana/Guest Suite
13'-0" x 13'-4"
10'-0" Clg.

WIC

Veranda
26'-6" x 10'-2"
Open to Above

Outdoor Grille

Guest Bath

Walk-In Shower

Living/Dining Room
21'-11" x 11'-9"
Open to Above

Two Sided Fireplace

Built-Ins

Library / Study
13'-3" x 15'-0"
9'-4" to 10'-0"
Stepped Clg.

Foyer
10'-0" Clg.

Elev.

Stor.

Up

Stor.

Entry
10'-0" Clg.

Porch
10'-0" Clg.

FIRST FLOOR

©THE SATER DESIGN COLLECTION, INC.

Master Retreat
17'-8" x 19'-11"
9'-4" to 10'-0" Tray Clg.

Master Porch
9'-4" Clg.

Balcony

Bedroom 1
13'-0" x 13'-8"
9'-4" to 10'-0" Tray Clg.

Whirlpool

M. Bath
9'-4" Clg.

Make-Up Area

Walk-In Shower

Master Foyer

WIC

Bath 3
Walk-In Shower

Stor.

Open to Below
23'-6" to 24'-2"
Stepped Clg.

WIC

Morn. Kit.

Walk-In Shower

Linen

Bath 1

Utility
7'-8" x 10'
9'-4" Clg.

Drip Dry

Bedroom 3
12'-4" x 13'-0"
9'-4" Clg.

WIC

Loft
24'-2" x 8'-6"
11'-10" Clg.

Elev.

Linen

Bath 2
8'-8" Clg.

Sun Porch
Barrel Clg.

Dn

Sun Porch
9'-4" Clg.

WIC

Bedroom 2
11'-4" x 13'-6"
9'-4" Clg.

SECOND FLOOR

Vasari

Plan No. 8025

A stunning window-lined turret, classic columns and repeating arches create a striking façade. An uninhibited spirit prevails within—where a gallery foyer and loft deepen the central living/dining room, allowing a stepped ceiling to soar above open vistas defined only by decorative columns. A two-sided fireplace warms the central area as well as a study that boasts a private porch. A view-oriented leisure room enjoys multiple connections with the outdoors.

Bedrooms: **5**	Width: **58' 0"**
Baths: **5½**	Depth: **65' 0"**
1st Floor: **1995 sq. ft.**	2nd Floor: **2165 sq. ft.**
Total Living: **4160 sq. ft.**	
Foundation: **Slab or Optional Basement**	

PDF **$2704**	Vellum **$2704**	CAD **$4784**

REAR ELEVATION

© Sater Design Collection, Inc.

Della Porta

Plan No. 8007

Carved brackets and balusters, stucco, glass panels and shingles surround a triple-arch entry—a grand start for this spacious villa. Designed for 21st-century living, the interior plan creates flexible spaces that are not formal or self-conscious, but simply comfortable. Defined by arches, columns and magnificent views that extend beyond the veranda, the living room opens to the dining room and shares a two-sided fireplace.

Bedrooms: **3**	Width: **106' 4"**
Baths: **3½**	Depth: **102' 4"**

1st Floor: **3653 sq. ft.**

Total Living: **3653 sq. ft.**

Foundation: **Slab or Optional Basement or Optional Walkout**

PDF **$1827**	Vellum **$1827**	CAD **$3288**

REAR ELEVATION

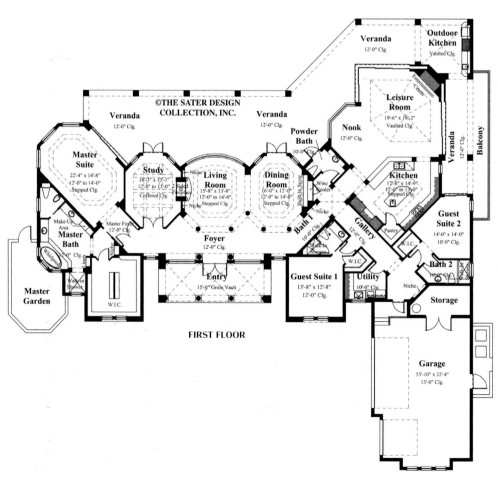

FIRST FLOOR

© Sater Design Collection, Inc.

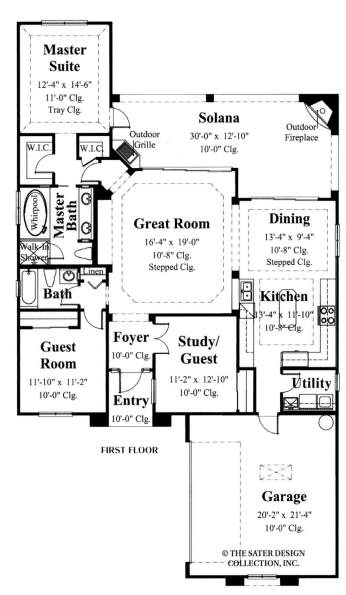

Master Suite
12'-4" x 14'-6"
11'-0" Clg.
Tray Clg.

Solana
30'-0" x 12'-10"
10'-0" Clg.

Outdoor Fireplace

W.I.C.   W.I.C.

Outdoor Grille

Whirlpool

Master Bath

Walk-In Shower

Linen

Bath

Great Room
16'-4" x 19'-0"
10'-8" Clg.
Stepped Clg.

Dining
13'-4" x 9'-4"
10'-8" Clg.
Stepped Clg.

Kitchen
13'-4" x 11'-10"
10'-8" Clg.

Guest Room
11'-10" x 11'-2"
10'-0" Clg.

Foyer
10'-0" Clg.

Study/ Guest
11'-2" x 12'-10"
10'-0" Clg.

Entry
10'-0" Clg.

Utility

Garage
20'-2" x 21'-4"
10'-0" Clg.

FIRST FLOOR

© THE SATER DESIGN COLLECTION, INC.

Cateena

Plan No. **6503**

Ideal for a view-oriented lot, this home offers scenic vistas from the master suite, great room and dining room, which border a rear solana complete with corner fireplace and outdoor grille. The master suite and guest room are secluded to one side, while the family living space connects easily to the kitchen and a private study.

Bedrooms: **2**	Width: **44' 0"**
Baths: **2**	Depth: **74' 0"**
1ˢᵗ Floor: **1608 sq. ft.**	
Total Living: **1608 sq. ft.**	
Foundation: **Slab**	

PDF **$875**	Vellum **$875**	CAD **$1447**

ALTERNATE ELEVATION - PLAN #6505

© Sater Design Collection, Inc.

Mercato

Plan No. **8028**

Spiral columns articulate an elegant arcade that's merely the beginning of this Mediterranean villa. Inside, a beamed ceiling contributes a sense of spaciousness to the heart of the home, while walls of glass draw the outdoors inside. Varied ceiling treatments and sculpted arches define the wide-open interior, permitting flexibility as well as great views. The great room is anchored by a massive fireplace flanked by built-in shelves.

Bedrooms: **3** Width: **62' 10"**

Baths: **2½** Depth: **73' 6"**

1st Floor: **2191 sq. ft.**

Total Living: **2191 sq. ft.**

Foundation: **Slab or Optional Basement**

PDF **$1097**	Vellum **$1097**	CAD **$1972**

REAR ELEVATION

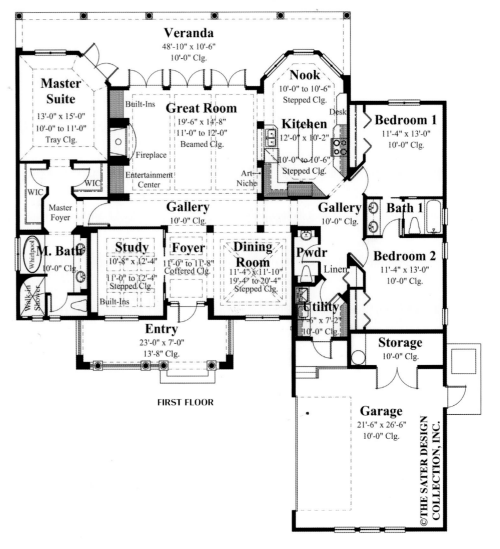

FIRST FLOOR

© Sater Design Collection, Inc.

Tamarron

Plan No. **6760**

This plan is perfect for move-up families or those looking for a home that can expand with their needs. Three large bedrooms plus a large kitchen/great room area with a breakfast nook provide plenty of space for family members and pets. The study with a walk-in closet could be turned into another bedroom as needed. Vaulted ceilings throughout the central part of this home provide openness and drama, while eight-foot ceilings throughout the rest of the home are anything but confining.

Bedrooms: **3**	Width: **58' 0"**
Baths: **2**	Depth: **59' 4"**

1st Floor: **1746 sq. ft.**

Total Living: **1746 sq. ft.**

Foundation: **Slab**

PDF **$875**	Vellum **$875**	CAD **$1571**

REAR ELEVATION

Bedroom 2
11'-10" x 11'-6"
8'-0" Clg.

Bath 1

Lanai
Vaulted Clg.

Nook
9'-2" x 7'-0"
Vaulted Clg.

Cl

Great Room
16'-0" x 11'-10"
Vaulted Clg.

Kitchen
9'-4" x 10'-0"
Vaulted Clg.

Master Suite
13'-2" x 15'-0"
8'-0" Clg.

Bedroom 1
11'-10" x 10'-4"
8'-0" Clg.

L

WIC

Study
12'-2" x 10'-2"
8'-0" Clg.

Foyer

WIC

Dining Room
11'-6" x 10'-6"
Vaulted Clg.

Cl

Util.
5'-8" x 7'-10"
8'-0" Clg.

WIC
8'-0" Clg.

M. Bath

Walk-In Shower

Whirlpool

Entry

FIRST FLOOR

Garage
20'-4" x 21'-6"
8'-0" Clg.

© THE SATER DESIGN COLLECTION, INC.

© Sater Design Collection, Inc.

Sondrio

Plan No. 6511

Multiple arched windows and varied rooflines add interest to the façade, while a smart floor plan gives style and function to the interior. Angled countertops and an island enhance the kitchen, while glass doors and windows brighten the adjoining leisure room and bayed breakfast nook. A spacious master retreat is tucked away from the secondary bedrooms and common living area, ensuring privacy and solitude.

Bedrooms: **3**   Width: **50′ 5″**

Baths: **2**   Depth: **69′ 4″**

1st Floor: **2010 sq. ft.**

Total Living: **2010 sq. ft.**

Foundation: **Slab**

| PDF **$1005** | Vellum **$1005** | CAD **$1809** |

ALTERNATE ELEVATION - PLAN #6512

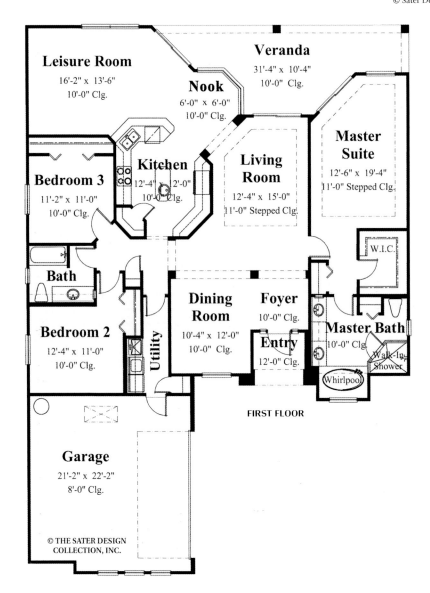

Leisure Room
16'-2" x 13'-6"
10'-0" Clg.

Veranda
31'-4" x 10'-4"
10'-0" Clg.

Nook
6'-0" x 6'-0"
10'-0" Clg.

Master Suite
12'-6" x 19'-4"
11'-0" Stepped Clg.

Kitchen
12'-4" x 12'-0"
10'-0" Clg.

Living Room
12'-4" x 15'-0"
11'-0" Stepped Clg.

Bedroom 3
11'-2" x 11'-0"
10'-0" Clg.

W.I.C.

Bath

Dining Room
10'-4" x 12'-0"
10'-0" Clg.

Foyer
10'-0" Clg.

Master Bath
10'-0" Clg.

Bedroom 2
12'-4" x 11'-0"
10'-0" Clg.

Utility

Entry
12'-0" Clg.

Walk-In Shower

Whirlpool

FIRST FLOOR

Garage
21'-2" x 22'-2"
8'-0" Clg.

© THE SATER DESIGN COLLECTION, INC.

© Sater Design Collection, Inc.

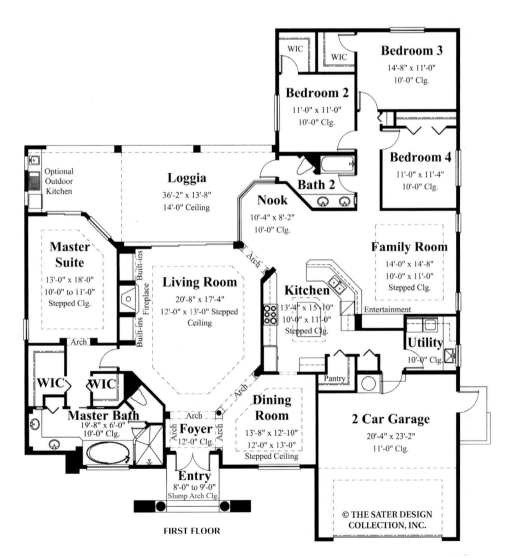

WIC

WIC

Bedroom 3
14'-8" x 11'-0"
10'-0" Clg.

Bedroom 2
11'-0" x 11'-0"
10'-0" Clg.

Bedroom 4
11'-0" x 11'-4"
10'-0" Clg.

Bath 2

Loggia
36'-2" x 13'-8"
14'-0" Ceiling

Nook
10'-4" x 8'-2"
10'-0" Clg.

Optional Outdoor Kitchen

Master Suite
13'-0" x 18'-0"
10'-0" to 11'-0"
Stepped Clg.

Living Room
20'-8" x 17'-4"
12'-0" x 13'-0" Stepped Ceiling

Built-ins Fireplace Built-ins

Arch

Kitchen
13'-4" x 15'-10"
10'-0" x 11'-0"
Stepped Clg.

Family Room
14'-0" x 14'-8"
10'-0" x 11'-0"
Stepped Clg.

Entertainment

Utility
10'-0" Clg.

WIC **WIC**

Master Bath
19'-8" x 6'-0"
10'-0" Clg.

Arch

Foyer
12'-0" Clg.

Arch Arch

Dining Room
13'-8" x 12'-10"
12'-0" x 13'-0"
Stepped Ceiling

Pantry

2 Car Garage
20'-4" x 23'-2"
11'-0" Clg.

Entry
8'-0" to 9'-0"
Slump Arch Clg.

© THE SATER DESIGN COLLECTION, INC.

FIRST FLOOR

Esperane

Plan No. **6759**

A slump-arch ceiling defines the elegant entryway into this Mediterranean family home. The living room is charming, with a fireplace surrounded by built-ins and disappearing glass walls to the loggia. The nearby kitchen, nook and leisure room make this floor plan ideal for both entertaining and family living. The master suite gets lots of privacy and space, as well as an utterly luxurious bathroom.

Bedrooms: **4**   Width: **63' 8"**

Baths: **2**   Depth: **72' 8"**

1st Floor: **2654 sq. ft.**

Total Living: **2654 sq. ft.**

Foundation: **Slab**

| PDF **$1327** | Vellum **$1327** | CAD **$2389** |

REAR ELEVATION

St. Thomas

Plan No. 6770

Open living areas under high ceilings give this home a large and airy feel. The arrangement of the common spaces makes it ideal for gatherings large and small. Sliding glass doors and bay windows connect the living room and dining nook to the outdoors. The master retreat enjoys seclusion to one side of the home and features French doors to the veranda and luxe bathroom amenities.

Bedrooms: **3**　　　　Width: **64' 0"**

Baths: **2**　　　　Depth: **55' 0"**

1st Floor: **1911 sq. ft.**

Total Living: **1911 sq. ft.**

Foundation: **Slab**

PDF **$957**	Vellum **$957**	CAD **$1720**

REAR ELEVATION

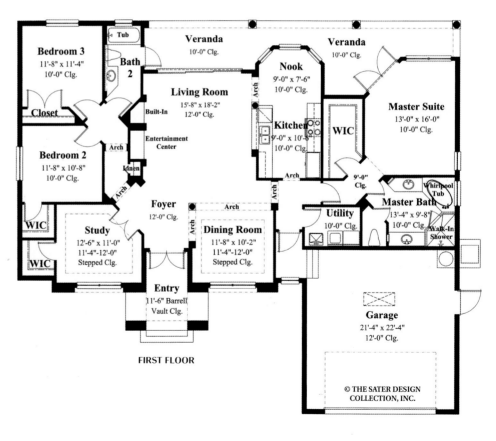

FIRST FLOOR

Sommerset

Plan No. **6827**

A Spanish tile roof and elegant portico combine to create this captivating Mediterranean villa. A gallery-style foyer leads to a powder room and a walk-in pantry, which enhances the efficiency of the kitchen. Angled counters, a center island and built-in desk or message center overlook the breakfast nook and offer views of the rear property. Upstairs the master suite shares the second floor with two additional bedrooms and a study.

Bedrooms: **3**	Width: **34' 0"**
Baths: **2½**	Depth: **63' 2"**
1st Floor: **1296 sq. ft.**	2nd Floor: **1354 sq. ft.**
Total Living: **2650 sq. ft.**	
Foundation: **Slab**	

PDF **$1325**	Vellum **$1325**	CAD **$2385**

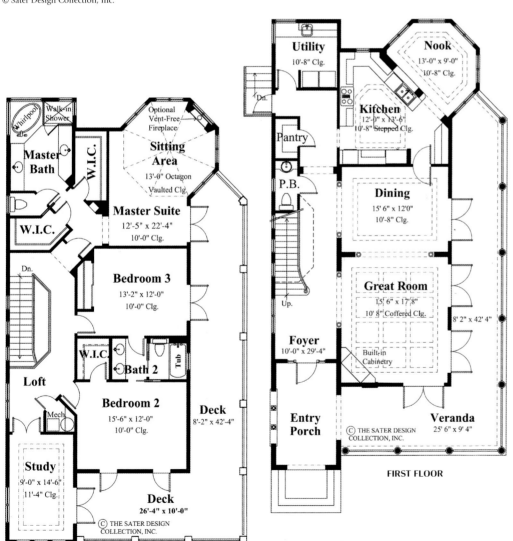

Master Bath

Whirlpool

Walk-in Shower

W.I.C.

Optional Vent-Free Fireplace

Sitting Area
13'-0" Octagon
Vaulted Clg.

W.I.C.

Master Suite
12'-5" x 22'-4"
10'-0" Clg.

Dn.

Bedroom 3
13'-2" x 12'-0"
10'-0" Clg.

W.I.C.

Bath 2

Tub

Loft

Mech.

Bedroom 2
15'-6" x 12'-0"
10'-0" Clg.

Deck
8'-2" x 42'-4"

Study
9'-0" x 14'-6"
11'-4" Clg.

Deck
26'-4" x 10'-0"

© THE SATER DESIGN COLLECTION, INC.

SECOND FLOOR

Utility
10'-8" Clg.

Nook
13'-0" x 9'-0"
10'-8" Clg.

Dn.

Kitchen
12'-0" x 13'-6"
10'-8" Stepped Clg.

Pantry

P.B.

Dining
15'-6" x 12'-0"
10'-8" Clg.

Up.

Great Room
15'-6" x 17'-8"
10'-8" Coffered Clg.

8'-2" x 42'-4"

Foyer
10'-0" x 29'-4"

Built-in Cabinetry

Entry Porch

Veranda
25'-6" x 9'-4"

© THE SATER DESIGN COLLECTION, INC.

FIRST FLOOR

REAR ELEVATION

© Sater Design Collection, Inc.

Ardenno

Plan No. **6500**

A corbelled roofline, arched windows and a columned entryway provide luxurious curb appeal to this moderately-sized home. A smart layout separates the master suite and secondary bedroom to one side. An open floor plan provides convenience and functionality to the home's core rooms. The eat-in kitchen features a pass-thru to the formal dining area. Retreating glass doors provide for easy access to the outdoors.

Bedrooms: **2**   Width: **40' 0"**

Baths: **2**   Depth: **63' 4"**

1st Floor: **1281 sq. ft.**

Total Living: **1281 sq. ft.**

Foundation: **Slab**

| PDF **$875** | Vellum **$875** | CAD **$1153** |

REAR ELEVATION

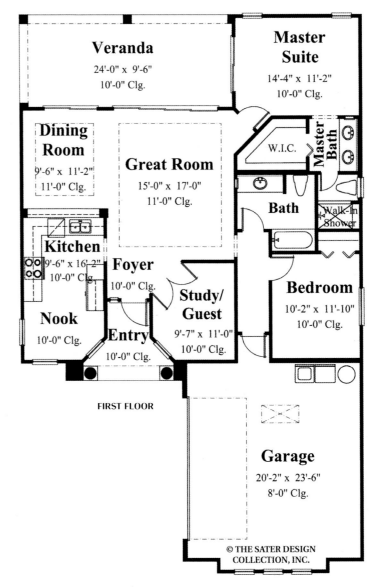

Veranda
24'-0" x 9'-6"
10'-0" Clg.

Master Suite
14'-4" x 11'-2"
10'-0" Clg.

Dining Room
9'-6" x 11'-2"
11'-0" Clg.

Great Room
15'-0" x 17'-0"
11'-0" Clg.

W.I.C.

Master Bath

Bath

Walk-In Shower

Kitchen
9'-6" x 16'-2"
10'-0" Clg.

Foyer
10'-0" Clg.

Study/ Guest
9'-7" x 11'-0"
10'-0" Clg.

Bedroom
10'-2" x 11'-10"
10'-0" Clg.

Nook
10'-0" Clg.

Entry
10'-0" Clg.

FIRST FLOOR

Garage
20'-2" x 23'-6"
8'-0" Clg.

© THE SATER DESIGN COLLECTION, INC.

© Sater Design Collection, Inc.

Mission Hills

Plan No. 6845

This enticing European villa combines Mediterranean influences with Italian design. Rising a few steps, this home offers banded stucco, columns and an arched, glassed entry leading into the main corridor, linking two wings that spread outward from the central great room. The kitchen with casual dining blends into the great room, with an eating bar that defines the spaces, still joined by expansive vaulted ceilings.

Bedrooms: **3**   Width: **60' 0"**

Baths: **3**   Depth: **60' 0"**

1ST Floor: **2350 sq. ft.**

Total Living: **2350 sq. ft.**

Foundation: **Island Basement**

| PDF **$1175** | Vellum **$1175** | CAD **$2115** |

REAR ELEVATION

FIRST FLOOR

©THE SATER DESIGN COLLECTION, INC.

Verandah
57'-4" x 9'-2"
Vaulted Clg.
10'-0" Clg.   10'-0" Clg.

Master Suite
13'-8" x 16'-8"
Tray Clg.

Nook
11'-10" x 11'-3"
Vaulted Clg.

Guest Suite 1
12'-2" x 12'-0"
Tray Clg.

Great Room
18'-8" x 18'-6"
Vaulted Clg.

Built-Ins

Entertainment Center

Kitchen
11'-4" x 12'-3"
Vaulted Clg.

Bath 1
10'-0"

Hers   His

Built-Ins

Pantry

Bath 2
10'-0" Clg.

Master Bath
10'-8" x 12'-4"
Vault Clg.

Walk-In Shower

Study
13'-6" x 11'-2"
Vault Clg.

Foyer
7'-0" x 9'-10"
15'-0" Clg.

Up
Dn.

Utility
8'-8" x 7'-2"
12'-0" Clg.

Guest Suite 2
13'-4" x 11'-2"
Tray Clg.

Balcony 1
12'-0" Clg.

Entry
15'-0" Clg.

Balcony 2
12'-0" Clg.

LOWER LEVEL

©THE SATER DESIGN COLLECTION, INC.

Lanai
57'-4" x 9'-6"
8'-4" Clg.

Storage
33'-4" x 16'-1"
8'-4" Clg.

Storage
25'-6" x 16'-8"
8'-4" Clg.

Storage
25'-2" x 18'-1"
8'-4" Clg.

Lower Foyer
13'-2" x 6'-5"
8'-4" Clg.

Storage
6'-8" x 10'-8"
Sloped Clg.

2-Car Garage
25'-6" x 22'-0"
8'-4" Clg.

© Sater Design Collection, Inc.

Fedora

Plan No. 6513

Multiple arched windows and varied rooflines add interest to the façade, while a smart floor plan gives style and function to the interior. The centerpiece of this home is the spacious great room that serves as the hub of activity. A kitchen generous with counter space is open to the dining room. The dining room and great room both feature sliding glass walls, that when open, provide a seamless transition to the outdoor living space.

Bedrooms: **2**   Width: **47′ 0″**

Baths: **2**   Depth: **74′ 0″**

1st Floor: **1727 sq. ft.**

Total Living: **1727 sq. ft.**

Foundation: **Slab**

PDF **$875**	Vellum **$875**	CAD **$1554**

ALTERNATE ELEVATION - PLAN #6514

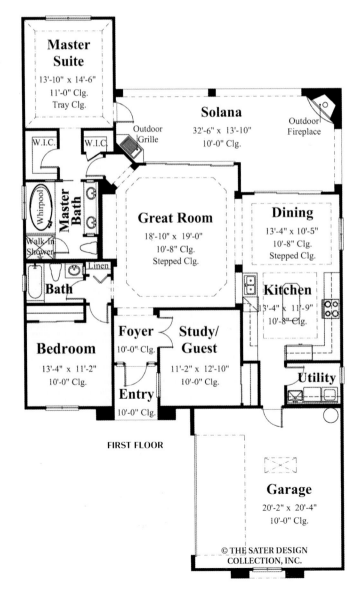

Master Suite
13'-10" x 14'-6"
11'-0" Clg.
Tray Clg.

Solana
32'-6" x 13'-10"
10'-0" Clg.

Outdoor Grille

Outdoor Fireplace

W.I.C.   W.I.C.

Whirlpool

Master Bath

Walk In Shower

Great Room
18'-10" x 19'-0"
10'-8" Clg.
Stepped Clg.

Dining
13'-4" x 10'-5"
10'-8" Clg.
Stepped Clg.

Linen

Bath

Kitchen
13'-4" x 11'-9"
10'-8" Clg.

Bedroom
13'-4" x 11'-2"
10'-0" Clg.

Foyer
10'-0" Clg.

Study/ Guest
11'-2" x 12'-10"
10'-0" Clg.

Utility

Entry
10'-0" Clg.

FIRST FLOOR

Garage
20'-2" x 20'-4"
10'-0" Clg.

© THE SATER DESIGN COLLECTION, INC.

© Sater Design Collection, Inc.

Terra Valley

Plan No. **6761**

From the covered entry, the foyer presents a vaulted great room, complete with amazing rear vistas. The vault continues to the galley kitchen and bayed breakfast nook, enhanced by floods of natural light. In the right wing, the master suite revels in a pampering whirlpool bath and access to the lanai that offers up over 400 square feet of outdoor relaxation. Two additional bedrooms are located on the far left and share a full bath.

Bedrooms: **3**   Width: **58' 0"**

Baths: **2**   Depth: **59' 4"**

1st Floor: **1515 sq. ft.**

Total Living: **1515 sq. ft.**

Foundation: **Slab**

| PDF **$875** | Vellum **$875** | CAD **$1365** |

REAR ELEVATION

FLOOR PLAN LABELS

Lanai
Vaulted Clg.

Nook
9'-2" x 7'-0"
Vaulted Clg.

Great Room
16'-0" x 11'-10"
Vaulted Clg.

Kitchen
9'-4" x 10'-2"
Vaulted Clg.

Master Suite
13'-2" x 15'-0"
8'-0" Clg.

Bedroom 1
11'-10" x 10'-6"
8'-0" Clg.

Bath 1

WIC

WIC

Bedroom 2
12'-2" x 10'-2"
8'-0" Clg.

Foyer

Dining Room
11'-6" x 10'-6"
Vaulted Clg.

Entry

Cl.

Util.
6'-8" x 7'-10"
8'-0" Clg.

WIC
8'-0" Clg.

M. Bath
Walk-In Shower
Whirlpool

Garage
20'-4" x 21'-6"
8'-0" Clg.

FIRST FLOOR

© THE SATER DESIGN COLLECTION, INC.

© Sater Design Collection, Inc.

Casina Rossa

Plan No. 8071

Columns, stucco and rough-hewn stone embellish the façade of this charming Tuscan villa. Inside, a beamed ceiling contributes a sense of spaciousness to the heart of the home, while walls of glass draw the outdoors inside. Varied ceiling treatments and sculpted arches define the wide-open interior, permitting flexibility as well as great views. The great room is anchored by a massive fireplace flanked by built-in shelves.

Bedrooms: **3**   Width: **62' 10"**

Baths: **2½**   Depth: **73' 6"**

1st Floor: **2191 sq. ft.**

Total Living: **2191 sq. ft.**

Foundation: **Slab or Optional Basement**

PDF **$1097**	Vellum **$1097**	CAD **$1972**

REAR ELEVATION

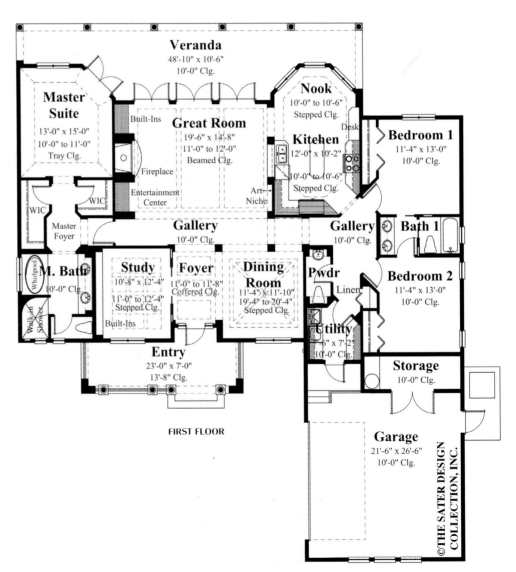

FIRST FLOOR

San Marino

Plan No. 6833

A fashionable sunburst transom adorns the arched entryway where pillars introduce the distinguished detailing found within. From the entry to the rear balcony, the wide-open vistas allow the warm, gentle breezes to flow through the house. The great room at the core of the plan is open to the dining room, which in turn is open to the gourmet kitchen and breakfast nook. The master retreat is separated from two guest suites by the common areas.

Bedrooms: **3**	Width: **70′ 2″**
Baths: **3**	Depth: **53′ 0″**

1st Floor: **2433 sq. ft.**

Total Living: **2433 sq. ft.**

Foundation: **Island Basement**

FIRST FLOOR

First Floor Plan Labels

- Veranda 38′-6″ x 12′-0″ 10′-0″ Clg.
- Nook 9′-0″ x 8′-0″ 10′-0″ Clg.
- Balcony 18′-8″ x 9′-0″ 16′-0″ Clg.
- Master Porch 13′-0″ x 12′-0″ 10′-0″ Clg.
- Guest 2 11′-2″ x 13′-4″ 10′-0″ Clg.
- Kitchen 10′-8″ x 14′-8″ 10′-0″ Clg.
- Dining 10′-0″ x 13′-6″ 12′-0″ Clg.
- Great Room 17′-8″ x 21′-0″ 16′-0″ Clg.
- Master Suite 12′-6″ x 15′-6″ 11′-4″ Tray Clg.
- DN
- Bath 2
- W.I.C.
- Closet
- Gallery 12′-0″ Clg.
- Foyer 16′-0″ Clg.
- W.I.C.
- Guest 3 12′-8″ x 11′-0″ 10′-0″ Clg.
- Bath 3
- Utility
- Walk-in Shower
- Elev.
- Up
- W.I.C.
- Master Bath 10′-0″ Clg.
- Whirlpool
- Entry Porch
- Walk-in Shower
- Built-ins
- Ent. Center
- Pantry

PDF **$1217**   Vellum **$1217**   CAD **$2190**

REAR ELEVATION

Lower Level Plan Labels

- Porch 70′-2″ x 15′-0″
- Up
- Storage 54′-0″ x 42′-8″
- Garage 27′-8″ x 24′-0″
- Elev.
- Storage

LOWER LEVEL

© Sater Design Collection, Inc.

Sunset Beach

Plan No. 6848

Just beautiful, this elegant manor of perfect proportion is long on views with a gazebo-styled front porch. A dramatic foyer opens to a sweeping circular staircase and views that extend the length of the house. The leisure room and nook create an open casual living area with the kitchen, which accesses the formal dining room through a butler's pantry. The master retreat encompasses the remainder of the main level, while three bedrooms share two full baths upstairs.

Bedrooms: **4**   Width: **74' 0"**

Baths: **3½**   Depth: **88' 0"**

1st Floor: **2083 sq. ft.**   2nd Floor: **1013 sq. ft.**

Total Living: **3096 sq. ft.**

Foundation: **Crawl Space**

PDF **$1548**   Vellum **$1548**   CAD **$2786**

REAR ELEVATION

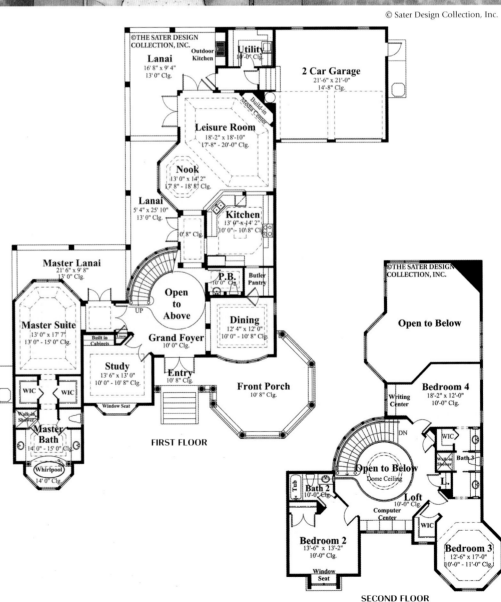

© Sater Design Collection, Inc.

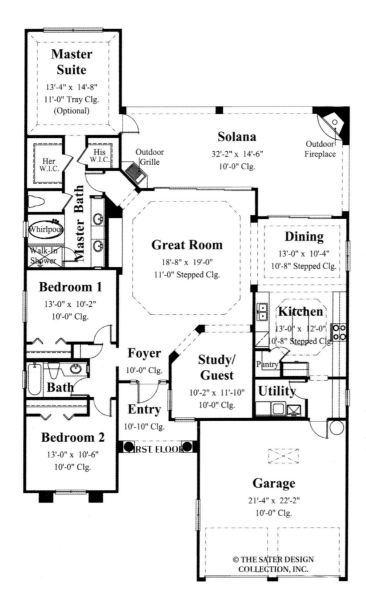

Master Suite
13'-4" x 14'-8"
11'-0" Tray Clg.
(Optional)

Her W.I.C.

His W.I.C.

Outdoor Grille

Solana
32'-2" x 14'-6"
10'-0" Clg.

Outdoor Fireplace

Master Bath

Whirlpool

Walk-In Shower

Great Room
18'-8" x 19'-0"
11'-0" Stepped Clg.

Dining
13'-0" x 10'-4"
10'-8" Stepped Clg.

Bedroom 1
13'-0" x 10'-2"
10'-0" Clg.

Kitchen
13'-0" x 12'-0"
10'-8" Stepped Clg.

Bath

Foyer
10'-0" Clg.

Study/ Guest
10'-2" x 11'-10"
10'-0" Clg.

Pantry

Utility

Entry
10'-10" Clg.

Bedroom 2
13'-0" x 10'-6"
10'-0" Clg.

FIRST FLOOR

Garage
21'-4" x 22'-2"
10'-0" Clg.

© THE SATER DESIGN COLLECTION, INC.

Tirano

Plan No. 6509

The turreted, recessed entry grants elegance to the façade of this Mediterranean charmer. The interior flows around a large central great room featuring a stepped ceiling. The central living space offers easy access to the master suite and two secondary bedrooms on one side of the home, the dining room and kitchen on the other, and a study near the foyer.

Bedrooms: **3**

Width: **47' 2"**

Baths: **2**

Depth: **75' 0"**

1st Floor: **1919 sq. ft.**

Total Living: **1919 sq. ft.**

Foundation: **Slab**

PDF $961	Vellum $961	CAD $1727

ALTERNATE ELEVATION - PLAN #6510

Charleston Place

Plan No. 6700

Louvered shutters, balustered railings and a Spanish tile roof blend with stucco and quoins in this Row House-style plan infused with a Mediterranean flavor. Entry stairs lead to the main-level living areas, defined by arches and columns that blend Old-World craftsmanship with modern space. A wall of built-ins and a warming fireplace lend a cozy feeling to the open, contemporary great room.

Bedrooms: **3**

Baths: **2½**

1st Floor: **1305 sq. ft.**

Total Living: **2520 sq. ft.**

Foundation: **Slab**

Width: **32' 6"**

Depth: **77' 6"**

2nd Floor: **1215 sq. ft.**

PDF $1260	Vellum $1260	CAD $2268

REAR ELEVATION

© Sater Design Collection, Inc.

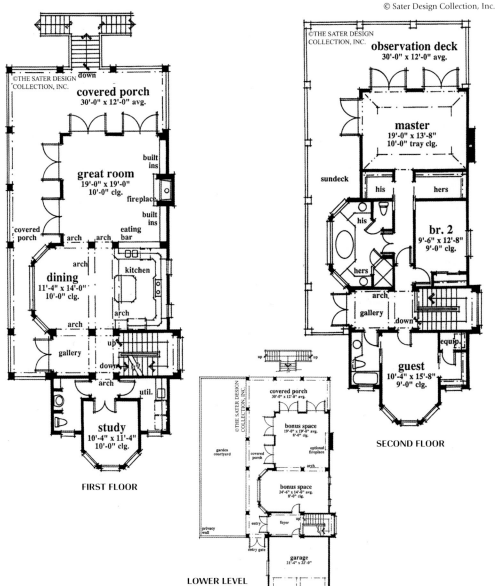

©THE SATER DESIGN COLLECTION, INC.

covered porch
30'-0" x 12'-0" avg.

down

built ins

great room
19'-0" x 19'-0"
10'-0" clg.

fireplace

built ins

eating bar

dining
11'-4" x 14'-0"
10'-0" clg.

arch

kitchen

arch

covered porch

arch

arch

gallery

up

down

util.

study
10'-4" x 11'-4"
10'-0" clg.

FIRST FLOOR

©THE SATER DESIGN COLLECTION, INC.

observation deck
30'-0" x 12'-0" avg.

master
19'-0" x 13'-8"
10'-0" tray clg.

sundeck

his

hers

his

br. 2
9'-6" x 12'-8"
9'-0" clg.

hers

arch

gallery

down

equip.

guest
10'-4" x 15'-8"
9'-0" clg.

SECOND FLOOR

up

up

©THE SATER DESIGN COLLECTION, INC.

covered porch
30'-0" x 12'-0" avg.

garden courtyard

bonus space
19'-0" x 19'-0" avg.
8'-0" clg.

covered porch

optional fireplace

arch

bonus space
24'-6" x 14'-0" avg.
8'-0" clg.

privacy wall

entry

foyer

up

entry gate

garage
21'-4" x 21'-0"

LOWER LEVEL

© Sater Design Collection, Inc.

Master Suite
13'-10" x 12'-4"
10'-0" Clg.

Verandah
27'-2" x 9'-8"
10'-0" Clg.

Walk-In Shower

Master Bath

W.I.C.

Great Room
15'-6" x 15'-10"
11'-0" Clg.

Dining
9'-4" x 11'-6"
11'-0" Clg.

Bath

Kitchen
9'-4" x 17'-4"
10'-0" Clg.

Bedroom
10'-2" x 10'-0"
10'-0" Clg.

Utility

Study/ Guest
9'-10" x 12'-8"
10'-0" Clg.

Foyer
10'-0" Clg.

Entry
Barrel Vault Clg.

Nook
10'-0" Clg.

Garage
20'-2" x 24'-2"
8'-0" Clg.

© THE SATER DESIGN COLLECTION, INC.

FIRST FLOOR

Bianca

Plan No. 6506

A turreted breakfast nook sits elegantly aside the entryway, which features a dramatic barrel vault ceiling. Inside, the foyer looks ahead through a disappearing wall of glass that opens the great room to the verandah. The master suite and dining room also have sliding doors to the rear living spaces, and a pass-thru bar makes the kitchen user-friendly.

Bedrooms: **2**   Width: **42' 8"**

Baths: **2**   Depth: **63' 4"**

1st Floor: **1404 sq. ft.**

Total Living: **1404 sq. ft.**

Foundation: **Slab**

| PDF $875 | Vellum $875 | CAD $1264 |

ALTERNATE ELEVATION - PLAN #6507

 **index** | Plans listed by square footage largest to smallest.

index

Plans listed by square footage largest to smallest.

WHAT'S IN A SET OF plans?

A set of plans is a collection of drawings that show the important structural components and how the home should be built. Architectural and construction terms are complex. If you have further questions about these terms, ask your builder or visit our glossary online at www.saterdesign.com.

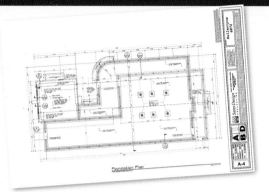

COVER SHEET, INDEX & SITE PLAN — The cover sheet features an elevation of the exterior of the house that shows approximately how the home will look when built. The index lists the order of the drawings included, with page numbers for easy reference. The site plan is a scaled footprint of the house to help determine how the home will be placed on the building site.

FOUNDATION PLAN — This sheet provides a fully dimensioned and noted foundation layout, including references to footings, pads, and support walls. For plans with a basement, additional walls and columns may be shown. Basement plans come with a floor framing layout which may be included in this section or the floor framing section, depending on the plan.

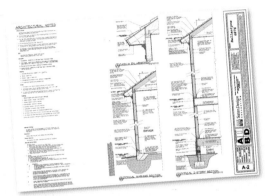

WALL SECTION & NOTES — This section shows section cuts of the exterior wall from the roof down through the foundation. These wall sections specify the home's construction and building materials. They also show the number of stories, type of foundation and the construction of the walls. Roofing materials, insulation, floor framing, wall finishes and elevation heights are all shown and referenced.

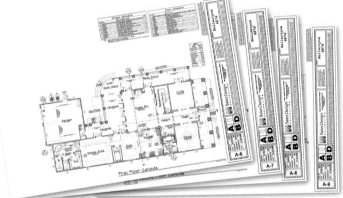

DETAILED FLOOR PLAN — This section provides detailed drawings and descriptions of all the elements that will be included on each floor of the home. The home's exterior footprint, openings and interior rooms are carefully dimensioned. Important features are noted including built-ins, niches and appliances. All doors and windows are identified. Typically this section also includes the square footage information.

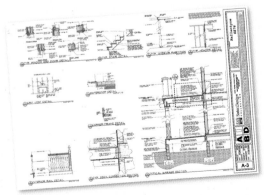

TYPICAL DETAILS & NOTES — This section addresses all the facets and details you will want to include in your home, with the exception of local building code requirements. Architectural and structural elements are detailed, including: window and door components, railings, balusters, wood stairs and headers, interior walls, interior partitions, concrete steps and footings (if applicable).

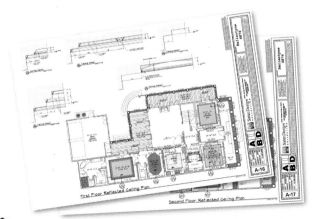

REFLECTED CEILING PLAN — One of Sater home's most distinguishable features is the highly detailed ceiling treatments. This section shows ceiling heights and treatments. It also shows the details, profiles and finishes of the ceiling treatments. Arches and soffits are also specified in this section.

bonus:

GREEN SOLUTIONS GUIDE — Guide designed to help make decisions about the level of green building you wish to implement in the construction of your home.

MATERIALS LIST — A Guide to assist in pricing and construction of a Sater home.

electronic plans:

Our plans are also available in an electronic format, supplied on a CD-ROM. All of the features explained below are included on this disk.

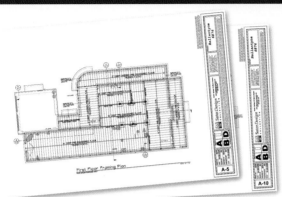

FLOOR FRAMING PLANS — Homes with a basement or crawl space will have a floor framing plan for the first floor. Multi-story homes will have floor framing plans for upper floors as well. The floor framing plans provide structural information such as the joist location, spacing and direction, as well as the floor heights and stair openings.

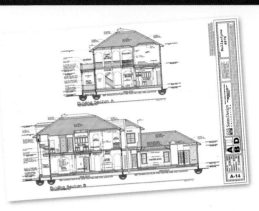

CROSS SECTION & DETAILS — This section will illustrate the important changes in the floor, ceiling and roof heights or the relationship of different floors to one another. Interior elements of rooms and areas, such as columns, arches, headers and soffits, are also discernible and easier to visualize in a cross section.

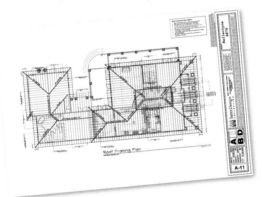

ROOF PLAN — The overall layout and necessary details for roof design are provided in this section. If trusses are used, we suggest using a local truss manufacturer to design your roof trusses to comply with your local codes and regulations.

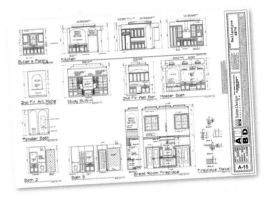

INTERIOR ELEVATIONS — These elevations show the specific details and design of the kitchen, bathrooms, utility rooms, fireplaces, bookcases, built-in units and other special interior features. The interior elevations vary based on the complexity of the home.

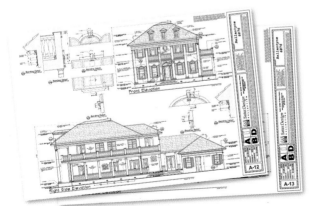

EXTERIOR ELEVATIONS — Elevations are drawings that show how the finished home will approximately look. In this section, elevations of the front, rear and left and right sides of the home are shown. Exterior materials, details and heights are noted on these drawings.

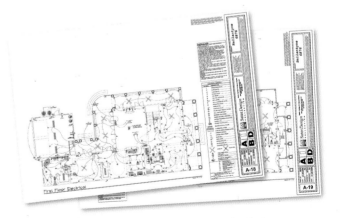

ELECTRICAL PLAN — This section shows an electrical plan that will enhance functionality and highlight the unique architectural features of the home.

QUICK TURNAROUND

If you place your order before 3:00 P.M. eastern time, we can usually have your plans to you the next business day. Some restrictions may apply. We cannot ship to a post office box, so please be prepared to supply us with a physical street address.

OUR EXCHANGE POLICY

We do not accept returns because each set of plans or disk is generated just for you at the time of your order. However, if you should find that the plan you purchased does not meet your needs, we do permit exchanges requested within sixty days of the date of purchase. At the time of exchange, you will be charged a processing fee of 20% of the total of your original order plus the difference in price between the plans (if applicable) and the cost to ship the new plans to you. Please call our customer service department if you have any questions or to request an exchange authorization number.

WHAT FORMAT OF PLANS SHOULD I GET?

Our plans are available in three formats: PDF plan sets, a reproducible vellum set and an electronic version on a disk. Most people select a format based on the changes they will make to their plan.

PDF plan sets are the fastest, most convenient way to get going. With a PDF file you can obtain the necessary copies (up to twenty) at your local print shop. This saves you shipping costs and time.

Vellum is a special type of paper that can be erased for small changes, such as moving kitchen appliances, or enlarging a shower. You will receive one set of plans on the special paper with permission to make up to twenty copies for the construction process.

Most customers, and engineers, prefer the electronic version of the plans. The AutoCAD file facilitates major modifications and dimensional changes. You will receive one disk with permission to make up to twenty copies for the construction process.

LOCAL BUILDING CODES AND ZONING REQUIREMENTS

Our plans are designed to meet or exceed the International Residential Code. Because of the great differences in geography and climate, each state, county and municipality has its own building codes and zoning requirements. Your plan may need to be modified to comply with local requirements regarding snow loads, energy codes, soil and seismic conditions and a wide range of other matters. Prior to using plans ordered from us, we strongly advise that you consult a local building official.

ARCHITECTURAL AND/OR ENGINEERING REVIEW

Some cities and states require a licensed architect or engineer review and approve any set of building documents prior to permitting. These cities and states want to ensure that the proposed new home will be code compliant, zoning compliant, safe, and structurally sound. Often, this architect or engineer will have to create additional structural drawings to be submitted for permitting. You can learn if this will be necessary in your area from a local building official.

DISCLAIMER

We have put substantial care and effort into the creation of our house plans. We authorize the use of our plans on the express condition that you strictly comply with all local building codes, zoning requirements and other applicable laws, regulations and ordinances. However, because we cannot provide on-site consultation, supervision or control over the actual construction and because of the great variance in local building requirements, building practices and soil, seismic, weather and other conditions, WE CANNOT MAKE ANY WARRANTY, EXPRESS OR IMPLIED, WITH RESPECT TO THE CONTENT OR USE OF OUR PLANS, INCLUDING, BUT IS NOT LIMITED TO, ANY WARRANTY OF MARKETABILITY OR OF FITNESS FOR A PARTICULAR PURPOSE. Please note that floor plans included in this magazine are not construction documents and are subject to change. Renderings are an artist's concept only.

IGNORING COPYRIGHT LAWS CAN BE A

$150,000 *mistake!*

Recent changes in Federal Copyright Laws allow for statutory penalties of up to $150,000 per incident for copyright infringement involving any of the copyrighted plans found in this publication. The law can be confusing. So, for your own protection, take the time to understand what you cannot do when it comes to home plans.

WHAT YOU CAN'T DO:

- **YOU CANNOT BUILD A HOME WITHOUT BUYING A LICENSE.**

- **YOU CANNOT DUPLICATE HOME PLANS WITHOUT PERMISSION.**

- **YOU CANNOT COPY ANY PART OF A HOME PLAN TO CREATE ANOTHER.**

- **YOU MUST OBTAIN A SEPARATE LICENSE EACH TIME YOU BUILD A HOME.**

CONSIDERATIONS IN ORDERING
A SATER DESIGN PLAN.

what is a license?

PRINT LICENSE

This license is issued in the form of either six sets of plan prints or as a single vellum set.
The licensee is entitled to build one home.

ELECTRONIC LICENSE

This license is issued in the form of an electronic (AutoCAD) file. The licensee is entitled to customize and build one time only.

HOW TO ORDER

ORDER BY PHONE
1-800-718-7526

ORDER ONLINE
www.saterdesign.com

SATER DESIGN COLLECTION
25241 Elementary Way, Suite 201
Bonita Springs, FL 34135

WHAT SETS A SATER PLAN APART?

In order to ensure that your home is built to look just as spectacular as the homes shown in this magazine, we have created highly detailed construction drawings. Our plans are the ultimate guide to building the home of your dreams. Some of the features that you'll find in Sater plans, but not other plans, are:

	SATER	OTHERS
Extensive Interior Elevations *Interior design-quality drawings, showing highly detailed elevations of architectural built-ins and cabinetry*	YES	NO
Detailed Materials List *To assist the owner and builder with estimating building costs (Some offer this for a fee, but with us it's free!)*	YES	NO
Reflected Ceiling Plans *With detailed sections of the numerous ceiling and soffit designs*	YES	NO
Separate Electrical Plans *Carefully designed lighting plans that contemplate your family's use and enjoyment*	YES	NO
Green Brochure *To help you make decisions about implementing green building practices in your home's construction .*	YES	NO
Detailed Plumbing Plans, Electrical Riser Diagram and Sanitary Riser Schematic *(Offered at no additional charge with Sater Reserve Plans)*	YES	NO
Unparalleled Customer Support *Our dedicated staff is committed to helping you in the decision process*	YES	NO

PLAN CUSTOMIZATION SERVICES

If you want to tweak the plan to better suit you and your family, we certainly understand and hope you'll let us make the changes for you. That way we can ensure that the plan with the changes is just as beautiful as the plan before the changes and that all changes are properly made. Call 1-800-718-7526 to speak with a customer service representative about your needs, we're happy to help!

ADDITIONAL ITEMS
Additional Plan Prints* (per set)...........$65.00
Full Reverse Plans*.................special order
*Call for availability and/or pricing.

POSTAGE AND HANDLING
Overnight.............................$55.00
2nd Day..............................$44.00
Ground $34.00
Saturday.............................$74.00
International deliveries: ..... *Please call for a quote.*

We DO NOT sell photography shown in this magazine for any purpose.
Prices of plans and of shipping are subject to change without notice.

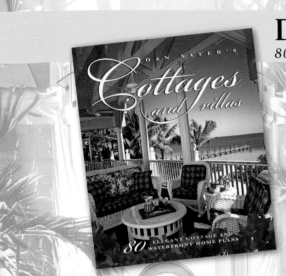

Dan Sater's Luxury Home Plans
over 100 view-oriented estate homes

A colorful and rich textured collection of more than 100 exquisite floor plans. This stunning display of unique Sater homes features more than 220 pages of exciting interior and exterior photography, with unique design ideas for the most gracious living. Whether you're seeking plans for a 6,000-square-foot estate or a 3,000-square-foot villa, you can find them in this truly inspirational portfolio of Dan's best luxury home plans.

2,700 to over 8,000 sq. ft.

$16.95   256 full color pages

Dan Sater's Cottages & Villas
80 elegant cottage & waterfront home plans

A photo tour of 8 stunning coastal homes previews a portfolio of eighty beautiful rendered and charming clapboard cottages and grand Mediterranean villas. These highly versatile designs are big on open porches and courtyards, while balancing function with style and brings to mind a relaxed attitude that can only come with view-oriented living.

2,200 to over 4,300 sq. ft.

$14.95   224 full color pages

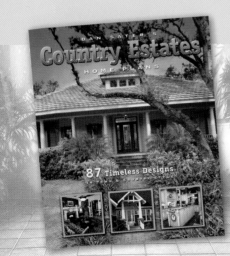

Country Estates Home Plans
87 timeless designs in Town & Country styles

Innovative designs beautiful photography and illustrated, these homes combine the casual feel and comfort of country living with today's most popular amenities, including entertainment-ready kitchens, inviting morning rooms, family gathering areas, home offices and media rooms. Each home has been designed with superb indoor-outdoor relationships and many feature full-width and wraparound porches to take advantage of country vistas and inspiring lake, ocean or golf-course views.

1,500 to over 4,100 sq. ft.

$14.95   160 full color pages